FATAL FUTURE?
TRANSNATIONAL TERRORISM AND

FATAL FUTURE?

TRANSNATIONAL

TERRORISM AND THE

NEW GLOBAL DISORDER

Richard M. Pearlstein

 UNIVERSITY OF TEXAS PRESS, AUSTIN

Requests for permission to reproduce material from this work should
be sent to Permissions, University of Texas Press, Box 7819, Austin,
TX 78713-7819.

⊗ The paper used in this book meets the minimum requirements of
ANSI/NISO Z39.48-1992 (R1997) (Permanence of Paper).

Library of Congress Cataloging-in-Publication Data

Pearlstein, Richard M. (Richard Merrill), 1953–
    Fatal future? : transnational terrorism and the new global disorder /
Richard M. Pearlstein. — 1st ed.
        p.   cm.
Includes bibliographical references and index.
    ISBN 0-292-70162-4 (hardcover : alk. paper)—ISBN 0-292-70265-5
(pbk. : alk. paper)
1. Terrorism.   2. Political violence.   3. Islam and terrorism.
I. Title.

    HV6431.P428   2004
    303.6'25—dc22

                                        2003020477

To my mother, who has always guided me with wisdom and love
To my darling wife Pamela, who is the love of my life
And to the memory of Barry Wolman and Nel Grannell

CONTENTS

PREFACE

IT IS A CRISP, SUNNY MORNING in America's heartland. The date is September 15, 1995. The place is the corner of Fifth and Robinson Streets, Oklahoma City, Oklahoma. I can see an enormous crater where a massive office building once stood. I also see the damage to nearby buildings, some of which appear near collapse. I can hear the bulldozers going about their grim work, the soft weeping of bystanders. I can touch the rubble, the fence festooned with poetry, prayers, and toddlers' sneakers. I can smell the diesel exhaust, the dust, the indescribable smells of disaster. It is nearly five months since the Oklahoma City bombing. I have never personally witnessed a scene such as this. Terrorism is no longer an abstract academic topic to me—it is a reality.

It is a warm, clear, and bright afternoon in America's largest city. The date is July 31, 2002. The place, a viewing platform along lower Manhattan's Church Street, is adjacent to a site now known simply as Ground Zero. I can see a sixteen-acre crater where mighty twin skyscrapers—once the most recognizable image of New York City—and other buildings once stood. Upon that crater stands a simple makeshift cross composed of rusty steel girders. I again see the damage to nearby buildings—dusty, abandoned skyscrapers now shrouded by dark mesh-like material. An enormous American flag and a banner conveying words of eternal remembrance for the victims, their families, and the city's gallant rescue workers are sewn to one of those shrouds. I also see hundreds of other visitors: a large church group from Portugal, a cluster of Muslims reading passages from the Quran, an impeccably dressed young businessman who clutches his briefcase and leans against the metal fence. Was he a friend or loved one of one of the nearly three thousand souls who perished here? Had he, long ago, resolved to make a daily visit to this now-hallowed ground? I do not know, and I cannot bring myself to ask. I can hear the Portuguese church group praying and singing, the Muslims softly murmuring their prayers. Again I touch the rubble. I can feel the pain in my teeth, which—perhaps in subconscious dread of this pilgrimage—I had been grinding in my sleep. The odor of burned buildings hangs in my nostrils. Again, I smell the diesel exhaust, the dust, those now all too horribly familiar odors of unimaginable tragedy. But this dust is much more than mere dust. I pause and remember the thousands of photographs posted by frantic family members and friends after the collapse of the towers. It is nearly eleven months since that hideous day in September.

Will the human race ever witness an end to this scourge? Most of us acknowledge that we cannot expect to eliminate terrorism, any more than we can expect to end other major crimes, such as rape or murder. Nonetheless, terrorism has undergone a dramatic evolution in recent years. What are the environment and nature of this evolution? What does this evolution tell us about the future of terrorism?

Do you remember where you were when you first learned of the terrorist attacks in Oklahoma City, New York, Washington, and Pennsylvania? Who did you immediately assume was responsible for these monstrous deeds? Given the growing number of attacks against Americans by foreign-based terrorists, most Americans, including me, assumed that foreign terrorists were to blame in each case. In the first instance, our assumptions were wrong. The fact that so horrible an act was planned and executed by American citizens was in itself profoundly shocking. Yet the foreign-based terrorist attacks of September 11 were many times more disturbing, for on that day our national home, our collective sanctuary, our safe haven was violated and desecrated by outside infiltrators. To a great extent, our very sense of "home" has been forever lost.

We ask: Why? There are no simple answers. A new form of terrorism is at our door. What led us to this point?

In addressing these questions, *Fatal Future? Transnational Terrorism and the New Global Disorder* focuses on two closely related themes. The first is the evolution of a global system once dominated by fairly predictable diplomatic or military relationships among dominant nation-state actors on a well-structured global stage. In recent years, this well-ordered system has been deliberately undermined by new actors—such as transnational terrorist organizations—which follow no clear rules. Second, *Fatal Future?* examines the gradual transformation of terrorism from a relatively restrained form of domestic, or intranational, conflict to a much more threatening form of transnational conflict, which, unlike its intranational predecessor, intentionally spills over the borders of nation-states.

Fatal Future? consists of seven chapters. Chapter One, "What Is Terrorism?" seeks, quite obviously, to define the term *terrorism*. This chapter also classifies and describes the various "generations" of terrorist organizations. Chapter Two, "The Rise of the New Global Disorder," analyzes the old global order's nature, demise, and replacement by a new global disorder marked by turbulent interactions between global actors—particularly new types of actors—on a new global stage. These major players include not only traditional nation-states, but also intergovernmental organizations and transnational organizations. Chapter Three, "Transnational Terrorism and the New Global Disorder," examines the evolution of terrorism from the old global order through the new global disorder. and also highlights the origins and nature of transnational terrorism. Chapter Four, "Ethnoterrorism: Menace from Within and Without," examines the continuing specter of ethnonationalist terrorism as well as how and why this form of terrorism now violates the borders of so many nation-states. Chapter Five, "Holy Rage," analyzes the political, religious, and ideological factors which have culminated in a new and even more formidable form of transnational terrorist organization. Most disturbingly, what the perpetrators of this new form of terrorism may have accomplished is to thrust upon the global stage a prototype or model for the transnational terrorist organization of the future. Chapter Six, "Superterrorism: What's in It for You?" probes the now widely accepted prospect that transnational terrorists will expand their use of nonconventional weapons of mass destruction. Chapter Six also explores the relative likelihood, and consequences, of the transnational terrorist employment of chemical, biological, radiological, and nuclear weapons. Chapter Seven, "After September 11: Responding to Transnational Terrorism," addresses some of the many efforts—some successful, some controversial—to combat transnational terrorism in the post–September 11 period.

ACKNOWLEDGMENTS

Even a book authored by a single individual is the product of tremendous collaboration and support. I particularly wish to acknowledge the love and guidance which my dear mother, Mollie Pearlstein, has provided throughout my life. My wife, Pamela, has been a tower of patience, strength, and intuitive wisdom throughout our more than ten years together. I also extend my love to my brother, Robert, to my sister, Elaine Wolman, and to my sister-in-law, Emily.

The person who certainly made the greatest contributions to this book is Theresa J. May, Assistant Director and Editor-in-Chief of the University of Texas Press. Theresa May's faith, patience, and support during the long process of making this work a reality are a model for every professional and have earned my deepest and most heartfelt thanks. In addition, the kind assistance and support of Allison M. Faust, Associate Editor at the University of Texas Press, are greatly appreciated.

I also wish to express deep gratitude to my great friends Robert and Barbara Eichorn. Robert, a retired U.S. Navy commander, read the first manuscript draft; his invaluable comments are sincerely appreciated. I also wish to thank three of my colleagues, all of Southeastern Oklahoma State University. They are Dr. Muhammad K. Betz, who offered valuable suggestions on Chapter Five; Dr. Sauri P. Bhattacharya, who was an early reader of Chapter Four; and Dr. John R. Wright, who read and made key suggestions on Chapter Six.

Many of my colleagues at Southeastern Oklahoma State University have been enormously supportive of my work over the years and deserve special mention. I particularly wish to salute Professor Bruce A. Johnson, Dr. L. David Norris, and my colleague and department chair, Dr. Kenneth Chinn, all of Southeastern's Department of Social Sciences. The longtime support of our dean, Dr. C. W. Mangrum; Southeastern's associate vice president for academic affairs, Dr. Douglas McMillan; our vice president for academic affairs, Dr. Jesse O. Snowden; and the president of Southeastern Oklahoma State University, Dr. Glen D. Johnson, are also greatly appreciated. My students, in particular Preston Harbuck and Thomas Gray, have also provided me with invaluable feedback on how to make this book a more useful text. Thank you all.

Some of us are profoundly fortunate to have had wonderful mentors over the years. I am particularly grateful for my association with Dr. Lawrence Zelic Freedman, M.D., of the University of Chicago and the Institute of Social and Behavioral Pathology; Dr. J. Garry Clifford of the University of Connecticut; and Dr. Lewis Lipsitz and the late Dr. Paul F. Kress of the University of North Carolina at Chapel Hill. Lastly, I shall never forget the intellectual influence of both the late Dr. William C. Hartel and the late Professor Robert H. Deets of Marietta College.

The staffs of many university libraries have been extremely helpful over the years. The respective staffs of Harvard University's Widener Library and various libraries at the Massachusetts Institute of Technology, Tufts University's Fletcher School of Law and Diplomacy, Stanford University, and the University of California at Berkeley deserve special mention. I also wish to thank Jeffrey Levy of the main library at the University of North Texas for his last-minute bibliographical assistance.

R.M.P.

FATAL FUTURE?
TRANSNATIONAL TERRORISM AND THE NEW GLOBAL DISORDER

CHAPTER ONE

What is Terrorism?

A great people has been moved to defend a great nation. Terrorist attacks can shake the foundations of our biggest buildings, but they cannot touch the foundation of America. These acts shattered steel, but they cannot dent the steel of American resolve.

U.S. PRESIDENT GEORGE W. BUSH, SEPTEMBER 11, 2001

IN HIS FIRST FORMAL RESPONSE to the events of September 11, 2001, U.S. President George W. Bush sought to reassure a nation abruptly and harshly confronted by one of the most horrifying and formidable threats of our age: terrorism. What is terrorism? Common understanding of this term is far too vague, broad, and simplistic. Terrorism is widely characterized, for example, as the "weapon of the weak," as "violence for effect," or as "violence for political purposes." Terrorism may be all of these things, but so are many other forms of violence. Further obscuring the issue is that far too many people use two very different terms, *terrorism* and *terror,* interchangeably. Heated debates over how to define terrorism are a staple at any conference on terrorism. Even various agencies within the same government are unable to agree on a common definition of terrorism. Some students of terrorism despair that a common definition is even possible.[1]

In order to counter a threat, it is essential to understand precisely what that threat is. The controversial and highly emotional threat of terrorism is no exception. It is certainly true that the same act of terrorism may be condemned by one observer and glorified by another. For example, although the destruction of the World Trade Center is vilified by most Westerners, that same event is celebrated by many non-Westerners. Whether acts of terrorism are condemned or extolled, however, is of no definitional relevance whatsoever.

The definition of terrorism is a technical issue, not an emotional one. Terrorism may be defined as a specific form of civil rebellion in which the use or threatened use of violence is imposed from below the governmental level against certain symbolic victims or objects. Terrorism is actual or threatened violence intended to indirectly coerce a primary target (typically, a government or a people) to accept a demanded outcome through the fomenting of intense fear or anxiety. Acts of terrorism have generally included, for example, means such as kidnappings for propaganda effect, hostage-takings, shootings, bombings, hijackings, sabotage, chemical and biological attacks, and threats of any of the above.[2]

Terror, on the other hand, may be defined as a specific form of official, governmental intimidation in which the use or threatened use of violence is inflicted from above, from the governmental level, against certain symbolic victims or objects. Like terrorism, terror is intended to indirectly coerce a primary target (typically, all or part of some population) to accept a demanded outcome due to the fomenting of intense fear or anxiety. Terror, however, differs from terrorism in that terror is the official act of a governmental body, whereas terrorism is the rebellious act of a discontented nongovernmental organization. Acts of terror have included, for example, means such as shootings, bombings, "disappearances," arrests, torture, amputation, imprisonment, execution, exile, and threats of any of the above.

It is certainly true that there have been all-too-frequent partnerships between certain governments and terrorist organizations. Not surprisingly, those same governments also frequently practice terror against their own populations. Governments and their official agencies also occasionally support, sponsor, or even control terrorist organizations. However, as long as those terrorist organizations maintain a clear degree of separate identity and independence from their official patrons, then those organizations are in fact practicing terrorism, rather than terror.

Terrorism is easily distinguished from direct violence, which takes place for personal, financial, or even political reasons. Common acts of direct violence include, for example, robbery, rape, and murder. When not meant as a means to convey a threat to some third party, the simple assassination of any prominent figure also constitutes an act of direct violence.

An act of direct violence involves only two distinct parties. One is the perpetrator, and the other is the victim, whose harm is the direct and sole aim of the perpetrator. It may also be noted that perpetrators of direct violence typically shun news media coverage of their actions and their actual identities.

An act of terrorism, on the other hand, involves at least three, and in almost every case four, distinct parties. These parties are the perpetrator, the victim, the primary target of the terrorist act, and, in almost every case, the messenger. Indeed, the role of the messenger is a crucial one. To ensure that a primary target may be made aware that it has been targeted, a messenger, most typically the news media, must somehow report an act of terrorism. For this as well as other reasons, perpetrators of terrorist violence typically crave news media coverage of their actions, if not of their identities.

Terrorist Generations

What are the major motivations, and types, of terrorist organizations? In terms of overall motivations, terrorist organizations may be classified as: (1) left-wing, (2) ethnonationalist, (3) right-wing, or (4) religious. It is far more useful, however, to classify terrorist organizations from the old global order period through the new global disorder period on a "generational" basis. From the early 1970s through the present, there have been three major generations of terrorist organizations. Each generation is characterized by whether or not a terrorist organization is financed or otherwise actively supported by a government, and whether or not its operations cross nation-state borders. These terrorist generations may be classified as

(1) *first generation:* intranational terrorist organizations
(2) *second generation:* international terrorist organizations
(3) *third generation:* transnational terrorist organizations (TTOs)[3]

There are important functional and organizational differences between these three generations of terrorist organizations. First-generation, intranational terrorist organizations confine their attacks within the boundaries of a single nation-state. They are funded and actively supported exclusively through private means; they thus neither require nor receive financial or other support from any nation-state. Equally significant is that this private funding or support is derived solely from within the organization's own nation-state borders.[4]

Both second-generation, international terrorist organizations and third-generation, transnational terrorist organizations routinely conduct their activities across nation-state borders. Yet international and transnational terrorist organizations also differ in certain important respects. Although international terrorist organizations typically require, and always receive, funding or other active support from nation-state sponsors, transnational terrorist organizations neither require nor receive nation-state sponsorship.

The issue of nongovernmental funding or other support is also significant. All three types of terrorist organizations may receive funding or other active support from private organizations or individuals. Unlike intranational terrorist organizations, however, international and transnational terrorist organizations may receive such funding or support from anywhere in the world.[5]

Each of these three generations of terrorist organizations may be further classified on the basis of underlying motivations. Left-wing terrorist organizations, for example, plagued many Western nation-states during much of the old global order period which existed prior to the disintegration of the former Soviet Union. The following is a partial list of those organizations, followed by the nation-states within which they operated:

Weather Underground (United States)
Symbionese Liberation Army (United States)
Sam Melville–Jonathan Jackson Unit (United States)
Red Army Faction (West Germany)
Revolutionary Cells (West Germany)
Red Brigades (Italy)
Front Line (Italy)
Armed Revolutionary Nuclei (Italy)
Direct Action (France)
Angry Brigade (Britain)
Fighting Communist Cells (Belgium)
November 17 (Greece)

The Weather Underground, Symbionese Liberation Army, Sam Melville–Jonathan Jackson Unit, Angry Brigade, and November 17 organizations serve as pure illustrations of the intranational generation. These organizations thus neither received financial or other active support from any nation-states nor pursued their activities outside of their own nation-state borders. Of the scores of left-wing terrorist organizations to plague the democracies of Western Europe and the United States, few remain in existence. November 17 operated as a major left-wing terrorist organization from the mid-1970s until at least the summer of 2002, when the Greek government declared the group defunct.[6]

The Red Army Faction, Red Brigades, Revolutionary Cells, Front Line, Armed Revolutionary Nuclei, Direct Action, and Fighting Communist Cells appear to have originated as intranational terrorist organizations. Due to their eventual acceptance of financial and other active support from nation-states such as the Soviet Union, East Germany, and

Czechoslovakia, however, these organizations gradually evolved into examples of the second, international generation.

Left-wing terrorist organizations generally subscribe to some form of anticapitalist ideology. During the old global order period, they attacked capitalism and extolled the interests and virtues of the working class. Left-wing terrorist organizations tended to engage in small-scale bombings of symbolic capitalist targets (e.g., business, military, or police interests) and in the kidnappings of certain high-profile business, military, or political figures (e.g., corporate executives, heiresses, NATO generals, political party leaders, or mayors). The supposed goal of these acts was to compel democratic nation-states to overreact in such a repressive manner that the latter's "democratic façades" would be exposed as fraudulent or hypocritical and would be so stripped away as to enable the working class to view its government as the repressive and autocratic force that it supposedly was. This realization would presumably lead to some form of popular uprising or revolt and, eventually, to some sort of "workers' revolution."

Perhaps the most enduring type is the ethnoterrorist organization, the basic purpose of which is to utilize terrorist tactics in order to ultimately foster new nation-states for stateless ethnic groups. Examples of ethnoterrorist organizations include the Corsican National Liberation Front, the Palestine Liberation Organization (PLO), the Puerto Rican Armed Forces of National Liberation (FALN), the Puerto Rican Los Macheteros, and the Puerto Rican Armed Revolutionary Movement.

Given the fact that the Corsican National Liberation Front has neither received state sponsorship nor attacked targets outside of France, that terrorist organization is a fine example of the pure intranational generation. The FALN, Los Macheteros, and the Armed Revolutionary Movement are organizations which have restricted their attacks within the borders of the United States (including Puerto Rico); however, they must be classed as second-generation, international terrorist organizations in that each has received financial and other active support from the government of Cuba. The PLO, which accepted financial and other active support from any number of Arab nation-states, and conducted its attacks across national boundaries, is another example of an international terrorist organization.[7]

Right-wing terrorist organizations have become an increasingly serious problem in the United States and Europe. Members are obsessed with an imagined "new world order," within which certain intergovernmental organizations (such as the United Nations and the World Bank), as well as certain minority groups, have supposedly "colonized" power-ful nation-states. These organizations and groups are thus obvious tar-gets for right-wing terrorists.

There is no evidence that any contemporary right-wing terrorist or-ganization receives nation-state support. Moreover, these organizations are not known to have conducted actual operations across national bor-ders. There is evidence, nonetheless, that the advent and growth of the Internet is leading to increased transnational communication between such organizations. For example, a shared sense of transnational racial identity, rather than specific national identity, is becoming an ideologi-cal link between right-wing terrorist organizations in the United States and Europe. Thus, such organizations may well evolve from almost purely intranational to more distinctly transnational. Examples of right-wing terrorist organizations and the nation-states within which they op-erate include the Aryan Nations and the Order (United States), Black Order and New Order (Italy), and S O S France (France).[8]

Religious, or "theoterrorist," organizations are motivated by reli-gious, cultural, and ultimately political issues. Theoterrorist organiza-tions are exemplified by groups as diverse as the radical Christian fun-damentalist Army of God, the radical Islamic fundamentalist al-Qaeda, and the radical Jewish Gush Emunim ("Bloc of the Faithful"). The Army of God and Gush Emunim are fairly clear examples of intranational ter-rorist organizations. Al-Qaeda, on the other hand, is perhaps the pre-mier example of a transnational terrorist organization.

The third generation of terrorist organization is the transnational. As one of the two primary subjects of this book, transnational terror-ist organizations merit special attention. Before turning to that topic, however, the global stage upon which transnational terrorist organiza-tions thrive—the other major theme of this book—needs to be set. That global stage, the new global disorder, is the focus of the next chapter.

CHAPTER TWO

The Rise of the New Global Disorder

The old order changeth, yielding place to new.
ALFRED, LORD TENNYSON, "THE PASSING OF ARTHUR"

A NUMBER OF RECENT DEVELOPMENTS in global politics have helped shape an entirely new type of global system. These developments have led to the replacement of the old global order by a new global disorder, the emergence of which illustrates the important principle of change in global systems. In order to grasp the nature of that change, it is first necessary to understand: (1) the basic types of global systems, and (2) the basic types of global actors which populate those systems.

Global Polarity

Global systems have traditionally been classified according to the number of system "poles," or power centers, which exist within them. Most scholars of global politics, such as John T. Rourke, believe that three such polar systems have been present at one historical moment or another. The first is the bipolar system, in which two nation-states, or alliances of nation-states, dominate global politics. The second is the tripolar system, or "triangular" relationship, in which three nation-states, or alliances of nation-states, dominate the global system. The third is the multipolar, or "balance-of-power" system, in which as few as four to as many as perhaps ten nation-states, or alliances of nation-states, dominate global politics.[1]

According to Rourke and other scholars of global politics, one of the best ways to understand the nature of any global system is to grasp the most important "rules of the game" for that system. For bipolar systems, the rules of the game are:

(1) Eliminate the other bloc by techniques including war, if it is necessary and the risks are acceptable.

(2) Increase power relative to the other bloc by such techniques as bringing new members into your bloc and preventing others from joining the rival bloc.

For tripolar systems, the rules of the game are:

>(1) Optimally, try to have good relations with both other players or, minimally, try to avoid having hostile relations with both other players.
>
>(2) Try to prevent close cooperation between the other two players.

For multipolar systems, the rules of the game are:

>(1) Oppose any actor or alliance that threatens to become hegemonic [i.e., overly dominant]. This is also the central principle of balance-of-power politics.
>
>(2) Increase power or, at least, preserve your power. Do so by negotiating if possible but by fighting if necessary.
>
>(3) Even if fighting, do not destabilize the system by destroying another major actor.[2]

Bipolar, tripolar, and multipolar global systems have been present during various periods during the pre-1991, old global order era.

A bipolar system dominated global politics from 1945 to 1972. During this period, the democratic nation-states of the West, led by the United States, and the communist nation-states of the East, led by the Soviet Union, fought what is customarily referred to as the cold war, which generally involved nonviolent conflict between the two sides. For example, the West sought to contain the East primarily through the stationing of defensive military forces in western Europe in order to counter the positioning of offensive military forces in eastern Europe.[3]

Cold war conflict also involved nonviolent skirmishes between East and West. Particularly dramatic examples included crisis "brinksmanship," such as the Berlin blockade of 1948, the Berlin Wall crisis of 1961, and the Cuban missile crisis of 1962. By going to the very brink of nuclear war, the two blocs demonstrated their desire, if not total dedication, to observe the first rule of bipolarity: eliminate the other bloc by whatever means possible.[4]

Cold war rivalry occasionally turned, however, into a "hot" or shooting war, as during the Korean and Vietnam conflicts. Throughout these primarily civil wars, the United States and her allies lent massive military and economic assistance to noncommunist South Korea and South Vietnam; the Soviet bloc states provided similar aid to communist North Korea and North Vietnam. In providing that aid, the two blocs observed, however roughly, Rourke's second rule of bipolarity: "Increase power relative to the other bloc by bringing new members into your bloc and preventing others from joining the rival bloc."[5]

From roughly 1972 to 1991, a triangular, or tripolar, system dominated the global stage. The poles of this relationship consisted of the two cold war adversaries, the United States and the Soviet Union, and the People's Republic of China, which had aligned herself with the Soviet Union from 1949 until the late 1950s. From 1972 to 1991, both the United States and the Soviet Union attempted to foster a more positive relationship with China. Each of the two superpowers also sought to discourage China from establishing a similar relationship with the other actor. This "playing of the China card" thus observed the major rules of tripolarity, which caution against both having hostile relations with the two other players and allowing close cooperation between them.[6]

Although the collapse of the Soviet Union in 1991 spelled the official end of this era of tripolarity, the United States, Soviet successor-state Russia, and China continue to pursue friendly relations with each other whenever possible. Moreover, each of these three nation-states attempts to prevent the remaining two actors from forming an alliance against itself.

The nation-states of Europe shared relations within an essentially multipolar, or balance-of-power, system from the mid-seventeenth century until 1945. During this roughly three-hundred-year period, four to as many as perhaps nine powers dominated the European regional system at any one time. As colonial powers, many of these European nation-states also served as masters of the global system as a whole. Spain, Sweden, Britain, France, Prussia (later Germany), the Austrian Empire (later Austria-Hungary), the Ottoman Empire, Italy, and Russia (later the Soviet Union) were the most notable such power centers during the long history of European, and global, multipolarity. During the waning years of multipolarity (1905–1945), two non-European nation-states, the United States and Japan, became major power centers, and colonial powers, in their own right.[7]

Nevertheless, none of these nation-states, or any alliance comprising these nation-states, was able to dominate either the European continent or the global system for any extended period of time. This was due largely to the commitment of Britain, and later the United States, to maintaining a balance-of-power system in which no single actor or combination of actors could dominate Europe. When first France during the Napoleonic Wars, and then Germany during the two world wars, threatened to destroy this balance-of-power system, Britain, and later the United States, successfully intervened in order to preserve a European balance of power. Hence, Rourke's first rule for multipolar systems, to "oppose any actor or alliance that threatens to become hegemonic," was successfully observed. Moreover, this was generally accomplished without the permanent destruction of any major actor (thus observing Rourke's third rule of multipolarity), a measure which might have permanently upset the European balance of power.[8]

A Nonpolar Moment

The advent of a new type of global system forces a thorough rethinking of the entire concept of polarity. Key trends forcing this reexamination include:

(1) the disintegration, deterioration, or extremely short lifespan of major military alliances
(2) the rise of scores of new small- and medium-size powers
(3) increasing permeability, and irrelevance, of nation-state borders
(4) the increasing influence of new types of global actors

These trends have all contributed in a major way to the dawning of what may be termed *the new global disorder.*[9]

The deterioration or disintegration of a number of major military alliances has also helped lead to the decline of the once-stable bipolar and tripolar global systems of 1945–1991. For example, the collapse of the Soviet Union led directly to the demise of the Soviet-imposed Warsaw Pact military alliance. These developments also doomed the once-thriving military and economic relationship between Eastern bloc patron-states such as the Soviet Union, East Germany, and Czechoslovakia and client-states such as Egypt, Syria, Iraq, North Korea, and Cuba. Another major standing military alliance, the North Atlantic Treaty Organization (NATO), is now plagued both by a seeming lack of clear purpose and by members who frequently refuse to suggest, advance, or even observe alliance policy. Other, once-major standing military alliances, such as the U.S.-led Southeast Asia Treaty Organization (SEATO) and Central Treaty Organization (CENTO), have in recent years become subjects for diplomatic history rather than global politics textbooks. Ad hoc, or special, temporary military alliances, such as the anti-Iraq "Gulf Coalition," have had, and should continue to have, a fairly short shelf life. The new global system thus richly illustrates former French president Charles de Gaulle's shrewd observation that "nation-states have no allies, only mutual interests."

Although the population of major military alliances has clearly dwindled, the number of influential nation-states has risen sharply. Many new small- and medium-size powers, such as Kazakhstan, Uzbekistan, the Czech Republic, a unified Germany, and Serbia, have emerged from the ranks of the former Soviet Union, her former Warsaw Pact members, other former Soviet bloc allies, and the former Yugoslavia. More such powers have risen from the likes of "rogue states" (i.e., nation-states which violate global norms of behavior), such as North Korea, Iraq, Iran, Libya, and Sudan. Many of these rogue states, such as North Korea and Iraq, are former client states of the now-defunct Soviet bloc.

The increasing permeability, and irrelevance, of nation-state borders is another factor contributing to the crumbling of the old global order. Factors spurring this trend include the creation of intergovernmental organizations such as the European Union (EU), within which travelers may freely cross once-restricted nation-state borders. Critical, too, is the development of the Internet and satellite technology, and the overall growth of global communications empires which serve to shrink the global village.

Finally, the increasing prominence of independent nonstate actors, such as intergovernmental and transnational organizations, has made the whole notion of polarity obsolete. Many international organizations, such as the United Nations, are by their very nature actors whose mission precludes gravitation around any particular pole. Transnational organizations, such as transnational terrorist organizations, corporations, or syndicates, are by their very nature independent actors whose formal presence around any fixed pole would be both inconvenient and undesirable.

The Polyplex Global System

These developments have culminated in a far more congested, complex, and disorganized global system in which the whole notion of polarity has lost a good deal of its past relevance. Indeed, the traditional concept of a polar global system may be discarded in place of an entirely new notion—that of a "polyplex" global system. The term *polyplex* combines the notions of *poly,* or many, and *plex,* from the word *complex,* to suggest extreme complication and disorder. The suffix *-plex* also suggests a tight interweaving of various "plaits" or "strands"—in this case, global actors. The term *polyplex* thus describes a global system in which many global actors, and many types of global actors, interact tightly in an exceedingly difficult, unruly, congested, shrinking, nonpolar, and swiftly evolving world.

Is this polyplex global system subject to any systemic rules? Nonpolar polyplex global systems, unlike polar global systems, are in all likelihood not governed by any particularly firm rules. Nonetheless, it is probably wise for both nation-state and nonstate actors within polyplex global systems to pay heed to certain flexible guidelines, if not outright rules:

(1) Formulate pragmatic, flexible new "rules of the game" drawn from actual experience with polyplex global systems.

(2) Try to create ad hoc—even if necessarily temporary—blocs, consisting of varying types of actors, to deal with threats posed by hostile actors or blocs.

(3) Attempt to prevent or otherwise discourage alliances between hostile actors or blocs.

What major actors populate this polyplex global system? Nation-states, which govern territory and remain the principal users of coercive force (e.g., military and public security forces), certainly remain among the most significant actors in any type of global system, including the evolving polyplex system. It is certainly true that the permeability and increasing irrelevance of nation-state borders and the rise of other types of actors are factors which have diminished the central role that nation-states once played. Nevertheless, nation-states enjoy unique privileges—such as sovereignty over territory and the possession of vast military arsenals—which are naturally denied to other types of global actors. Yet nation-states, which during the heyday of polarity had held a virtual monopoly on global power, must now share power with other types of actors within a polyplex system.

Intergovernmental organizations, whose members are nation-states, and which require agreement among nation-states, have become important actors since the conclusion of the Second World War. Examples include the United Nations (U.N.), NATO, the North American Free Trade Agreement (NAFTA), and the EU. Intergovernmental organizations have enjoyed various levels of achievement. Despite the fact that many U.N. resolutions, or statements of policy, are routinely ignored by large numbers of nation-states, on many recent occasions, U.N.-

sponsored military actions (e.g., Operation Desert Storm) and economic sanctions (e.g., against South Africa, Iraq, and Libya) have enjoyed varying degrees of success. Although NATO has seemingly become less relevant since the disintegration of the Warsaw Pact, it has played a major role in helping to resolve ethnic conflicts in the Balkans. Indeed, the evolving relevance of NATO has been evidenced by the fact that many former Warsaw Pact nation-states have sought, and in certain cases received, membership within the ranks of their old adversaries. Despite complaints from some quarters of American society, the continued implementation of NAFTA reflects the increasing importance of international economic integration. And the European Union continues to unify much of Europe along not only economic but also political and military lines.

Even more critical, however, are transnational organizations— wholly nonstate actors. Transnational organizations are self-sufficient, privately supported organizations that transcend both nation-state borders and any need of nation-state sponsorship. Moreover, these organizations pursue their own transnational interests across the territorial borders of numerous nation-states.[10]

Intergovernmental organizations and transnational organizations are very different forms of global actors. One way to distinguish between them is that intergovernmental organizations require accord among nation-states in order to pursue their aims. Transnational organizations, which lack territory of their own, require access to nation-states in order to pursue their aims. Since only nation-states or military alliances may resort to overt military invasion, this particular type of access includes either invitation or infiltration.

There are at least eight types of transnational organizations. These include corporations; crime syndicates; professional, humanitarian, environmental, and religious organizations; religious cults; and terrorist organizations.

Transnational corporations are business firms which are based in one nation-state, yet do business in many nation-states. Significant examples (with their major products in parentheses) include General Motors and Toyota (motor vehicles), ExxonMobil (petroleum products), and Philip Morris (tobacco products). Transnational corporations have tremendous economic power—and, by extension, political power. For example, the gross revenues, or total earnings, of certain transnational corporations are consistently greater then the combined gross domestic product of several of the world's medium-size nation-states.

Transnational crime syndicates are organizations which produce and distribute illegal drugs, arms, and other goods and services on a global basis. Contemporary examples include the Sicilian mafia, the Russian mafiya, and the Chinese triads. Other examples include the Medellín and Cali drug cartels, which, although based in Colombia, distributed their products through global networks. It might also be noted that the line between terrorism and drug trafficking sometimes becomes blurred. This dynamic, sometimes termed *narco-terrorism*, occurs when: (1) transnational crime syndicates resort to terrorist tactics, (2) terrorist organizations themselves resort to drug trafficking, or (3) terrorist organizations forge interorganizational alliances with transnational crime syndicates in order to help finance their activities.[11]

Other examples of transnational organizations include transnational professional, humanitarian, environmental, and religious organizations, religious cults, and terrorist organizations. Transnational professional organizations represent and promote professional interests on a global basis. Examples include the International Olympic Committee, the International Political Science Association, and the International Studies Association. Transnational humanitarian organizations promote human rights concerns on a global basis. Examples include the International Red Cross and Amnesty International. Transnational environmental organizations are organizations which (for the most part legally and peacefully) promote ecological concerns on a global basis. Examples include the World Wide Fund for Nature and the International Wildlife Coalition. Transnational religious organizations seek to peacefully promote their religious beliefs and interests on a transnational basis. Examples include both mainstream religious organizations, such as the Presbyterian Church, and transnational religious cults. (It is interesting to note that one such mainstream organization, the Roman Catholic Church, is also a nation-state—Vatican City.) Transnational religious cults are tightly knit and united by total devotion to a leader who serves as the source of the organization's ideology. Examples include Aum Shinrikyo (which might also be considered as both a transnational corporation and a transnational terrorist organization), the People's Temple, and the Solar Temple.

Transnational terrorist organizations, which are among the most frightening illustrations of transnational organizations functioning within a polyplex global system, are the topic of the next chapter.

CHAPTER THREE

Transnational Terrorism
and the New Global Disorder

*Take, for instance, a twig and a pillar, or the ugly person and the great
beauty, and all the strange and monstrous transformations. These are all
leveled together by Tao. Division is the same as creation; creation is the
same as destruction.* CHUANG TZU, "ON LEVELING ALL THINGS"

THE THOROUGH TRANSFORMATION of the global system roughly parallels the dramatic
evolution of terrorism. Just as nation-states once functioned as supreme
actors dominating a highly structured global order, the typical terrorist
organization once operated within the clearly defined borders of a single
nation-state. Since the first rumblings of the new global disorder, however, nation-states have had little choice but to grudgingly and awk-
wardly share the global stage with relatively new types of actors. One
such new type of actor is the transnational organization, and one of the
most significant examples is the transnational terrorist organization.

The transformation of the old polar global order into a new polyplex
global disorder was examined in the previous chapter. This chapter explores a number of related questions:

(1) What methods are used by transnational terrorist organizations to
become dynamic, self-sustaining global actors which so significantly
contribute to the new global disorder?

(2) In what ways has the new global disorder itself contributed to the
problem of transnational terrorism?

(3) What is the specific nature of transnational terrorism?

Transnational Terrorism: Means and Opportunities

The transnational terrorist organization (TTO) is by no means a com-
pletely different form of transnational, or terrorist, actor. Like all transnational organizations, TTOs (1) are self-sufficient, privately supported
organizations that transcend both nation-state boundaries and any need
of nation-state sponsorship; (2) pursue their own transnational interests
across the territorial borders of numerous nation-states; and (3) lacking
sovereign territory of their own, require access to nation-states in order

to pursue their aims. Like all terrorist organizations, TTOs (1) use, or threaten to use, violence imposed from below against certain symbolic victims or objects, and (2) utilize these means in order to indirectly coerce a primary target (typically, a nation-state or nation-states) to accept some demanded outcome through the fomenting of intense fear or anxiety.

As previously noted, there are, on the other hand, important functional and organizational differences between the three generations of terrorist organizations. First-generation, intranational terrorist organizations, which neither require nor receive financial or other support from nation-states, conduct their operations entirely within the boundaries of a particular nation-state. Second-generation, international terrorist organizations and third-generation, transnational terrorist organizations routinely conduct their activities across nation-state borders. Unlike international terrorist organizations, however, TTOs neither require nor receive nation-state sponsorship. TTOs are thus genuinely transnational in nature, in that they are independent, privately financed organizations whose global operations—like those of transnational corporations or crime syndicates—necessitate only some degree of access to a nation-state's territory in order to plan and conduct their operations. Operations within these territories, moreover, may be readily shifted across national borders as circumstances favorable to the TTO, rather than any particular nation-state, may dictate.[1]

Three basic tactics enable transnational terrorist organizations to secure access to a nation-state's territory. These tactics are brought into play when transnational terrorist organizations exploit

(1) common ideological beliefs or political interests shared with the ruling regime of a nation-state or substate region

(2) the decline or disintegration of a nation-state's legitimate central authority, or effective challenges to that authority by religious, ethnic, or political strife

(3) various covert methods used to penetrate the borders of nation-states whose central governments may possess no, weak, or even strong degrees of authority

In the first instance, transnational terrorist organizations frequently share ideological beliefs and political interests with the ruling regime of a particular nation-state or substate region. For example, al-Qaeda, a loosely structured, far-flung TTO, was once welcomed by Islamic fundamentalist regimes which shared some or all of that organization's religious, political, and social beliefs. One of those regimes continues to govern most of Sudan; the other once governed much of Afghanistan.

In the second instance, TTOs (like transnational crime syndicates) are able to base or otherwise conduct their operations in nation-states where fierce political, religious, or ethnic conflict has caused central authority to be seriously challenged. As Stephen Sloan notes, transnational terrorists

> . . . move in what has been called the "gray areas," those regions where control has shifted from legitimate governments to new half-political, half-criminal powers. In this environment the line between state and rogue state, and rogue state and criminal enterprise will be increasingly blurred. Each will seek out new and profitable targets through terrorism in an international order that is already under assault.[2]

The growing number of nation-states which are vulnerable to TTO (and transnational crime syndicate) penetration is a source of increasingly serious concern to a variety of global actors, including nation-states, intergovernmental organizations, and transnational corporations.[3]

Lastly, TTOs are also able to gain access to nation-state territory through various covert means. In some cases, TTOs pay secret bribes to government officials. There are strong indications that al-Qaeda may have utilized this tactic in order to gain bases of operation in Sudan and Afghanistan. The positioning of covert operatives under false pretexts is another favorite tactic. Entering a target nation-state by carrying false student, business, or travel identification is a tactic that can be used effectively against weak and powerful nation-states alike. These tactics are particularly effective in penetrating the borders of the great democracies of the world, as Americans learned to their horror after September 11, 2001. They are effective because of relatively little restriction on the movement of foreign visitors who enter these nation-states for what appear to be legitimate purposes. Transnational terrorists have also used these methods to enter nation-states as diverse as Canada, France, Britain, Germany, Belgium, Argentina, Jordan, Kuwait, Bangladesh, Australia, Russia, Zaire, and even China and Iran. One example is that of Aum Shinrikyo, a Japanese-based organization which was part transnational religious cult, part transnational corporation, and part transnational terrorist organization. In 1992, members of Aum Shinrikyo traveled to Zaire in order to obtain Ebola virus samples. In entering Zaire, this organization claimed to be on a "relief" or "humanitarian" mission.[4]

Despite the views of some observers, international terrorist organizations, which must constantly defer to the political, military, and economic interests of their nation-state sponsors, are not transnational in nature, due to their inability to transcend their need for nation-state sponsorship. For example, the interests of nation-states such as Sudan, Jordan, Tunisia, Libya, and the former Soviet Union have almost always taken precedence over the goals of their clients, such as the Palestine Liberation Organization (PLO), the Popular Front for the Liberation of Palestine (PFLP), the Popular Front for the Liberation of Palestine–General Command, the Palestine Liberation Front (PLF), the Abu Nidal organization, the Red Army Faction, and the Red Brigades. In these cases, whenever the relationship between client and sponsor proved to be too much of a political, military, or economic burden to the sponsor, the relationship was always severed, sometimes bloodily. Moreover, the termination of that relationship was almost always structured along terms favorable to the nation-state involved, rather than to the terrorist organization.

There are a number of examples, some quite dramatic, that illustrate this stubborn pattern. The Abu Nidal organization was expelled from Sudan in 1970 after it had begun to recruit exiled Palestinian students who had taken up residence there. In September 1970, the PFLP, then supported by Jordan, hijacked to Jordan or otherwise attacked four commercial jetliners. Jordan's King Hussein responded to these humiliating events by quelling the uprising, ordering the killing of hundreds of Palestinian terrorists, and expelling various Palestinian terrorist organizations from Jordan. In 1985, when the PLO's headquarters in Tunisia were bombed during an Israeli air raid, the Tunisian government quickly seized upon the raid as an opportunity to discard its client. When the Libyan cities of Tripoli and Benghazi were subjected to U.S. air raids in retaliation for Libyan leader Moammar Qadafy's sponsorship of a 1986 West Berlin nightclub bombing, Qadafy promptly and drastically scaled back his overt patronage of numerous international terrorist organizations. When various Palestinian and left-wing terrorist organizations backed by the Soviet Union and other Eastern bloc nation-states no longer served the interests of those nation-states, sponsorship was abruptly withdrawn.[5]

The fact that TTOs may place their own needs at the top of their own agendas clearly demonstrates their ability to function fairly autonomously within the new global disorder. An excellent example occurred after the September 11, 2001, attacks against the World Trade Center and the Pentagon. Seizing upon clear evidence of al-Qaeda involvement, President George W. Bush demanded that Afghanistan's former Taliban regime "hand over the terrorists" to U.S. officials. Although it was clearly in the interest of the Taliban regime to expel al-Qaeda from Afghanistan, that regime was either unwilling or unable to do so. With respect to autonomy, TTOs may thus actually bear a closer resemblance to first-generation, intranational terrorist groups than to second-generation, international ones. In at least this respect, it appears that the evolution of terrorist organizations has come full circle.

The Nature of Transnational Terrorism

What, in more specific terms, is the nature of transnational terrorism? In order to better understand the nature of TTOs, it is first necessary to analyze three elements which provide identity for them (and, as a general matter, for any terrorist organization). These elements include (1) motivations, (2) behavior and structure, and (3) choice of incidents and targets.

First-generation (and, to some degree, earlier second-generation) terrorist organizations were easily identified as durable and static, with goals—such as the payment of ransom or the release of imprisoned members—which were generally clear and relatively limited. Such goals were, if not justifiable, at least comprehensible to external observers. Transnational terrorist organizations, on the other hand, fail to communicate realistic or clear-cut goals. Many TTOs, in fact, issue no verbal communications related to their attacks, or, in certain cases, their existence itself.

Unlike previous generations of terrorist organizations, many TTOs also tend to have extremely short life spans. Most TTOs are in fact small, ad hoc entities, or cells, created for the ultimate purpose of contributing to a single act of terrorism. These cells typically serve as subunits of larger, more permanent TTOs. Operational secrecy between, and even within, individual cells means that the apprehension of specific members or even entire cells may pose little or no threat to other cell members, other cells, or the TTO as a whole.

Moreover, factionalism within larger TTOs occasionally leads to the establishment of splinter organizations, which may or may not continue to associate with—or may actually turn against—their parent TTOs. Alliances or coalitions between similar or even diverse TTOs, between TTOs and transnational crime syndicates, or between TTOs and international terrorist organizations also naturally lead to multiple centers of decision-making.

The issue of TTO membership must also be noted. Transnational terrorist organizations make heavy use of so-called sleeper cells, whose members remain inactive—and, most critically, unnoticed—until they receive their operational orders. TTOs also welcome the efforts of so-called amateurs, individuals who have neither prior terrorist experience nor criminal records. Also known as "freelancers," these individuals may independently subcontract their services to various TTOs (or transnational crime syndicates). TTOs also utilize "cut-outs"—unwitting patsies or pawns. A TTO may even consist of a "lone wolf," a single individual whose sinister aims are virtually undetectable, and whose rudimentary organization is almost impossible to infiltrate.

Given the peculiar structure, personnel characteristics, and personnel dynamics of most TTOs, it should come as no surprise that they are extremely effective in carrying out their specific activities. The old global order counterterrorist had the luxury of focusing on a more-or-less known quantity of homogeneous individuals who were members of a relatively durable and static terrorist organization. For now understandable reasons, counterterrorists enjoy no such luxury in the new global disorder.

Like more recent international terrorists, transnational terrorists tend to engage in indistinct, indiscriminate, and almost incomprehensible acts of violence resulting in large numbers of casualties. They have also begun to make more and more frequent use of what are commonly referred to as weapons of mass destruction (WMDs). Thus far, those weapons have included: (1) large, sophisticated, conventional explosive devices, (2) nonconventional chemical and biological substances, and even (3) large makeshift weapons. Furthermore, there is general consensus, if not universal agreement, that TTOs (as well as other types of terrorist organizations) will execute future nonconventional or "superterrorist" scenarios, which would involve the further deployment of chemical or biological weapons as well as the use of radiological or even nuclear arms.

What is most relevant about the willingness of TTOs to use weapons of mass destruction is that they typically exhibit little restraint in selecting their targets. Earlier terrorist organizations had indeed observed the dictum that terrorists "want a lot of people watching, not a lot of people dead." These groups preferred to limit the numbers and types of casualties produced by their acts. Later international, and transnational, terrorist organizations have tended to demonstrate no such restraint. Indeed, while the number of terrorist incidents has actually decreased in recent years, the number of terrorism-related casualties (both deaths and injuries) has dramatically increased during the same period. Moreover, more recent transnational terrorist targets have come to include high-profile, highly populated physical symbols of Western—and particularly American—influence.[6]

Lastly, transnational—like more recent international—terrorists rarely claim responsibility for their behavior. First-generation and earlier second-generation terrorist organizations frequently claimed credit or responsibility for their acts via lengthy communiqués or brief statements, generally issued through the news media. On the other hand, anonymous terrorism has become the norm, rather than the exception, during the last fifteen to twenty years. What, for instance, were the stated goals of the 1993 World Trade Center bombing, the nearly simultaneous bombings of the U.S. embassies in Nairobi, Kenya, and Dar es Salaam, Tanzania, in 1998, the bombing of the destroyer USS *Cole* in 2000, or the suicide hijackings of September 11, 2001? What was the stated purpose of the release of lethal sarin nerve gas in the cities of Matsumoto and Tokyo, Japan, in 1994 and 1995? Although intensive investigation revealed that these horrific acts were the work of transnational terrorists, no organization ever made demands clearly associated with those acts. Moreover, it was not until after arrests were made for these attacks that responsibility for their commission was even acknowledged, let alone claimed.

Later international and transnational terrorists have not wished to be identified for a number of entirely rational reasons. First, there is increasing determination among many nation-states to seek out, capture, prosecute, and punish terrorists. Coupled with this determination is a new level of sophistication in counterterrorist strategies, tactics, and equipment. Openly claiming responsibility for major terrorist attacks simply invites further unwanted exposure, public outrage, and, potentially, the very destruction of the entire organization.

There are a number of other reasons why transnational terrorists no longer feel a need to claim authorship for their acts. These include:

(1) the growing strength of transnational terrorist organizations

(2) the increasing refusal or inability of nation-states to grant the demands of terrorists

(3) the tremendous and widespread publicity automatically generated by any employment of weapons of mass destruction

(4) the fact that anonymous terrorist acts may be even more terrifying to the public than acts for which authorship is formally claimed

(5) the fact that transnational terrorists who have religious motivations may feel that their act alone serves as a means of communication with the only audience which matters—i.e., God[7]

There are certain specific factors which have served to increase the number of TTOs. The five most important factors contributing to the growth of transnational terrorism during the new global disorder period are:

(1) the development of religious issues which transcend nation-state boundaries

(2) the increasing permeability of nation-state borders

(3) the development of new sources of funding and other support

(4) the growing availability of weapons of mass destruction

(5) dramatic advances in communications technology

First, many religious issues transcend nation-state borders. For example, radical Islamic fundamentalists who demand nothing less than a total Western retreat from the entire Islamic world feel compelled to attack Western interests throughout the world. These attacks have taken place in Asia, Africa, Europe, North America, and South America.

Second, nation-state borders are becoming increasingly permeable or even irrelevant. In Europe, the advent of the European Union (EU) is gradually bringing about the virtual tearing down of many European border crossings. One may only speculate as to whether the disintegration of Europe's borders will be accompanied by an equivalent increase in trust and cooperation among those best equipped to counter transnational terrorists—that is, Europe's national intelligence agencies. If cooperation continues to increase, then the maturation of the EU will greatly enhance Europe's ability to deal with TTOs operating on that continent. Travel across the borders separating Canada, the United States, and Mexico—still relatively easy—also satisfies the mobility requirements of transnational terrorists and simplifies their task of obtaining access to large areas of nation-state territory. The disintegration of the former Soviet Union, Yugoslavia, and other nation-states, and the accompanying advent of newly established (and vaguely defined) nation-state borders, further serves the needs of TTOs. The development of the Internet also makes the notion of nation-state borders increasingly irrelevant. This shrinking of the global village greatly, albeit unintentionally, contributes to the scourge of transnational terrorism.[8]

Third, as nation-states have become more reluctant to finance or otherwise support terrorist organizations, the specter of international, state-supported terrorism has declined. As always, money is the lifeblood of terrorist organizations; all terrorist organizations, without exception, need some source of financing and support. Like the intranational terrorist organizations of an earlier era, transnational terrorist organizations are largely self-sufficient because they have been able to turn to nonstate sources for financing and support. These sources include other TTOs, other types of transnational actors (e.g., transnational crime syndicates), and miscellaneous private sources.

Fourth, weapons of mass destruction have become cheaper and easier for terrorist organizations to acquire. This fact provides TTOs with additional options to consider when engaging in their activities. The prospect of chemical, biological, radiological, or even nuclear weapons obtained by transnational terrorists from within the former Soviet republics, or other nations, is an issue which is taken very seriously by nation-states throughout the world. Chemical and biological weapons are also available to transnational terrorists from any number of other public sources; this too is a matter which haunts global policymakers. Surface-to-air missiles, such as American-made Stingers, and surface-to-surface missiles have been available to various types of terrorist organizations for years. In addition, surface-to-surface missiles may be guided to their targets by inexpensive global positioning systems (GPS).

Lastly, dramatic advancements in communications technology allow terrorists to transmit messages to one another much more easily, much more cheaply, and in greater secrecy than in the past. The development of the Internet and of cellular telecommunications makes it considerably easier for transnational terrorists and their allies to engage in global communications. It has also been speculated that transnational terrorists utilize "embedded" Internet or video—so-called messages-within-messages. Equally alarming is the growing availability of advanced encryption technology, which makes it possible for terrorists to convey sensitive, coded information in greatly increased secrecy. And, of course, when all else fails, TTOs may (as al-Qaeda has since at least 1998) employ simple human means of communication.[9]

CHAPTER FOUR

Ethnoterrorism:
Menace from Within and Without

In friendship false, implacable in hate,
Resolv'd to ruin or to rule the state.

JOHN DRYDEN, "ABSALOM AND ACHITOPHEL"

THE NEW GLOBAL DISORDER is rich with irony, paradox, and contradiction. On the one hand, the dawning of the twenty-first century has been hailed as a period of increasing "globalization." On the other hand, the advent of the millennium is condemned as an era of renewed "tribalization." Globalization is the technological and cultural shrinking of the global community, leading to the presumed emergence of some broad form of global identity, or even global citizenship. Tribalization, on the other hand, is the fragmentation of nation-state populations along relatively narrow ethnic, religious, or other such "tribal" lines.

In his provocative and highly influential book, *Jihad vs. McWorld,* Benjamin R. Barber argues convincingly that civilization is being reshaped not by globalization or tribalization alone, but by both. As Barber puts it,

> . . . our world and our lives are caught between what William Butler Yeats called the two eternities of race and soul: that of race reflecting the tribal past, that of soul anticipating the cosmopolitan future. . . . The first scenario rooted in race holds out the grim prospect of a re-tribalization of large swaths of humankind by war and bloodshed: a threatened balkanization of nation-states in which culture is pitted against culture, people against people, tribe against tribe. . . . The second paints that future in shimmering pastels, a busy portrait of onrushing economic, technological, and ecological forces that demand integration and uniformity and that mesmerize peoples everywhere with fast music, fast computers, and fast food—MTV, Macintosh, and McDonald's—pressing nations into one homogenous global theme park, one McWorld tied together by communications, information, entertainment, and commerce.[1]

Barber is quite correct. The new global disorder is characterized not merely by globalization or tribalization, but rather, by both of these powerful forces.

Ethnoterrorism, or terrorism intended to foster new nation-states for stateless ethnic groups, is one of the more dramatic and frightening consequences of tribalization. Ethnoterrorism is also one of the most common and widespread forms of contemporary terrorism, as well as the oldest and most enduring form of transnational terrorism. In analyzing the problem of ethnoterrorism, this chapter addresses four essential questions:

(1) What is meant by the terms *ethnicity* and *ethnic group*?

(2) What factors lead to violent conflict between ethnic groups?

(3) Why are ethnicity and ethnic conflict fundamentally transnational phenomena?

(4) How do major ethnoterrorist organizations illustrate that ethno-terrorism has become, in large part, a transnational issue?

What Is Ethnicity?

Many observers find that the terms *ethnicity* and *ethnic group* are excruciatingly difficult to define. In suggesting what is perhaps the best single definition for the term *ethnic group*, renowned sociologist Talcott Parsons states:

> In spite of the difficulty of being specific about criterial features and components, what social scientists have called ethnic groups do belong to a relatively distinctive sociological type. This is a group the members of which have, both with respect to their own sentiments and those of non-members, a distinctive identity which is rooted in some kind of a distinctive sense of its history. It is, moreover, a diffusely defined group sociologically quite different from collectivities with specific functions. For the members it characterizes what the individual *is* rather than what he *does*.[2]

Parsons goes on to observe that ethnicity

> . . . is a primary collective aspect concerning the identity of whole persons, not of any particular aspect of them. Common culture is probably the most important general core, but it is a culture which has some feature of temporal continuity often reaching into an indefinite past. An ethnic group is, of course, always a group consisting of members of all ages and both sexes and ethnicity is always shared by forebears at some level. It is thus a transgenerational type of group.[3]

On the individual level, ethnicity enables a person to answer the question, Who am I *as a whole person?* rather than, Why is this *part of me* like it is? A sense of ethnicity allows an individual to answer this question with rejoinders such as, I am a Pole, I am a Basque, or I am a Jew. A sense of ethnicity does not, however, enable an individual to answer questions such as, Why do I have blond hair? or, Why do I have a fair complexion? or, Why do I have blond hair and a fair complexion? Ethnicity also allows an individual to understand who he or she is, rather than what he or she does. It enables an individual to understand that he or she is of Polish, Basque, or Jewish descent, but not why he or she pursues a particular career or hobby.

Parsons is quite correct. On the collective level, an ethnic group is a group of individuals who share the same ethnicity. Poles, Basques, and Jews are three such groups. An ethnic group, as a whole, also has a distinct shared identity and sense of history, and a common culture rooted in that history. Lastly, as may be observed in these three examples, all ethnic groups are comprised of individuals of both genders and of all ages.[4]

The terms *ethnicity* and *nationalism* are frequently used interchangeably, or in combination. Taking a more useful approach, Michael Ignatieff clearly distinguishes between "civic nationalism" and "ethnic nationalism." For Ignatieff, civic nationalism

> . . . maintains that the nation should be composed of all those—regardless of race, color, creed, gender, language, or ethnicity—who should subscribe to the nation's political creed. This nationalism is called civic because it envisages the nation as a community of equal, rights-bearing citizens, united in patriotic attachment to a shared set of political practices and values.[5]

Ethnic nationalism implies, on the other hand,

> . . . that an individual's deepest attachments are inherited, not chosen. It is the national community that defines the individual, not the individuals who define the national community. This psychology of belonging may have greater depth than civic nationalism's, but the sociology that accompanies it is a good deal less realistic.[6]

Ignatieff's perspectives are entirely sound. He views civic nationalism—which may be chosen—as far more artificial than ethnic nationalism, which is inherited.[7]

The term *race* has also been used either synonymously or in combination with the term *ethnicity,* as in the use of the compound term *ethnic race*. Rather, the term *race* should apply to physical characteristics, usually in combination—such as blond hair and fair complexion—which are inherited, rather than chosen. These physical characteristics tell us about parts of a person's appearance, which are readily observable, or about aspects of a person's physiological makeup, which may or may not be readily visible. Finally, race is typically—albeit not universally—a poor indicator of how a person may view his or her own whole identity.[8]

Ethnic Conflict: An Analysis

What factors lead to violent conflict between ethnic groups? Long-standing—and typically mutual—hatreds between ethnic groups almost always underlie violent ethnic conflict. These hatreds may be based on religious or racial differences, perceptions of ethnic superiority, or ethnic scapegoating (i.e., the placing of blame for any or all unpleasant political, social, or economic circumstances or events upon a specifically targeted ethnic group). Violent conflict between ethnic groups may be traced to four political, economic, and religious factors: (1) political and economic crises, (2) the revival of long-standing ethnic hatreds by ultranationalistic political leaders, (3) religious disputes that are manipulated by religious fundamentalists, and (4) territorial disputes.[9]

There are untold examples of violent ethnic conflicts brought about by political crises. The disintegration of once-stable nation-states and international warfare are two dynamics which are likely to bring ethnic conflicts to the surface. The political, economic, and military disintegration of the former Soviet Union, the bloody dismantling of Yugoslavia, Indonesia's grudging granting of independence to East Timor, and the remarkably peaceful division of Czechoslovakia have led to the creation of new nation-states for a limited number of fortunate ethnic groups. The peoples of the Ukraine, Lithuania, Georgia, Armenia, Slovenia, Macedonia, East Timor, the Czech Republic, and Slovakia thus now govern their own nation-states. Developments like these, however, have also led to understandable frustrations among other ethnic groups whose desires for nation-state status continue to be thwarted. The Chechen, Kurdish, Basque, Puerto Rican, Sikh, Tamil, and Kashmiri peoples, to cite but a few examples, continue to lack full-fledged nation-state status.[10]

Warfare between nation-states also provides opportunities for inter-ethnic violence. It was in the midst of the First World War (1914–1918) that the undercurrent of ethnic conflict between the Irish and the English came to a boil. The result was the Irish-led Easter Rebellion of April 24–May 1, 1916. One of the primary causes of the Easter Rebellion was the resistance of many Irish people to fighting in what was viewed as "England's war" against Germany, Austria-Hungary, and the Ottoman Empire. The Irish rebellion was renewed when riots broke out in Dublin on June 10, 1917. These events ultimately led to the creation of the Irish Free State and the evacuation of the last British troops from that newly established nation in December 1922. Another example of international conflict leading to ethnic violence took place in 1915, when more than one million Armenians were slaughtered by the ruling Turkish majority of the warring—and disintegrating—Ottoman Empire. It was also during the First World War that a small number of innocent German-Americans were tarred, feathered, and beaten—or, in one case in Illinois, lynched by a drunken mob. Another example is the devastating war waged by Japan against China from 1931 to 1945, which led to the massacre of millions of Chinese civilians by the occupation forces of the Imperial Japanese Army. The most glaring, and horrifying, example of ethnic violence during international conflict was the wholesale extermination of nearly all of Europe's Jewish population in the Nazi-engineered Holocaust during the Second World War.

Ethnic violence also results, in many instances, when ultranationalistic political leaders stir up long-standing ethnic hatreds in order to achieve short-term political aims. In many cases, this type of political manipulation takes place during political crises like those discussed above. For example, it was during the last gasps of Germany's politically and economically chaotic Weimar Republic period (1918–1933) that Jews, Gypsies, and other ethnic groups began to be persecuted by the Nazi Party. An even more recent example took place during the collapse of Yugoslavia, when Serbian ultranationalists, such as Yugoslav president Slobodan Milosevic and Bosnian Serb leader Radovan Karadzic, promoted so-called ethnic cleansing against Croatians and Muslims in the breakaway regions of Croatia and Bosnia. Later, these ruthless war criminals used the same tactics against ethnic Albanians in the restive region of Kosovo. Milosevic's and Karadzic's orders led to the torture, rape, and slaughter of hundreds of thousands of Croats, Muslims, and ethnic Albanians. In south Asia, on the other hand, bloody ethnic conflict between Sri Lanka's Sinhalese and Tamils does not seem to have been precipitated by any specific political, economic, or social crisis. Rather, it appears that that conflict was instigated solely by opportunistic, ultranationalistic political leaders on both sides of the struggle.[11]

When ultranationalistic political leaders whip up violent ethnic conflict, they seek to manipulate what Timur Kuran refers to as "public ethnic behaviors," as opposed to "private ethnic preferences." Kuran refers to this dynamic as "ethnic preference falsification":

> By definition, ethnic preference falsification entails an incongruity between private ethnic preferences and the preferences conveyed by public ethnic behaviors. It occurs when, for example, a Croatian-Yugoslav turns against her neighbors of Serbian extraction in order to appear supportive of Croat separatism, even though privately she remains committed to the ideal of Yugoslav unity. Private ethnic preferences are not directly observable, so the privately felt demand for ethnically meaningful behavior cannot be measured, except perhaps through controlled experiments. By contrast, public ethnic behaviors are observable. In terms of these concepts, ethnic dissimilation raises aggregate ethnic activity as individuals undertake more and more actions that emphasize, celebrate, or deepen ethnic divisions. Because of the possibility of preference falsification, a rise in aggregate ethnic activity can occur even without changes in private ethnic preferences, although such changes can be a contributing factor. Individuals engage in ethnic preference falsification when they come under real or imagined social pressures to undertake, or to avoid, particular ethnic behaviors.[12]

As Kuran correctly notes, the interethnic violence which ultranationalistic political leaders seek to elicit from members of their own ethnic groups may not represent the genuine forms of behavior privately preferred by members of those groups.

The third path toward violent ethnic conflict may be aggravated, or even precipitated, when such conflict is compounded by religious disputes between ethnic groups. This is particularly the case when religious fundamentalists intentionally fan the flames of ethnic conflict. For example, chronic ethnic conflict between Jews and Palestinians became further inflamed when Islamic fundamentalist groups such as Hamas and Hizbollah and Jewish extremist groups such as Gush Emunim lent a radical religious dimension to the already bitter Israeli-Palestinian conflict. In another case, the drive for Kashmiri separatism received new urgency when Hindu nationalists, who largely ignored Hindu attacks against Muslims (such as those who wish to govern an independent Kashmir), gained power in India. The drive for an independent Sikh nation-state (which would be named "Khalistan") carved out of the present borders of India is based upon both ethnic and religious hatreds between Hindu nationalists and radical Sikhs. The violent interethnic conflict between majority Buddhist Sinhalese and minority Hindu Tamils in Sri Lanka is another tragic example of religious preferences exacerbating underlying ethnic conflict. The decades-old "troubles" which continue to plague Northern Ireland (a region also known as Ulster) is both an ethnic conflict between Ulsterites of Irish and non-Irish ancestry and those of the Catholic and Protestant religious faiths.[13]

Lastly, virtually all violent conflict between ethnic groups stems from disputes over which group will govern or in extreme cases even inhabit a specific territory. This ethnic violence frequently occurs when a formerly intact, multiethnic nation-state disintegrates or is otherwise dismantled. Ignatieff's differentiation of civic nationalism from ethnic nationalism is particularly pertinent here. The demise of such nation-states results in an obvious breakdown in civic nationalism and an accompanying rise in ethnic nationalism. These dynamics compel ethnic group members, who had faithfully adhered to the ideal of civic nationalism, to now lay claim to fully independent ethnic homelands. As Myra H. Immel observes,

> . . . feelings of being different from and superior to another ethnic group do not in and of themselves lead to violent conflict. Some other factor usually comes into play, such as disputes between . . . ethnic groups over territory. . . . The breakdown of the existing social or political order can also unleash ethnic warfare, especially in the breakup of multinational states such as the Soviet Union. In the not-too-distant past, people tended to identify themselves foremost by their nationality, their political citizenship. For example, although Yugoslavia was made up of several different ethnic groups, these people primarily identified themselves as Yugoslavs. As the nation began to fall apart, the Yugoslav people became more and more likely to base their identities on their ethnicity—the combination of cultural factors that bind people together as a permanent group. Instead of considering themselves Yugoslavs, they began to identify themselves as Serbs, Croats, Albanians, and so forth. In situations such as this, each group makes its own claim to territory and seeks political dominance

or autonomy. Hostile feelings grow and fester; neighbors watch each other nervously and some eventually take sides; and, before long, violence erupts.[14]

Ethnic demands for territorial independence arise in other settings as well. Insult was added to injury when those ethnic groups which continued to be unwillingly incorporated within the Russian Federation—such as the Chechens—were treated to the added affront of seemingly selective independence for certain ethnic groups residing in other regions of the former Soviet Union, such as the Ukraine, Armenia, and Moldova. Chechen demands for a fully independent Chechnya have resulted in years of brutal interethnic violence. This fighting has included full-scale conventional warfare and massive terrorist attacks involving military troops and civilians on both the Russian and Chechen sides. Chechen-Russian ethnic conflict has also spilled over into the neighboring region of Dagestan, which, like Chechnya, seeks full independence from Moscow.

Territorial independence may also be sought by ethnic groups who reside within intact nation-states. India, Spain, Turkey, and Britain are all fine examples of reasonably to extremely viable nation-states which have experienced ethnic violence over territorial disputes.

Ethnicity and Ethnic Conflict as Transnational Issues

Why are ethnicity and ethnic conflict fundamentally transnational phenomena? Immigration, fleeing refugees, and a variety of other travel flows account for the fact that most of the world's thousands of ethnic groups are spread far beyond the boundaries of any single nation-state. Not coincidentally, the vast majority of nation-states are populated by significant numbers of ethnic groups. Many of these nation-states provide some form of haven to ethnic groups whose members number in the hundreds of thousands, millions, or, in certain cases, tens of millions.[15]

One of the most notable examples of ethnicity as a transnational phenomenon is the diaspora, which may itself become a source of transnational ethnic conflict. What is a diaspora, and why are diasporas inherently transnational in nature? According to Milton J. Esman,

> Diasporas are ethnic communities of immigrant origin that maintain themselves in their host country because they decline to assimilate or are prevented from doing so. Although they remain in their adopted

country, diasporas normally sustain sentimental and material links to their country of origin. They organize initially for mutual assistance and to provide for their common social, recreational, religious and cultural needs. As they become politicized, their energies focus mostly on the defence and promotion of collective interests in their host country, usually non-discriminatory access to housing, employment, education and other economic opportunities and the right to maintain various elements of their inherited culture. They may also attempt to determine outcomes in their former home country, by the direct provision of resources—weapons, funds, personnel—or by influencing the foreign policy of their host country. By the assertion of interests that extend beyond their host country, diasporas become transnational actors.[16]

It is supremely ironic that certain means of globalization have enabled otherwise scattered and isolated ethnic group members to discover newfound cohesion, solidarity—and, ultimately, retribalization! As Esman again notes,

> Modern technologies that permit long-distance communications and rapid, low cost, reliable transportation have facilitated the extension of ethnic networks and their operations across and often in defiance of international borders. Some of these networks conduct legitimate business, some have political objectives, others engage in underworld criminal activities. What unites their members are a sense of common interest or purpose, reenforced by mutual trust, suspicion of outsiders, and ease of communications derived from a common collective identity and cultural heritage.[17]

Ted Robert Gurr points to two means through which ethnic conflicts become transnational in nature. These are what Gurr terms the diffusion of political action among transnational kindred and the contagion of communal activism. For Gurr,

> Diffusion refers to the "spillover" processes by which conflict in one country directly affects political organization and action in adjoining countries. The most important spillover effects in communal conflict occur among groups that straddle interstate boundaries. Political activists in one country often find sanctuary with and get support from their transnational kindred.[18]

Not surprisingly, a specific ethnic conflict may be inspired by other such conflicts. For Gurr, this contagion of communal activism

> refers to the processes by which one group's actions provide inspiration and strategic and tactical guidance for groups elsewhere: the diffusion of conflict is direct, contagion is indirect. While there is some evidence that internal conflict is generally contagious, we think the strongest force of communal contagion occurs within networks of similar groups. . . . More precisely, networks of communication, political support, and material assistance have developed among similar groups that face similar circumstances. . . . Groups that are tied into these networks acquire better techniques for effective mobilization: plausible appeals, good leadership, and organizational skills. Equally or more important, they benefit from the inspiration of successful movements elsewhere, successes that provide the images and moral incentives that motivate activists.[19]

Ethnoterrorism as a Transnational Phenomenon

In what ways do the activities of major ethnoterrorist organizations illustrate that ethnoterrorism is in large part a transnational phenomenon? An analysis of leading ethnoterrorist organizations might yield an answer to this question. Examples of major, well-known ethnoterrorist organizations which have been responsible for sustained, and relatively recent, transnational terrorist campaigns include the following:

(1) the Irish Republican Army (IRA) and the Irish National Liberation Army (INLA)
(2) the Kurdish Workers' Party (PKK)
(3) Basque Land and Liberty (ETA)
(4) various Armenian ethnoterrorist organizations, including the Armenian Secret Army for the Liberation of Armenia (ASALA) and the Justice Commandos of the Armenian Genocide (JCAG)
(5) the Liberation Tigers of Tamil Eelam (LTTE)
(6) various Sikh ethnoterrorist organizations, such as Dal Khalsa and Dashmesh Regiment
(7) various Chechen ethnoterrorist organizations[20]

Each of these major organizations functions, or has functioned, as a transnational terrorist organization, which is to say that each is an autonomous, privately funded organization that transcends both national boundaries and any need for nation-state sponsorship.[21]

Founded in 1916, the Irish Republican Army stubbornly endured as a terrorist organization for most of the twentieth century. For much of the last three decades, the IRA mounted a terrorist campaign on behalf of Ulster's Catholic minority and against that subnational region's Protestant majority as well as British interests. The ultimate goal of IRA terrorism was the withdrawal of British forces from Northern Ireland and the reunification of Ulster with the majority Catholic Irish Republic. If successful, this reunification would have automatically reduced Ulster's current Protestant majority to minority status.[22]

The terrorist campaign against British rule of Northern Ireland was originally confined to targets within the United Kingdom (UK). By 1980, however, the IRA began to assault targets outside the UK. Some of these external attacks included terrorist acts against British military personnel in the Netherlands and Germany. In November 1979, members of another Irish ethnoterrorist organization, the Irish National Liberation Army, bombed the British Consulate in Antwerp, Belgium. In August 1982, INLA members were arrested in Paris as they were assembling a bomb intended for use against a British target somewhere in Europe.

For many years, fugitive IRA members successfully sought refuge in Ireland and in the substantial Irish diaspora within the United States. IRA fugitives have also found safe haven in the Netherlands and other nations. In addition, IRA members have been apprehended for smuggling arms through nations such as France. Lastly, the IRA long received private financial support from Irish-American organizations like the Northern Ireland Aid Committee (NORAID).[23]

The signing of the Good Friday Agreement between the British government, Ulster's Protestant community, and the Irish Republican Army in April 1998 has led to a virtual cessation of the IRA's ethnoterrorist campaign. The Good Friday Agreement provides for joint rule in Ulster by Britain and Ireland in return for a surrender of arms by both the IRA and Protestant paramilitary forces. The agreement has been largely effective in ending IRA-related violence against British interests. Nevertheless, other, more militant terrorist organizations, such as the "Real IRA" and "Continuity IRA," have sprung up in place of the IRA itself. These organizations, which reject the Good Friday Agreement, continue to conduct sporadic and bloody acts of ethnoterrorism against Protestant interests.

Another example of a long-standing transnational terrorist organization is the Kurdish Workers' Party, or PKK (an acronym for Partia Karkaris Kurdistan). This organization, which was founded by the now-imprisoned Abdullah Ocalan in 1978, seeks an independent Kurdish nation-state in southeastern Turkey. For its brutal acts of terrorism, the PKK has selected targets in Turkey, the Middle East, Europe, and Asia. The PKK has also targeted certain Kurds whom the organization views as insufficiently pro-PKK within the large Kurdish diaspora in Europe and elsewhere.

Approximately twenty-two million Kurds inhabit a region of three hundred and ten thousand square miles (about the size of Texas and Louisiana combined). Upon this large expanse of land, the Kurds represent a substantial majority of the total population. This Kurdish region, however, is apportioned among a number of nation-states, including Turkey, Iraq, Iran, Armenia, and Syria. When the Kurdish population is divided among these autonomous states, the Kurds become a minority within each, and their opportunity for self-rule becomes far more remote. The Kurds are thus one of the world's largest stateless, transnational ethnic groups. Indeed, the concept of "Kurdistan" is itself a transnational one.[24]

The Kurdish Workers' Party has selected Turkish targets for its terrorist attacks throughout the world. From 1993 to 1995, most PKK terrorist attacks targeted Turkish diplomatic and commercial personnel in dozens of Western European cities. For example, non-PKK Kurdish activists who had been murdered in the Netherlands and Germany were later denounced as "traitors" in the PKK publication *Serxwebun* ("Independence"). The PKK has also conducted terrorist bombings and kidnappings against foreign tourists on Turkish soil. These attacks originated from territorial bases in Syria and Iran, nations which are relatively hostile to Turkey, as well as to the Kurds. PKK assaults have also been launched from northern Iraq, where the Kurds have enjoyed a substantial degree of autonomy since Operation Desert Storm ended in 1991. In February 1998, PKK leader Abdullah Ocalan was captured in Kenya by Turkish intelligence agents. After his return to Turkey, Ocalan was tried, convicted of treason, and sentenced to death in June 1999. To date, Ocalan's death sentence has yet to be carried out. Despite these events, the PKK's ethnoterrorist campaign continues.[25]

The Basque Land and Liberty terrorist organization, or ETA (an acronym for Euzkadi ta Askatasuna), limits most of its terrorist attacks to Spain proper. Nevertheless, like many other ethnoterrorist organizations, ETA exhibits selective respect for national borders. The process of diffusion also applies here, because, like the Kurds, the Basques inhabit a territory which spills over national boundaries. In this case, Basque territory includes much of northeast Spain and southwest France. Many Basques demand an independent nation-state within the present borders of Spain. During the long fascist regime of Spanish dictator Francisco Franco (1939–1975), ETA operations were openly based in France, which also provided safe haven for fugitive ETA members. Many observers believe that ETA continues to operate from the large Basque diaspora in France. Under pressure from Spain and the global community, however, the French government recently intensified its cooperation with Spanish police in order to eliminate this tactic. During the last few years, French authorities increased their hunt for Basque weapons caches on French soil, as well as for the extradition of ETA members to Spain. This has led to retaliation by ETA in the form of terrorist attacks against French interests in Mondragon, Bilbao, Lasarte, Durango, and Pamplona, Spain. In July 1990, a Spanish bank in Amsterdam was bombed by ETA members operating in the Netherlands. The process of contagion, which is also applicable in the instance of ETA, has resulted in formal contacts between ETA and other European ethnoterrorist organizations, such as the Irish Republican Army. Despite a September 1998 cease-fire agreement between ETA and the Spanish government, Basque ethnoterrorism resumed in November 1999. Since 2000, there has been a sharp rise in ETA-related violence.[26]

Since the granting of Armenian independence by Russia in 1991, the Armenian Secret Army for the Liberation of Armenia and the Justice Commandos of the Armenian Genocide have ceased their respective ethnoterrorist campaigns. During the 1970s and 1980s, however, terrorism conducted by the ASALA and the JCAG represented the most thoroughly transnational—and intense—ethnoterrorist activity in recent history. These organizations were primarily founded to avenge the Turkish genocide of Armenians during the First World War. From 1975 to 1987, the ASALA conducted numerous terrorist assaults, primarily against Turkish diplomatic and commercial interests in Lebanon, Britain, Italy, France, Belgium, Denmark, Iran, and Turkey itself. The ASALA also selected secondary targets in Europe and the Middle East. The World Council of Churches in Beirut, Lebanon, for example, was targeted for its role in assisting Armenians to emigrate to other nations. The Swissair office and the Swiss consulate in Milan, Italy, were also assaulted in retaliation for the arrest of Armenian nationals in Geneva, Switzerland. In Beirut, the French Embassy was targeted in order to force the French government to release ASALA prisoners held in France. From 1975 to 1985, the JCAG, too, was responsible for killing scores of Turkish diplomatic, commercial, and other personnel in Austria, France, Vatican City, Spain, Switzerland, the United States, Australia, Portugal, Canada, Yugoslavia, and Turkey.[27]

The Liberation Tigers of Tamil Eelam are yet another major example of a transnational ethnoterrorist organization. The LTTE was founded during the early 1970s in response to the oppressive treatment of the Tamil minority by the Sinhalese majority in Sri Lanka. The LTTE's goal is the establishment of an independent Tamil nation-state. In pursuit of this goal, the LTTE has conducted hundreds of terrorist attacks in Sri Lanka as well as in neighboring India, which too hosts a substantial Tamil diaspora in its southernmost region. India became embroiled in the conflict when it sent "peacekeeping" forces to Sri Lanka during the late 1980s. In 1991, former Indian prime minister Rajiv Gandhi was killed by an LTTE suicide bomber as he campaigned in southern India. Like the IRA, the LTTE relies on aid from large overseas diasporas in North America, Europe, and Asia. Over the last decade, the LTTE has relentlessly continued its ethnoterrorist campaign. In July 2001, for example, Sri Lanka's international airport and main air base were attacked in a bloody assault by the LTTE.[28]

The Sikhs, who are native to the Punjab region of northwestern India, are another important example of a stateless ethnic group which yearns for its own independent nation-state: "Khalistan." Like their Irish, Kurdish, Basque, Armenian, and Tamil counterparts, Sikh militants have engaged in numerous acts of transnational terrorism. Both an ethnic and a religious group, Sikhs throughout the world were outraged when the Indian Army stormed the sacred Sikh Golden Temple in Amritsar, India, in June 1984. In attempting to defend its action, the Indian government claimed that the Golden Temple had become a haven and arsenal for Sikh militants. As a direct result of this act, Indian Prime Minister Indira Gandhi (the mother of Rajiv Gandhi) was assassinated by her own Sikh bodyguards in October 1984. Yet even before the bloody takeover of the Golden Temple, numerous Sikh ethnoterrorist organizations had already been formed. The most significant of these organizations are the Dal Khalsa (founded in 1978) and the Dashmesh Regiment (founded in 1982). The Dashmesh Regiment claimed responsibility for the planting of two bombs aboard two Air India jetliners in June 1985. The first such device was placed on an Air India jetliner at Narita International Airport in Tokyo and exploded prematurely, killing two baggage handlers at the airport. The second bomb was planted on an Air India jetliner bound from Toronto to London. This bomb, which exploded over the Irish Sea, killed three hundred and twenty-nine passengers and crew onboard. In May 1986, Sikh terrorists of unknown affiliation also attempted to kill an Indian official visiting in Canada. Since 1986, Sikh ethnoterrorism has declined, although it has not totally ceased.[29]

The Chechens are native to the Caucasus region of southern Russia. Like the Kurds, the Basques, the Tamils, and the Sikhs, the Chechens also demand an independent nation-state. Unlike the Basques, the Tamils, and the Sikhs, however, and much like the Kurds of northern Iraq, the Chechens actually secured limited autonomy, if not outright independence. This took place in August 1996, when, after fierce warfare between the Russian army and Chechen forces, the Russian government was compelled to agree to a ceasefire. The Khasavyurt Agreement, as it came to be known, included the following critical provision: "An agreement on the basis of mutual relations between the Russian Federation and the Chechen Republic, defined in accordance with universally recognized principles and norms of international law, must be reached by 31 December 2001."[30]

The Khasavyurt Agreement did little to quell Chechen transnational ethnoterrorism, and terrorist acts continued against Russian targets. In November 1995, Chechen militants led a Russian television news crew to a cache of radioactive material buried in a Moscow park. In January 1996, nine gunmen seized control of a Turkish ship in the Black Sea in protest of Russia's attempt to rein in the Chechens. In March 1996, a Turkish Cypriot jetliner was hijacked; gunmen describing themselves as "pro-Chechens" forced the plane to land in Sofia, Bulgaria, and then in Munich, Germany. In July 1996, a bus bomb exploded in Moscow, a city which former Russian president Boris Yeltsin complained was "polluted with terrorists." Fingers were soon pointed at the sizable Chechen diaspora in Russia, as well as at Russian criminal syndicates, groups which (either alone or together) appeared to be likely suspects in the blast. In November 1996, fifty-nine people were killed when a nine-story apartment building in Dagestan, a southern Russian republic neighboring Chechnya, collapsed after a massive bombing. In this attack as well, the Chechen diaspora came under ever-increasing suspicion. Again in 1999, at least three powerful bombs in Moscow and Dagestan led to the deaths of no fewer than three hundred civilians and military personnel. Russian officials were by then convinced that the bombings had been instigated by Chechens eager to secure independence not only for themselves but also for Dagestan, a neighboring (and fellow Muslim) republic. In retaliation, the Russians attacked Chechnya with devastating force. In January 2000, the Russian Embassy in Beirut was assaulted when several men, one of whom carried a statement protesting Russia's reinvasion of Chechnya, fired rocket-propelled grenades at the compound. In May 2002, a Russian military parade in Dagestan was ripped by a powerful bomb. Scores of paraders and spectators ultimately died, and hundreds were wounded. Although no claims of responsibility were made, authorities were quick to blame separatists in nearby Chechnya. In October 2002, Chechen terrorists captured and held seven hundred hostages in a Moscow theater. In a disastrous attempt by Russian security officials to incapacitate the terrorists and free the hostages, over one hundred already weakened hostages fatally succumbed to a nerve agent employed by authorities.[31]

It is clear that there is an abundance of excellent examples of transnational ethnoterrorism. It is also clear that two extremely potent forces seem to be opposing one another on the global stage. On the one hand are the forces of globalization, cooperation, and economic growth. On the other hand are the forces of transnational ethnoterrorist organizations, which spawn division, destruction, and retribalization. The concept of globalization—"McWorld," if you will—is powerfully opposed by the desire of many ethnic groups to preserve or even redefine their ethnicity in its purest form. Perhaps Isaac Newton's statement of fact about the scientific world—that "for every action, there is an equal and opposite reaction"—is equally applicable to the new global disorder.

CHAPTER FIVE

Holy Rage

*A deafening explosion and a searing blast of heat ripped through the lobby.
The air turned black with smoke. Flames burst out of elevators. Walls and
the ceiling crumbled into a foot of debris on the floor. Shards of glass flew
like thrown knives. The blast threw people like dolls, tearing their bodies
apart. No one knew it was a plane.*

MARTHA T. MOORE AND DENNIS CAUCHON, IN *USA TODAY*, SEPTEMBER 4, 2002

THE SEPTEMBER 11, 2001, SUICIDE ATTACKS on the World Trade Center and the Pentagon are nothing less than the bloodiest terrorist outrage in world history. Most Americans, and many citizens in much of the rest of the
world, hoped, and reasonably expected, that the end of the cold war and
the dawning of a new millennium might bring forth a safer and more
peaceful world. In point of fact, however, we now dwell in a far more
dangerous and violent global environment. Throughout the late twentieth and early twenty-first centuries, ethnoterrorism has brought frequent horrors to the world. Yet religious terrorism, or theoterrorism,
presents an even more terrifying threat. That threat, moreover, is now
the most thoroughly transnational menace on the global stage. What has
brought the world to this astonishing juncture? What might theoterrorism portend for the future of terrorism itself?

Religious Moderates and Fundamentalists

Almost every major religion is divided into more moderate, or mainstream, and more militant, or fundamentalist, movements, wings, or
sects. Christianity, Hinduism, Islam, and Judaism all serve as illustrations of this rule. A majority of individuals embracing each of these four
faiths may be accurately characterized as "moderate" or "mainstream."
Most moderate religious sects are peaceful, law-abiding, and nonviolent. These moderate sects seem to agree on the following principles:

(1) that religion and government can remain separate
(2) that a "live and let live" posture toward other religious sects, other
religious faiths, and nonbelievers should be maintained
(3) that their own religion's sacred text or texts allow diverse interpre-
tation, rather than one literal meaning

A minority of individuals adhering to each of these four faiths, however, have been described as "fundamentalist," "militant," "radical," or "extremist." These religious adherents generally reject any firm separation between religion and government, and maintain varying degrees of hostility toward other religions. They harbor particular scorn for moderates within their own faiths, and particularly for apostates (i.e., former fellow believers who have formally or informally renounced their faith). Lastly, religious fundamentalists or extremists tend to overemphasize select parts of their sacred texts in order to justify their actions.

Terrorist activity fostered by fundamentalists or extremists within most major religious faiths has become increasingly commonplace with each passing decade. During the 1980s, the Gush Emunim Underground, an Israel-based terrorist organization led by fanatical Jewish rabbis hoping to hasten the arrival of the Messiah, plotted to blow up the sacred Muslim Dome of the Rock on Jerusalem's Temple Mount. In 1995, moderate Israeli prime minister Yitzhak Rabin was assassinated by an extremist Israeli Jew. Since the 1980s, numerous bombings and assassinations aimed at abortion providers in the United States have been traced to a loosely based terrorist organization known as the "Army of God." Members of this group claim to be acting on behalf of certain Christian fundamentalist beliefs. For decades, terrorist activity instigated by Hindu militants against Muslims, including the 1992 razing of the huge Babri mosque in Ayodhya, India, and countless other acts, has haunted the Asian subcontinent.[1]

Radical Islamic Fundamentalism

Predictably, Islam is no exception to this stubborn rule. The majority of the world's more than one billion Muslims can be properly described not only as moderate or mainstream, but as peaceful, law-abiding, and nonviolent. A minority of Muslims, on the other hand, have come to embrace what has been termed radical Islamic fundamentalism, or radical Islam. Like members of other militant religious movements, radical Islamic fundamentalists possess a kind of "holy rage" against those whose religious and political beliefs differ from their own. Moreover, certain adherents of radical Islam have actively taken up arms in pursuit of their ends.[2]

Islamic holy rage has led to radical Islamic attacks against targets on every continent of the world. Indeed, radical Islam provides the religious and political impetus for the most serious, sustained, and wide-ranging transnational terrorist campaign in contemporary global politics. Radical Islamic terrorism has targeted or otherwise involved scores of nations, including the United States. During the last decade, successful attacks against U.S. interests have included the following:

(1) In 1993, the World Trade Center was seriously damaged by a massive truck bomb.

(2) In 1995, a building operated by American military trainers in Riyadh, Saudi Arabia, was car bombed.

(3) In 1996, Khobar Towers, a high-rise apartment building housing American military personnel in Dhahran, Saudi Arabia, was gutted by a huge truck bomb.

(4) In 1998, U.S. embassies in Nairobi, Kenya, and Dar-es-Salaam, Tanzania, were very heavily damaged by nearly simultaneous car bombings.

(5) In 2000, the Navy destroyer USS *Cole* was bombed in the port of Aden, Yemen.

(6) On September 11, 2001, both World Trade Center towers were leveled by two hijacked jetliners; the Pentagon was heavily damaged by a third hijacked jetliner.

(7) In 2002, a U.S. consulate in Karachi, Pakistan, was heavily damaged by a car bomb.

(8) In 2003, three residential compounds in Riyadh, Saudi Arabia, housing scores of Americans, were destroyed by nearly simultaneous suicide bombers.[3]

Radical Islamic fundamentalists have conducted terrorist attacks within and against many other nation-states. These attacks include:

(1) a long series of suicide bombings and shootings both within Israel proper and against Jewish and Israeli interests in Argentina, Panama, Britain, France, Tunisia, Kenya, and other nations

(2) an extensive 1995–1996 terrorist campaign against subways, airliners, trains, schools, and other public places throughout France

(3) the continuing killings of Hindus in Kashmir and other parts of India

(4) a series of bus bombings and other terrorist attacks in Beijing and northwest China

(5) the car bombing of a crowded nightclub on the Indonesian island of Bali

(6) five nearly simultaneous suicide attacks against various civilian targets in Casablanca, Morocco.[4]

In recent years, similar acts of terrorism have also been directed against the historically pro-Western, or insufficiently fundamentalist, governments of three predominantly Muslim nation-states—Algeria, Egypt, and Pakistan. In Egypt, bombings and shootings have claimed the lives of hundreds of civilians, including foreign tourists, ordinary Egyptian citizens, and others. The radical Islamic fundamentalist campaign in Algeria has spilled over that nation-state's borders into neighboring Morocco, Tunisia, and France. It has targeted teachers, judges, labor union leaders, entertainers, foreign journalists, missionaries, business personnel, unveiled women, and many others. Pakistan has also witnessed a long string of car bombings, truck bombings, shootings, and other acts of terrorism.[5]

In seeking to analyze the complex reasons for, and ultimate meaning of, these horrific terrorist acts, this chapter seeks to answer four key questions:

(1) What, precisely, is radical Islamic fundamentalism?

(2) How can deeply held religious beliefs be used to justify seemingly wanton acts of terrorism?

(3) What is the relationship between radical Islamic fundamentalism and transnational terrorism?

(4) In what ways does a particular radical Islamic terrorist organization, al-Qaeda, serve as a prototype, or model, for the transnational terrorist organization of the future?

Understanding Radical Islam

What is the nature of radical Islam? In order to determine what radical Islamic fundamentalism is, it is necessary to first define the broader terms *fundamentalism* and *Islamic fundamentalism*. In general, the term *fundamentalism* is used to distinguish a system of beliefs held by religious movements or sects which, in order to justify their actions, selectively emphasize specific "fundamental" themes or issues drawn from a larger body of religious teachings. Fundamentalists clash with more moderate, mainstream believers who, they claim, have strayed from the true teachings of their religion. In general, religious moderates hate and fear religious fundamentalists, who are variously depicted as militant, radical, extremist, fanatical, or worse.

Islamic fundamentalists, like many other fundamentalists, selectively emphasize certain themes and issues taken from their faith's most holy work, the Quran, as well as from other Islamic religious teachings. Unlike their Christian counterparts, who emphasize a literal, cover-to-cover reading of their own holy work, the Bible, Islamic fundamentalists tend to emphasize and interpret only those Muslim teachings relevant to their own purposes.

Observers of Islamic fundamentalist sects frequently remark upon their seeming obsession with political rather than religious matters. Nonetheless, Islamic fundamentalism is not merely a political ideology; it is also a comprehensive system of religious beliefs. Johannes J. G. Jansen, one of the world's foremost students of Islamic fundamentalism, notes for example that "Islamic fundamentalism is both fully politics and fully religion," and that, although "[Islamic f]undamentalism is a religion narrowed down to a [political] ideology . . . it is undeniably a religion too." Jansen also emphasizes:

> Islamic fundamentalism is a religion and not a mere political ideology. It is a religion concerned with earthly power. At the same time, it is also a political movement and an ideology. Modern political science categories do not fit and are irrelevant.[6]

Islamic fundamentalists, as well as more moderate Muslims, accept the following beliefs:

(1) Allah's (God's) ultimate teachings or revelations are contained within Islam (which may be loosely translated as the "complete surrender of the believer to Allah").

(2) These teachings were expressed by Allah's messenger, or prophet, Muhammad, as holy law, or shari'a.

(3) Muhammad conveys the revealed word of Allah in the Quran, and the prophet relates his own teachings, proverbs, and sayings in another holy work, the Hadith.

(4) Islam provides for a comprehensive code of law which regulates all aspects of both religious and secular life.[7]

Where more moderate Muslims and fundamentalists differ is on the question of precisely who shall rule Islamic society. More moderate Muslims believe that the sultan or caliph (i.e., the civil or secular ruler) may be censured, or criticized harshly (albeit not directly removed), by the Ulama (Islamic scholars) when Allah's holy law, the shari'a, is improperly carried out. Islamic fundamentalists, on the other hand, believe that the Ulama rule, and directly carry out the shari'a themselves. Hence, the central question dividing moderate and fundamentalist Muslims becomes one of who ultimately governs—a civil authority or a religious clergy. For moderate Muslims, only a secular ruler, advised by—but not truly responsible to—the Ulama, may govern. For Islamic fundamentalists, only the clergy may rule, and they must do so directly.[8]

Islamic fundamentalists wish to establish a kind of modern theocracy rather than any type of secular government. And it is very important to bear in mind that Islamic fundamentalism is a *modern* political ideology as well as a system of religious beliefs. Islamic fundamentalism should therefore not be confused with previous historical examples of Islamic "revivalism," although the two terms are sometimes used interchangeably. Jansen emphasizes for example that "[t]he mere acceptance of the modern nation-state is something relatively new in the world of Islam." In this new "attempt at Islamisation of the modern nation-state," Jansen claims, "Islamic law would be the law of the land."[9]

What events were responsible for precipitating this notably modern movement? The first was the founding of the Majallat al-Ikhwan al-Muslimin, or Muslim Brotherhood, in Egypt during the late 1920s. This transnational organization advocated the establishment of a modern Islamic nation-state whose law would be the shari'a. To this day, the Muslim Brotherhood maintains a genuinely transnational presence throughout the Middle East, but particularly in Egypt, Iran, Lebanon, and the Palestinian territories.

The second event propelling Islamic fundamentalism was the Iranian revolution of 1979, which provided a model for the Islamic nation-state and support for Islamic fundamentalists throughout the world. As Jansen puts it,

> The 1979 Islamic Revolution in Iran, despite its anti-Western rhetoric, similarly accepted the existence of the modern Western nation-state as legal—its use of the word "republic" [to describe the new Iranian regime] betrays this. Up till the twentieth century, the world of Islam was ruled by dynasties, whose rule was accepted—or not ac-

cepted—by Muslim religious leaders, the "Ulama" and Ayatollahs. In founding an *Islamic republic,* [the Ayatollah Ruhollah] Khomeini [the spiritual leader of the Iranian revolution] carried out his most daring and perhaps most lasting innovation.[10]

According to many Islamic fundamentalists, nation-states—particularly Muslim nation-states—whose governments do not conform to the basic model set forth by the Iranian republic are an affront to Allah. Nonfundamentalist Muslim rulers (who govern most of the remainder of the Muslim world) are particularly offensive since, as Muslims, rather than infidels (nonbelievers), these rulers cannot claim ignorance of their true duties to Allah.

Radical Islamic fundamentalists believe that these rulers, their followers, and their supporters throughout the world must be eliminated, banished, or converted through a kind of modern religious warfare, or jihad. As Jansen so aptly states, these Islamic fundamentalists

. . . reproach mainstream Muslims for underestimating the importance of the gihad, the armed struggle against unbelief, and for not attaching great value to waging war against the enemies of God. To true fundamentalists, the other, more spiritual meanings of gihad are unimportant, or at least much less important than the specific martial [i.e., military] meanings of the term. . . . [Islamic fundamentalists] expect a better world to come, which they believe can only be reached through armed struggle. Consequently, they are at war with the world and may well die waging war against it and its unbelief. If they do, they will be compensated by being blessed in paradise and obtain an exceptional place in the other world.[11]

In general terms, what radical Islamic fundamentalists demand is an upheaval in the Muslim world in which all nonfundamentalist regimes are overthrown and replaced by a pure, revitalized Islam where religion and government become one. According to Islamic fundamentalists, these new regimes will have no use for the non-Islamic world. These true Islamic nation-states will provide a model for the non-Islamic world, which, upon seeing the true way, will ultimately embrace the fundamentalist beliefs of Islam. In order to accomplish their goals, however, all nonfundamentalist "temptations" must be banished from every Islamic society. This requires that Western—and particularly American— influences be purged from these new societies. To accomplish this, Islamic fundamentalists must wage jihad not only against Muslim moderates and apostates, but against these nonfundamentalists' most powerful supporters as well. As Jansen states,

> The West, many fundamentalists believe, has forced the Muslim community to betray the shari'a, [and] now fears the Islamic movements. The pious are convinced that the West is afraid of what will happen to the world when the shari'a is again implemented.[12]

The United States is specifically targeted because of its status as a political, military, economic, and cultural superpower. Because of the vast influence of the United States throughout most of the world— and, in particular, the Islamic world—the United States represents the "great Satan" to Islamic fundamentalists. This has especially been the case since the disintegration of the world's only other superpower, the Soviet Union, in 1991. Above all, since the U.S.-led victory in Operation Desert Storm, the 1991 military operation which expelled Iraqi forces from Kuwait, the United States has maintained a sizable force of military advisors in Saudi Arabia, the home of two sacred cities of Islam: Mecca and Medina. The United States also maintains military and civilian personnel elsewhere in the Muslim world. Lastly, the United States is the chief economic and military supporter of Israel, which governs lands (in particular, Jerusalem) also considered holy to Muslims. In the eyes of many Islamic fundamentalists throughout the world, these conditions are intolerable.

The increasingly radical demand for Islamic fundamentalist armed struggle is skillfully conveyed in five mid- to late-twentieth-century works, none of which is widely read by, or available to, non-Muslims. The first is a work by Muslim Sheik Mohammed Hussein Fadlallah, *Islam and the Logic of Force* (1984). The second, issued in 1988, is *The Covenant of the Islamic Resistance Movement*. The third is Sayyid Qutb's *In the Shade of the Quran*. The fourth is another work by Qutb, *Milestones*. The last is a lengthy pamphlet by Abd Al-Salam Faraj, *Al-Faridah al-Gha'ibah*, or *The Neglected Duty*. Fadlallah's work, which offers a fairly narrow defense of Islamic fundamentalist terrorism, has been quite influential among followers of the radical Islamic fundamentalist organization Hizbollah (the "Party of God"). *The Covenant of the Islamic Resistance Movement* is also a somewhat narrow justification of, in this case, the radical Islamic fundamentalist Hamas organization's terrorist campaign against Israel.[13]

Although written some four to five decades ago, Qutb's *In the Shade of the Quran* and *Milestones* have been widely read throughout the Muslim world. His *Milestones* remains an influential work in that it thoroughly rejects the concept of a solely defensive jihad in favor of a fully offensive struggle against the *jahiliyyah,* or non-Islamic world. This struggle, Qutb maintains, must be initiated by a "vanguard" of truly and fully committed Muslim believers. *Milestones* also offers a particularly impassioned rhetorical condemnation of the "cheap worldly pleasures" which the "large brothel" of non-Muslim society represents to radical Muslims. Like his fellow Egyptian Abd al-Salam Faraj, Qutb, the chief ideologist of the Muslim Brotherhood, was also executed for his anti-government activities. Qutb is thus a kind of spiritual and philosophical forefather to later radical Islamic theorists such as Faraj.[14]

Understanding the Neglected Duty

Many students of radical Islam believe that Abd Al-Salam Faraj's pamphlet, *The Neglected Duty,* is the most enduringly significant of these five works. As noted Islamic authority Charles J. Adams puts it, *"The Neglected Duty* is the only authentic and extended statement of radical Muslim resurgence views." Adams also notes that Faraj's work "presents the radical world view in a forceful and vividly clear way." Jansen, who translated *The Neglected Duty* in 1986, states that this work "offers a comprehensive view of the history of Islam which is based on all relevant sources, and it does so impressively." Pertinent too is that Faraj—who hailed from the majority Sunni Muslim community— helped lead the Islamic Group of Egypt (popularly known as "Al-Jihad," or "armed movement against unbelief") and was subsequently executed for the Al-Jihad-sponsored assassination of Egyptian President Anwar Sadat in 1981.[15]

The Neglected Duty is indeed an impressive and thorough work which repeatedly attempts to justify two basic themes: First, jihad, or armed struggle against moderate Muslims, apostates, and infidels, has been neglected by most Muslims throughout the world. Second, a united Islamic world governed by the shari'a must be achieved. This duty, too, has been neglected by a majority of Muslims.

Faraj begins his treatise with an attack upon the Ulama and other Muslim moderates:

> Jihad (struggle) for God's cause, in spite of its extreme importance and its great significance for the future of this religion, has been ne-glected by the ulama (leading Muslim scholars) of this age. They have

feigned ignorance of it, but they know that it is the only way to the return and the establishment of the glory of Islam anew. . . . There is no doubt that the idols of this world can only be made to disappear through the power of the sword. . . . Whosoever did not comply and accept the unity of God, being called upon to do so by the text of the Qur'an, by arguments and by proof, would then be called upon with the sword.[16]

Faraj further insists that only through jihad may Muslims overcome their weakness and internal conflict. For "[n]eglecting jihad is the cause of the lowness, humiliation, division and fragmentation in which the Muslims live today."[17]

Like most radical Islamic fundamentalists, Faraj demands that an Islamic nation-state be introduced throughout the Muslim world:

The establishment of an Islamic State . . . [was] not only predicted by the Apostle of God [i.e., Muhammad]—God's peace be upon him—but they are, moreover, part of the Command of the Lord—Majestic and Exalted He is—for which every Muslim should exert every conceivable effort in order to execute it.[18]

The issue of precisely how far this Islamic nation-state is to extend is also addressed:

. . . the establishment of the Rule of God *over this earth* . . . must be considered to be obligatory for all Muslims. . . . If, moreover, such a state cannot be established without war, then this war is an obligation as well.[19]

It must be noted, however, that, although the creation of a global Islamic society is certainly desirable to Islamic fundamentalists as an ultimate goal, the purification and revitalization of existing Muslim societies must be accomplished first. As Jansen puts it,

Islamic fundamentalists represent a serious danger, but to their own compatriots and coreligionists. Except in Palestine and Israel, fundamentalism propagates the concept of an Islamic struggle against an internal enemy.[20]

In other words, jihad must first be conducted against nonfundamentalist Muslims before, perhaps long before, the time comes for armed struggle against the non-Muslim world. According to Faraj, "apostasy is worse than rebellion against the prescripts of a religion which comes from someone who has always been outside this religion [i.e., resistance by infidels, or those who have never accepted Islam]." [21]

Although Islamic fundamentalists do not insist upon the immediate creation of a global Islamic nation-state, Faraj is nevertheless firm in his demand that jihad must be waged against both apostates and those infidels who assist them. In *The Neglected Duty,* he excerpts the following from noted fourteenth-century Islamic scholar Ibn Tamiyah's writings on jihad:

> Every army commander and every soldier who goes over to them is to be judged like them. They are as much apostates from the prescripts of Islam as they (themselves) are apostates from the prescripts of Islam. When the Pious Forefathers used to call apostates the [non-Muslim] people who [disobeyed some Muslim laws yet] did not fight the Muslim community, how much more must we regard as apostates those who became in the same camp as the enemies of God and His Apostle and who kill Muslims? [22]

This statement makes clear that both apostates and infidels must be targeted, and banished or destroyed through the conduct of jihad. Hence "when the infidels descend upon a [Muslim] country, it becomes an individual duty for its people to fight them and drive them away." For without internal collaborators (i.e., apostates) among the ranks of the Muslims, the external infidel becomes powerless. Radical Islamic fundamentalists further believe that Allah will always favor Muslims who wage jihad no matter what the odds may be. [23]

Jihad is the duty of all Muslims who are physically capable of carrying arms and conducting war against moderate Muslims and infidels. Faraj emphasizes the following quotation from the eighth-century Muslim scholar Abu Hanifah:

> It is a well-established rule of Islamic Law that the punishment of an apostate will be heavier than the punishment of someone who is by origin an infidel (and has never been a Muslim), and this in many respects. For instance, an apostate has to be killed even if he is unable to carry arms and go to war. Someone, however, who is by origin an infidel and who is unable to carry arms and go to war against the Muslims should not be killed. [24]

What manner of fighting is permitted in this jihad? According to Faraj, virtually any strategies and tactics are permitted. For "Muslims are free to choose the most suitable method of fighting so that deception, which is victory with the fewest losses and by the easiest means possible, is realized." Any type of deception, even lying, "is essentially permitted," although "it is better to limit oneself to speaking ambiguously, and God knows best." Muslim fighters are even permitted to kill the children of their enemies if they "do not do it on purpose without need for it," which is to say, when such casualties are unavoidable during a justifiable attack. Given certain circumstances, even suicide attacks may be permitted. But above all, Muslim fighters must never allow themselves any form of weakness. Quoting from the Quran, Faraj emphasizes the following:

> Missions which further the cause of Islam require solid, straightforward, steady, and healthy constitutions which can withstand a long and difficult strife. Military ranks which are permeated with the weak and the soft cannot effectively resist because these weak and soft soldiers will abandon the ranks in the hour of difficulty. They will cause failure, weakness, and confusion to spread through the ranks. It is necessary to banish those who are weak and stay behind far away from the military ranks, in order to protect these from becoming disjointed and being put to flight. Indulgence towards those weak people is a crime towards the whole army.[25]

These, then, are the most significant general rules on how to conduct the type of transnational terrorist campaign favored by radical Islamic fundamentalists.

Before continuing, it is necessary to keep three very significant points in mind:

(1) Not all Islamic fundamentalists are in agreement about precisely what these goals, and the tactics necessary to achieve them, should be.

(2) Many Islamic fundamentalists agree that they must place some limitations upon the types of tactics which they may utilize in order to achieve their goals.

(3) Like any movement, Islamic fundamentalism is unlikely to achieve all, or even most, of its goals.

Islamic fundamentalism is thus neither monolithic nor all-powerful. Although many Islamic fundamentalists agree with the writings of Faraj, Fadlallah, and Qutb, many others have come to different conclusions.[26]

Firm generalizations may be drawn about how radical Islamic fundamentalist religious beliefs are used to justify seemingly indefensible acts of terrorism. By analyzing a seminal work such as *The Neglected Duty*, it is possible to understand how radical Islamic fundamentalists believe that a prolonged and wide-ranging terrorist campaign is not only justified, but entirely appropriate, given present circumstances. Most critically, these radical Islamic fundamentalists insist that God not only permits, but actually demands these acts of violence.

In summary, *The Neglected Duty* presents the following key themes:

(1) An Islamic society, encompassing the Islamic world and then, ultimately, the world as a whole, must, and will, be established.

(2) An initial focus upon the Islamic world is necessary because internal enemies (apostates) must be defeated before external enemies (infidels) may be ultimately vanquished.

(3) Although any individuals residing within the ranks of the apostates may be directly targeted, infidels, particularly those who provide support to the apostates, must be targeted as well.

(4) Only those infidels who are physically capable of carrying arms and conducting war against Muslims may be directly targeted; however, unavoidable casualties against the defenseless are permitted.

(5) God will grant ultimate victory to true Muslims regardless of the size or strength of their opponents.

(6) Virtually any tactics are allowed, particularly those which serve to bring about the most rapid and easy victory.

(7) Weakness of any kind is prohibited among the ranks of true Muslims.

In essence, these seven rules provide guidance to those radical Islamic fundamentalists who wage war, through terrorist means, against their opponents.

A better appreciation of these rules might assist in answering the other key questions posed earlier in this chapter. One is the issue of how deeply held religious beliefs may be used to justify seemingly wanton acts of terrorism. The other is the relationship between radical Islamic fundamentalism and transnational terrorism.

Performing One's Neglected Duty

How may deeply held religious beliefs be used to justify seemingly indefensible acts of terrorism? If God's demand that an Islamic society be es-

tablished, originally encompassing the present Islamic community and eventually the entire world, is to be met, then it is believed necessary to first rid the Islamic community itself of apostates and infidels. Although no rules restrain the elimination of apostates, certain limited rules govern the treatment of those infidels who provide support to apostates. Recall that, within the boundaries set by those rules, virtually any tactics, particularly those which speed victory, are allowed. Recall, too, the belief that God will grant ultimate victory to true Muslims regardless of whether they are outnumbered or outarmed. Also remember that weakness of any kind is prohibited among the ranks of Muslim warriors. Given the necessity to use the most efficient tactics, the fact that the West is numerically and physically stronger than the Muslim world, and God's prohibitions against weakness, it becomes clear that even the most seemingly savage acts of terrorism are not only allowed, but demanded. Terrorism, and terrorism alone, is that form of warfare which fulfills each of these requirements. Since the Muslim world does not possess the conventional military might of the West, unconventional tactics—particularly those which produce the most efficient results—are required. And terrorism—the "weapon of the weak"—is in fact the most efficient means available to an outnumbered, outarmed opponent whose tactics, even brutal ones, can know no bounds. Only a sustained, wide-ranging, and unlimited campaign of terrorism, then, can provide Islamic fundamentalism with the victory that God guarantees.

A related issue is the relationship between radical Islamic fundamentalism and transnational terrorism. First, although Islamic fundamentalists do favor the establishment of modern nation-states within the Muslim world, the boundaries between these nation-states have little real meaning. This is because many Islamic fundamentalists also adhere to a "pan-Islamic" ideology that recognizes the brotherhood of all Muslims regardless of where they may happen to reside, and to the eventual establishment of a single—and ultimately global—Islamic society.[27]

For radical Islamic fundamentalists, the perception is that the enemies of Islam, both apostates and their allies, the infidels, reside throughout the world. Their struggle must, therefore, be waged on a truly transnational basis within Muslim and non-Muslim nation-states alike. Throughout the last decade, most radical Islamic terrorist attacks were confined to targets within the Middle East. During that same period, however, a growing number of terrorist operations were also executed (with varying degrees of success) within the United States—the "great Satan" itself. Moreover, nations spanning every continent of the globe

(Russia, China, India, Britain, France, Kenya, Tanzania, Argentina, and Panama are but a few examples) have endured terrorist attacks with firm links to radical Islamic TTOs.

Masterminding the Performance

Most of these attacks have been traced to a single individual, Osama bin Laden, and a single organization, al-Qaeda. The relationship between the two is both instructive and fascinating. Bin Laden has played the leading role in establishing an extraordinarily well-financed, carefully organized, highly disciplined, superbly equipped, unusually resourceful, and extremely secretive terrorist organization. Al-Qaeda, with its links to many other like-minded radical Islamic fundamentalist organizations on every continent, is also the first terrorist organization with a truly global reach. The result has been nothing less than the creation of an organization which may well serve as a model for the transnational terrorist organization of the future.[28]

Al-Qaeda and Osama bin Laden bear major responsibility for a substantial number of deadly terrorist attacks during the last decade. Major examples of these attacks include: (1) the 1993 World Trade Center bombing, (2) the 1995 and 1996 bombings of two U.S. military facilities in Saudi Arabia, (3) the 1998 bombings of the U.S. embassies in Kenya and Tanzania, (4) the 2000 bombing of the USS *Cole,* (5) the September 11, 2001, terrorist attacks against the World Trade Center and the Pentagon, and (6) the 2002 bombing of a U.S. consulate in Karachi, Pakistan. Al-Qaeda is also clearly linked to the 1995–1996 terrorist campaign within France, the 2002 suicide bombing of a historic synagogue in Djerba, Tunisia, and dozens of other bloody acts. Scores of attempted al-Qaeda-supported terrorist operations have also been thwarted in recent years. Even more ominously, Western intelligence reports based upon recovered videotapes and documents and testimony furnished by captured members suggest that al-Qaeda may have trained, funded, or otherwise supported as many as 110,000 radical Islamic fundamentalists now operating within the borders of up to ninety nation-states.[29]

It is widely acknowledged that al-Qaeda in effect declared war against the United States and her allies on February 23, 1998. On that date, an organization identifying itself as the World Islamic Front for the Jihad against Jews and Crusaders issued a fatwa (religious edict or judgment) to all Muslims. This fatwa, signed by Osama bin Laden and other radical Islamic fundamentalists, warned that "[t]he ruling to kill the Americans and their allies—civilian and military—is an individual duty for every Muslim who can do it in any country in which it is possible to do it." The fatwa then went on to warn:

> We—with God's help—call on every Muslim who believes in God and wishes to be rewarded to comply with God's order to kill the Americans and plunder their money wherever and whenever they find it. We also call on Muslim Ulema, leaders, youths, and soldiers to launch the raid on Satan's U.S. troops and the devil's supporters allying with them, and to displace those who are behind them so that they may learn a lesson.[30]

Who is Osama bin Laden? In what ways have he and al-Qaeda served to reshape the very nature of global terrorism?

There is fairly wide concurrence about the basic facts of bin Laden's life. Osama bin Laden was born on July 30, 1957, in Riyadh, Saudi Arabia. He is the seventeenth son of fifty-two children fathered by Muhammad bin Laden, a Saudi Arabian construction firm magnate who was of Yemeni origin. In accordance with Muslim practice, Muhammad bin Laden had no more than four wives at any one time. On various occasions during Muhammad bin Laden's life, he married and divorced a number of other women, and also had numerous concubines, or mistresses. Osama's mother, Hamida, who remarried after Muhammad's death in a 1968 helicopter crash, is of Syrian origin. She played the major role in raising the future al-Qaeda leader, who in turn would marry one of his mother's distant Syrian relatives.[31]

The bin Laden family, one of the wealthiest in Saudi Arabia, has an estimated net worth of at least $5 billion. After his father's death, Osama bin Laden received an inheritance share of $25–30 million. Most of this sum was placed in careful and hugely profitable investments outside of Saudi Arabia. How much did bin Laden earn from these investments? According to Rohan Gunaratna's fine analysis, "Swiss [authorities], with access to superior banking information, opt for a [net earnings] figure of $250–500 million." These figures are in line with other government estimates.[32]

The course of Osama bin Laden's university education may have served as something of a harbinger of his future activities. Apparently intending to join his family's construction business, he studied economics

and management at one of Saudi Arabia's finest schools, King Abdul
Aziz University in Jedda. Although undistinguished in these disciplines,
bin Laden demonstrated a keen interest in government, global politics,
and, in particular, Islamic studies. Whatever his college-age experiences
may have been in the unusually cosmopolitan seaport of Jedda and the
particularly vice-filled environment of Beirut, Lebanon, during the mid-
1970s, Osama bin Laden was clearly persuaded by the arguments of
strict Islamic fundamentalists. He seems to have been particularly in-
fluenced by two men. The first was Muhammad Qutb, the brother of
Sayyid Qutb, one of the chief ideologists of the Muslim Brotherhood in
Egypt. The other was Abdullah Azzam, the original founder of al-Qaeda.
Perhaps as a result, bin Laden abandoned his formal educational plans
during his third year at King Abdul Aziz University.[33]

A few short years later, bin Laden joined those thousands of Muslims
who had journeyed to Afghanistan during the early 1980s in order to resist the Soviet occupation of that unfortunate land. It was in the rugged
Hindu Kush mountains of eastern Afghanistan and western Pakistan
that bin Laden's already fervent acceptance of strict Islamic belief became stronger still. During his early years in Pakistan, bin Laden encountered again the man who would become his chief mentor: radical
Islamic ideologist Abdullah Azzam, whose lectures bin Laden had already attended at King Abdul Aziz University. The two set up an organization intended to recruit and train foreign resistance fighters. This organization, the Maktab al-Khidmat lil Mujahidin al-Arab (MAK, or
Afghan Service Bureau), was led by the two men for several years after
its establishment in 1984. In 1988, Azzam personally founded another
organization, al-Qaeda al-Sulbah ("the Solid Base"). Azzam laid down
eight principles—which endured long beyond his death—by which this
"pious group" and "pioneering vanguard" was to be guided:

> [They] must jump into the fire of the toughest tests and into the
> waves of fierce trials.
>
> The training leadership shares with [its recruits] the testing march,
> the sweat and blood. The leadership must be like the motherly
> warmth of a hen whose chicks grow under its wings, throughout the
> long period of hatching and training.
>
> This vanguard has to abstain from cheap worldly pleasure and
> must bear its distinct stamp of abstinence and frugality. In like man-
> ner, it must be endowed with firm belief and trust in the ideology, in-

stilled with a lot of hope for its victory. There must be a strong determination and insistence to continue the march no matter how long
it takes.

Travel provision is among the most important items on this march.
The provision consists of meditation, patience and prayer.

Loyalty and devotion.

They must be aware of anti-Islam machinations all over the world.[34]

After the Soviet withdrawal from Afghanistan in 1989, MAK and al-
Qaeda al-Sulbah merged into what has now become known as al-Qaeda.
For a few months, Azzam and his designated successor, Osama bin
Laden, shared the leadership of al-Qaeda. The organization provided
refuge to those thousands of Afghan resistance fighters who, after re-
ceiving billions of dollars in U.S. financial and material aid during these
last gasps of the cold war, had been abruptly abandoned by their former
American patrons. Following a power struggle between Azzam and bin
Laden, the former was killed by a powerful bomb almost certainly set
off on bin Laden's orders. By this point, bin Laden had already come under the influence of a new, even more radical faction in al-Qaeda led by
Egyptian Islamic Jihad founder Ayman al-Zawahiri, who would become
al-Qaeda's chief ideologist. Following the Afghan war, bin Laden returned to Saudi Arabia.[35]

Operation Desert Storm led to the stationing of hundreds of thousands of American troops in Saudi Arabia. Bin Laden, who had unsuc-
cessfully offered his al-Qaeda forces in place of these "infidels," became
particularly enraged when thousands of American military personnel
continued to "occupy" Saudi soil. It was not long before bin Laden's
loud and incessant anti-American rhetoric and activities forced the fire-
brand from his homeland. Bin Laden eventually settled in Sudan. The
radical Islamic fundamentalist beliefs which bin Laden shared with Sudanese president Omar Hassan Ahmed al-Bashir enabled the al-Qaeda
leader to remain in Sudan until American and Saudi Arabian demands—
spurred by major anti-American terrorist attacks on Saudi soil—ef-
fected a second exile. In 1996, bin Laden returned to Afghanistan, where
he was reunited with thousands of joyous al-Qaeda loyalists. It was also
at this time that bin Laden was joined by Al-Jihad (also known as Islamic Group of Egypt) leader Muhammad Atef, who would become al-
Qaeda's "chief of operations."[36]

At this juncture, Osama bin Laden oversaw the unprecedented creation of a vast, loosely arranged network of transnational terrorist or-

ganizations. Dissecting this organization is similar to peeling away the layers of an onion. At its outer reaches, bin Laden's network consisted of layer upon layer of other radical Islamic terrorist organizations, as well as other groups which were useful to his purposes because of their hostility to Western, particularly American, interests. The next layer consisted of Atef's Islamic Group of Egypt, which had largely merged with bin Laden's primary organization. (It is interesting to note that this merger constituted a kind of organic link between Osama bin Laden and Abd Al-Salam Faraj, author of *The Neglected Duty* and one of the executed leaders of Al-Jihad.) Next was al-Qaeda itself, which served as bin Laden's own vehicle for the authorization and financing of a radical Islamic transnational terrorist campaign. At the center of the entire network was bin Laden's personal organization. During al-Qaeda's heyday in Afghanistan, bin Laden was surrounded by an entourage of some three thousand fully committed followers, many of them battle-hardened veterans of the struggle against the former Soviet occupation of Afghanistan. These forces were—and to large extent probably still are—armed with relatively advanced artillery, rocket launchers, and other sophisticated weapons left over from that campaign, as well as from much more recent sources.[37]

What is most striking about Osama bin Laden's vast transnational network of organizations is how little is precisely known about its surviving membership, sponsorship, past activities, and future plans. Even less is known about bin Laden's own role. This is due to several factors:

(1) Osama bin Laden may have had few if any direct ties to, and in all likelihood may have never had the need to personally order, any al-Qaeda-related terrorist acts.

(2) Although a growing number of individuals responsible for al-Qaeda-linked terrorist acts have been apprehended, many more simply disappear—or seem to disappear—after their missions have been completed.

(3) These amorphous, relatively obscure organizations have few if any links to one another; furthermore, the cells, or semi-independent subunits of these organizations, have extremely brief shelf lives.

(4) Osama bin Laden's most important roles in this campaign clearly seem to be those of authorizer and fund-raiser, rather than those of chief ideologist or tactical commander.

(5) Above all, bin Laden's organizational network is financed primarily through private sources.

In reference to al-Qaeda's networking structure, Gunaratna astutely observes:

> The conventional wisdom among intelligence specialists was that the emerging pattern of terrorism was one based on autonomous cells acting independently of each other, largely because we were unaware of how Al Qaeda and other groups had cleverly reverted to one-to-one contact, primarily via couriers, as a means of keeping in touch that circumvented governments' technical means of intelligence-gathering. This explains why the fact that Al Qaeda's German, British, Spanish, Dutch and Belgian cells were acting in concert was overlooked, something discovered only during [the investigation into the September 11, 2001, terrorist attacks].[38]

Another factor which makes al-Qaeda and its transnational activities so difficult to counter is that a growing number of radical Islamic fundamentalists are already agreed upon basic ideology, strategy, and tactics. Thus it is perfectly understandable that bin Laden's key role was primarily financial, rather than ideological or operational. Indeed, what bin Laden did, in effect, was to set up a kind of "terrorist foundation" to which radical Islamic fundamentalists might apply for what amount to "grants" to fund their activities.

An excellent example of this activity occurred during 1998 and 1999 when bin Laden provided financing to Harkat-ul-Jihad, a large yet obscure radical Islamic fundamentalist organization based in Bangladesh. After Harkat had recruited students from local Muslim seminaries, they received bin Laden–financed training in southeastern Bangladesh. Bin Laden was then able to provide his Taliban partners with reinforcements for use in fighting against other factions in the continuing Afghan civil war.[39]

It is firmly believed that al-Qaeda continues to help finance radical Islamic fundamentalist activities in India, Pakistan, China, Russia, and even Iran. Other obvious targets for bin Laden's efforts are the former Soviet Muslim republics of Azerbaijan, Uzbekistan, Kazakhstan, Turkmenistan, Tajikistan, and Kyrgyzstan. It has also been reported that bin Laden has financed an Albanian-based TTO which has infiltrated various European nations.[40]

This "foundation for terrorists" was originally funded from bin Laden's own pockets. After many of his personal resources were seized, frozen, or clandestinely "transferred" out of his hands, bin Laden turned not to nation-state sponsors but to new private funding sources. Until Saudi Arabian authorities reputedly stepped in to halt the practice, these sources—primarily Saudi Arabian and other Persian Gulf business-men—may have provided bin Laden with hundreds of millions of dol-lars. Other reported sources of al-Qaeda funding include (sometimes unwitting) Islamic charitable organizations, the diamond and gold trade, stock investments, and even drug trafficking and cigarette running.[41]

The uncanny endurance of al-Qaeda illustrates the enormous difficul-ties of effectively countering a transnational terrorist organization with true global reach. After Afghanistan's former Taliban regime failed to obey a U.S. ultimatum to extradite al-Qaeda's leadership following the September 11, 2001, terrorist attacks, U.S.-led Operation Endur-ing Freedom helped quickly topple that regime. Yet the fall of the Tal-iban by December 2001 in no way resulted in the destruction of al-Qaeda. By late 2001, the al-Qaeda leadership—and most of its forces, only some hundreds of whom had been captured and detained by the United States—had already hastily fled much of its main Afghan base. The reported death of Mohammad Atef during American bombing raids and the subsequent captures of "operations director" Abu Zubay-dah and September 11 mastermind Khalid Shaikh Muhammad in Paki-stan appear to have been the only losses sustained by al-Qaeda's top leadership.[42]

Prior to September 11, 2001, Western and pro-Western experiences with al-Qaeda had already indicated the difficulty of countering terror-ist organizations whose activities both cross nation-state boundaries and are sponsored privately, rather than by nation-states. Privately spon-sored intranational terrorist organizations, which conduct their activi-ties within the borders of a single nation-state, are relatively easy for that nation-state to counter. International terrorist organizations, which conduct their activities across nation-state boundaries, are the concern of several, sometimes many, nation-states. Given, however, (1) proper intelligence concerning which nation-states sponsor particular inter-national terrorist organizations, and (2) international agreement upon how to proceed, it is a relatively straightforward matter for nation-states targeted by such organizations to impose relatively effective economic, military, or other forms of retaliation against their nation-state sponsors.

Transnational terrorist organizations, which transcend both nation-state boundaries and nation-state sponsorship, present an entirely new type of problem. The fact that TTOs tend to operate within, and target, multiple nation-states means that broad international agreement upon how to counter them is a necessary first step. Yet in the case of privately sponsored TTOs, those nation-states which fall prey to them have to look long and hard when deciding against whom to retaliate.

One example was the American attempt to punish al-Qaeda for its role in the massive bombings of U.S. embassies in Kenya and Tanzania. On August 20, 1998, dozens of U.S.-launched Tomahawk cruise missiles were directed against what was reported to be bin Laden's "terrorist university" in Afghanistan and an apparently civilian pharmaceutical factory in Sudan. This provoked angry protests, particularly from the Sudanese government, whose links to bin Laden were then even weaker than civil war–wracked Afghanistan's. Producing what appeared to be credible evidence, the Sudanese government strongly denied that its pharmaceutical plant was producing chemicals used in the production of VX nerve gas. In addition, questions were raised about just how willingly Taliban authorities in Afghanistan had tolerated bin Laden's presence. These reactions led the Clinton administration to claim an even broader U.S. right to retaliate against nation-states which either sponsor international terrorist organizations or (willingly or unwillingly) host TTOs such as al-Qaeda. In helping topple the former Taliban regime, the administration of President George W. Bush demonstrated that mere retaliation could, and would, be transformed into full regime change. Yet Operation Enduring Freedom, too, has led to unavoidable casualties among innocent Afghan civilians.[43]

Since September 2001, al-Qaeda has planned and executed—in several cases successfully—several terrorist attacks against the United States, as well as other Western and pro-Western targets. This is despite the fact that no confirmed sightings of, or new videotaped appearances by, top al-Qaeda leaders Osama bin Laden or Ayman al-Zawahiri have been released since late 2001. A small number of audiotaped messages from bin Laden and al-Zawahiri were, however, released in 2002 and 2003. A number of mid-level al-Qaeda operatives, who are remolding the TTO into an even looser and more decentralized organization, continue to seriously menace U.S. and other interests. Its new leaders now include three Egyptians, Muhsin Musa Matwalli Atwah, Mustafa Mohamed Fadhil, and Abdullah Ahmed Abdullah; a Saudi, Saif al-Adel; Fazul Abdullah Muhammad, a native of the Comoro Islands; and Fahid Muhammad Ally Msalam (nationality unknown). This remodeled TTO continues to maintain links throughout the world, but is particularly well represented in a vast area from north Africa to southeast Asia. For example, the newly restructured al-Qaeda has forged a firm alliance with Jemaah Islamiyah, a major Islamic transnational terrorist organization in its own right. Although it presently lacks true global reach, Jemaah Islamiyah operates cells in numerous southeast Asian nations, including Malaysia, Indonesia, and Singapore.[44]

Gunaratna's analysis of the post–September 2001 al-Qaeda organization paints a richer and even broader portrait:

> Since the U.S. intervention in Afghanistan in October, 2001, Al Qaeda has lost its main base for planning and preparing terrorist operations. Hence the Al Qaeda leadership is relying on a wider network to plan and execute new operations with the support of its associate groups. After relocation, the current, or new, leadership will reorganize the group's lines of command and communication. Al Qaeda is structured in such a way that it can operate without a centralised command. Its regional bureau[s] function as the nodal points of its horizontal network outside Afghanistan and liaise with associate groups and Al Qaeda cells. . . . The severe disruption to Al Qaeda's command and communication structures in 2001/2 has only emphasized the usefulness of such a decentralised structure. To adjust to the new reality, Al Qaeda is rapidly learning from its mistakes. With the sustained targeting and hunting down of its cells, their cadres are bringing forward many operations. Other Al Qaeda cells have tactically retreated, either "sleeping" for the time being or seeking the protection of their allies operating in disrupted zones in Asia, Africa and the Middle East. . . . Functional and regional compartmentalisation of the organisation—both in its infrastructure and networks—ensures that the highest standards of operational security are maintained. [Al Qaeda] also has a proven capacity to regenerate new cells: its networks are intertwined in the socioeconomic, political, and religious fabric of Muslims living in at least eighty countries.[45]

As noted at the beginning of this chapter, the major religions of the world have all given rise to radical fundamentalist sects which have all too frequently embraced terrorist tactics. It is not insignificant that the holy rage borne by radical Islamic fundamentalists has spawned the most profound, unremitting, and extensive transnational terrorist campaign in contemporary global politics. Yet the single most enduring contribution which holy rage may have made to the new global disorder is to provide the model for the transnational terrorist organization of the future.

CHAPTER SIX

Superterrorism: What's in It for You?

> *Above ground it was pandemonium. Hundreds of commuters streamed*
> *from subway exits into the bright morning sun. The pavements and soon*
> *the roads were blanketed with casualties lying where they had fallen, or*
> *clutching tissues to staunch blood flowing from their noses and mouths.*
> *It was an eerie kind of chaos. The commuters made little noise, since the*
> *nerve gas had crippled their lungs and stolen their voices. On this subway*
> *line alone, eight people would soon be dead, and nearly 2,500 injured.*
>
> DAVID E. KAPLAN AND ANDREW MARSHALL, *THE CULT AT THE END OF THE WORLD*

THE MARCH 20, 1995, CHEMICAL ATTACK against the Tokyo subway system was a watershed event in the history of terrorism. This single terrorist act aroused a new kind of collective horror from which, it seems, no one is immune. Granted, this was by no means even close to being the most deadly of recent terrorist attacks. Nor, for that matter, was the Tokyo subway attack the first instance of chemical terrorism. Nevertheless, the Tokyo incident, and the anthrax attacks of late 2001, have compelled us all to grudgingly accept an entirely new perspective—not merely toward terrorism, but toward our own physical, and ultimately emotional, security. For we are now forced to acknowledge the long-dreaded onset, rather than the merely frightening prospect, of what has come to be known as "superterrorism." [1]

Since the Tokyo subway attack, the global news, entertainment, and academic media have directed steadily increasing attention toward the threat of superterrorism. Several acclaimed television documentaries, such as *Frontline*'s "Plague War"; numerous best-selling novels, such as Richard Preston's *The Cobra Event;* and a growing number of motion pictures, such as *The Peacemaker* and *Twelve Monkeys,* are but a few examples. The popular success of these works indicates that the theme of superterrorism will continue to entertain and frighten—if not always responsibly inform—a greatly intrigued, yet bewildered and apprehensive, global audience. Most significant, the issue of superterrorism now receives very serious attention from government policymakers, scientists, and the academic community. [2]

The purpose of this chapter is to analyze—seriously, yet soberly—the fiercely debated problem of superterrorism. In examining this controversial issue, the following key questions will be addressed:

(1) What is meant by the term *superterrorism?*

(2) What is meant by the term *weapons of mass destruction?*

(3) What are the differences between conventional and nonconventional weapons of mass destruction?

(4) What arguments have been made for and against the general likelihood of future terrorist use of nonconventional weapons of mass destruction?

(5) What are the major types of superterrorism?

(6) What is the nature of, and what are the prospects for, chemical terrorism?

(7) What is the nature of, and what are the prospects for, biological terrorism?

(8) What is meant by the terms *radiological terrorism* and *nuclear terrorism?* What are the prospects for radiological terrorism and nuclear terrorism?

(9) Why is superterrorism such an attractive option for transnational terrorist organizations?

Superterrorism and Weapons of Mass Destruction: An Analysis

Superterrorism is the terrorist use of nonconventional weapons of mass destruction. Weapons of mass destruction (WMD) are weapons which are capable of causing mass, or large-scale, total casualties (deaths plus injuries). There seems to be no general civilian or even military agreement upon precisely where the respective thresholds between small-scale, medium-scale, and large-scale casualties lie. Let it be understood, then, that the term *mass casualties* implies a minimum of one thousand total casualties per attack.

Conventional weapons of mass destruction are, quite simply, commonly used weapons which lead to large-scale casualties. Nearly every nation-state possesses conventional WMD, and many nation-states have used them against enemy military and, in somewhat more limited cases, civilian targets. Among the most powerful of these conventional weapons are trinitrotoluene (TNT), cyclonite, high-brisance explosive, ammonium picrate, and tetryl explosives housed in artillery shells, demolition charges, bombs, torpedoes, and missile warheads. Since the invention of TNT during the 1890s, these conventional WMD have been widely deployed against military targets. By the First World War, these fearsome weapons were beginning to cause large-scale civilian casualties as well. During the Second World War, the use of conventional

WMD actually caused more civilian than military deaths. Examples of nation-state use of conventional WMD against civilian targets during the Second World War include:

(1) German aerial bombings and missile launches against British cities
(2) British, American, and Russian aerial bombings of German cities
(3) American aerial bombings of Japanese cities
(4) German, British, American, Russian, and Japanese torpedoing of civilian shipping[3]

Actual cases involving the successful terrorist use of weapons of mass destruction, however, remain extremely few in number. The 1993 World Trade Center bombing, which led to six deaths and nearly one thousand injuries, and the 1998 bombing of the U.S. Embassy in Nairobi, Kenya, which led to a total of more than two hundred deaths and more than five thousand injuries, appear to be the closest that terrorists have (so far) actually come to the successful use of conventional WMD. And, until September 11, 2001, no single terrorist attack of any kind had ever led to a total of one thousand or more fatalities.

Nonconventional WMD are far less commonly used weapons which, like conventional WMD, lead to mass casualties. Nonconventional WMD are chemical, biological, radiological, and nuclear (CBRN) weapons. An increasing number of nation-states possess varying stockpiles of certain CBRN weapons. Moreover, both Western and non-Western armies have resorted to the sporadic use of crude chemical and biological weapons for many centuries. The first truly large-scale nation-state use of chemical WMD was the deployment of chlorine gas, sulfur mustard, phosgene, hydrogen cyanide, chloropicrin, and other deadly chemical agents by Germany, France, and Britain against enemy military personnel during the First World War. These chemical WMD attacks led to many tens of thousands of deaths and many hundreds of thousands of injuries. More recently, chemical WMD were deployed by both Iran and Iraq during the Iran-Iraq War (1980–1988). These attacks led to many tens of thousands of casualties. The first and only successful nation-state use of biological WMD came during the Second World War, when Imperial Japanese forces released fifteen million fleas, infected by plague-ridden rats, over Changteh and other Chinese civilian targets. The Changteh attack alone reportedly led to approximately ten thousand casualties. The Japanese, however, endured thousands of self-inflicted casualties when their own forces were infected while developing and deploying these weapons. This deployment of biological WMD would soon be followed by the American nuclear bombing of Hiroshima and Nagasaki, Japan. Despite the primitive nature of the nuclear bombs dropped over Hiroshima and Nagasaki, each of the two weapons deployed in these attacks led to many tens of thousands of deaths and many hundreds of thousands of injuries due to nuclear bomb blast effect and radiation exposure. These acts, which still constitute the sole nation-state use of nuclear (or for that matter radiological) WMD "in anger," against either a military or civilian target, brought a swift end to by far the bloodiest war in world history.[4]

The Prospect of Superterrorism

Since the 1995 Tokyo subway attack, superterrorism has become a fiercely debated topic among government policymakers, scientists, and academicians alike. Curiously, and although the study of superterrorism is almost as old as the existence of recent terrorism itself, the debate over superterrorism has actually become a particularly bitter one since, rather than before, superterrorism finally reared its ugly head. This seemingly paradoxical development is in part due to the fact that, since the Tokyo subway attack, more and more counterterrorist funding has been designated for the threat of superterrorist rather than conventional terrorist scenarios. Some terrorism analysts warn that this new funding emphasis is coming at the expense of programs to counter the far more likely prospect of continued conventional terrorist attacks. For these observers, the conventional bomb and gun, rather than more exotic weapons, should continue to be the chosen stock-in-trade of terrorists.[5]

Since the attacks of September 11, 2001, considerable concern has also been expressed about a new form of terrorism which is neither conventional nor nonconventional in nature. In this type of terrorism, objects which are not normally viewed as weapons (commercial jetliners, for example) are used as delivery devices for dangerous substances also not typically regarded as weapons (such as large amounts of jet fuel) against a civilian or military target. The net result, however, remains the same: mass destruction. This third and newest category of terrorist weaponry may be termed *quasi-conventional weapons of mass destruction*.

In recent years, numerous arguments have been made both for and against the inevitability of future terrorist attacks involving nonconventional WMD. Although this debate has become a sharp and polarized one, it cannot be overemphasized that the threat of superterrorism must, as Chemical and Biological Arms Control Institute president Michael L. Moodie has put it, "neither be hyped nor ignored." Richard A. Falkenrath, Robert D. Newman, and Bradley A. Thayer put it well in their superbly researched and highly influential work, *America's Achilles' Heel:*

> For decades, public discourse on [CBRN] terrorism and covert attack has been dominated by two opposing schools of thought. At one extreme is the alarmist view, which considers future terrorist use of weapons of mass destruction a virtual certainty. Complacency characterizes the other extreme, a conviction grounded in assumptions about terrorist motivations and the technical difficulty of acquiring [CBRN] weapons. Each school of thought contains grains of truth, but the correct view lies somewhere between the two extremes.[6]

What arguments—both for and against—have been made regarding the general likelihood of continued terrorist use of nonconventional WMD? In essence, arguments warning of the inevitability of further superterrorist attacks are predicated on these points:

(1) Terrorists have a long history of technological innovation.

(2) Given extremely significant recent political, military, and technological trends, a growing range of terrorist organizations have developed abundant, albeit varying, capabilities of acquiring CBRN materials and of fashioning these substances into crude yet functional weapons.

(3) In engaging in a number, however limited, of actual chemical, biological, and radiological incidents, terrorists have already violated what had appeared to be the grave taboo against the use of these weapons.

(4) The evolving nature and motivations of today's terrorist organizations make the use of nonconventional WMD an increasingly attractive and likely option.

(5) Higher and higher body counts may be necessary to compel attention from a global audience which has become jaded by and desensitized to overused, and perhaps even shopworn, traditional terrorist tactics.

(6) A wide range of terrorist organizations have already demonstrated an increasing willingness to cause larger and larger numbers of casualties against softer (i.e., less secure) targets.

(7) It appears to be difficult for terrorist organizations to cause large-scale total casualties (i.e., deaths and injuries totaling over one thousand), and impossible to cause mass deaths (i.e., deaths totaling over one thousand), through the use of conventional WMD.

(8) Increasing urbanization drastically expands the range of particularly vulnerable potential CBRN targets.

(9) In most democracies, respect for civil liberties makes it difficult to counter terrorist organizations seeking, acquiring, and deploying nonconventional WMD.

(10) There is little or no effective proactive defense against superterrorist attacks.

(11) Public panic over the terrorist use—or even credible threatened use—of CBRN weapons will accomplish many of the short-term goals of certain terrorist organizations.[7]

By contrast, positions against the likelihood of additional superterrorist attacks are based on these arguments:

(1) Although terrorists do indeed have a long history of technological innovation, the number of actual superterrorist attacks to date is minuscule compared to the number of conventional terrorist attacks.

(2) Despite undeniably profound recent political, military, and technological trends, few terrorist organizations possess the capability of acquiring CBRN weapons, let alone causing large-scale casualties with them.

(3) Despite a substantial number of CBRN threats and hoaxes, there have been a mere handful of publicly documented incidents of superterrorism.

(4) Despite the evolving nature and motivations of today's terrorist organizations, terrorists tend to regard nonconventional WMD (which are generally more expensive and technologically challenging than conventional weapons, and with which terrorists are relatively unfamiliar) as too difficult to handle safely.

(5) Terrorists are perpetually awaiting that actual first use of superterrorist weapons which both leads to mass fatalities and may be replicated; the implied tautology is that no first use leads to no first use.

(6) The achievement of sufficiently high body counts through the deployment of conventional—and, certainly, quasi-conventional—weapons continues to compel intense attention by a global audience.

(7) Despite the willingness of many terrorist organizations to impose much larger numbers of casualties against softer targets, the use of CBRN weapons continues to constitute the breaching of a kind of threshold which many terrorist organizations (and indeed, most nation-states) may still remain reluctant to cross.

(8) There are many means of making the acquisition and deployment of nonconventional WMD by terrorist organizations a far more difficult task even in democratic nation-states.

(9) There are varyingly effective means of reactive defense against threatened or actual superterrorist attacks.

(10) Public reaction to the use of CBRN weapons by terrorists would ultimately be one of profound and counterproductive rage against the perpetrators.

(11) The deployment of superterrorist weapons would lead to massive counterterrorist strikes and other actions—perhaps in certain cases even the use of nuclear weapons—by targeted nation-states and their allies.[8]

The major types of superterrorism are, as noted above, chemical, biological, radiological, and nuclear. Chemical terrorism is the terrorist use of lethal or otherwise toxic chemicals, usually in gaseous or aerosol form, as nonconventional WMD. Biological terrorism is the terrorist deployment of either naturally existing or artificially engineered bacteria, viruses, or biotoxins as nonconventional WMD. Radiological terrorism is the terrorist dispersal of deadly radioactive materials, particularly plutonium or highly enriched uranium, against human targets. Nuclear terrorism is the deployment of either stolen or terrorist-manufactured nuclear weapons against mass human and other physical targets.[9]

Thus far, the only nonconventional act of terrorism leading to mass casualties has been the 1995 Tokyo subway attack by Aum Shinrikyo. Other major instances of actual CBRN weapons deployment not leading to mass casualties include

(1) a June 1994 chemical attack in Matsumoto, Japan, which, although leading to eight deaths and over two hundred injuries, received little public attention until linked to the Tokyo subway attack

(2) the September 1984 biological contamination of salad bars by the Oregon-based Rajneeshee religious cult, which led to the *Salmonilla typhosa*–induced sickening of 751 victims

(3) the November 1995 planting of a radioactive canister in a Moscow park, probably by Chechen terrorists, who later claimed responsibility and issued threats of further radiological attacks

(4) the fall 2001 dispersal of anthrax spores through the U.S. mail by as-yet-unidentified perpetrators, which led to five deaths and dozens of nonfatal casualties[10]

Bad Chemistry

Thus far, only chemical weapons have served as true superterrorist WMD. Chemical weapons are either natural or, more typically, artificially engineered chemical agents which are intended to cause widespread deaths or injuries. There are six important characteristics and properties underlying the multitude of potential chemical weapons. According to Michael L. Moodie, these include:

(1) *Lethality:* the extent to which the agent will cause fatalities

(2) *Mode of action:* the route by which the agent causes its effects (inhalation, dermal [skin] exposure, mucous membrane, or oral ingestion)

(3) *Speed of action:* the time between exposure and effect

(4) *Stability:* the resistance of the agent to degradation [loss of chemical strength], which is important during storage and dissemination

(5) *Persistence:* the length of time an agent remains a hazard once it is released into the environment

(6) *Toxicity:* the quantity of a substance required to achieve a given effect[11]

According to Moodie, chemical weapons are classified into the following five categories:

(1) *blister agents,* which are delivered in vapor, aerosol, and liquid form, have a high persistency, and attack the lungs, eyes, and skin [e.g., pure mustard, lewisite]

(2) *blood agents,* which are delivered in vapor form, have a low persistency, and attack the lungs [e.g., hydrogen cyanide, cyanogen chloride]

(3) *choking agents,* which are delivered in vapor form, have a low persistency, and attack the lungs, eyes, and skin [e.g., chlorine, phosgene]

(4) *incapacitants,* which are delivered in aerosol or liquid form, have a low persistency, and attack the lungs and skin [e.g., lysergic acid diethylamide, or LSD; BZ]

(5) *nerve agents,* which are delivered in vapor, aerosol, or liquid form, have a low to high persistency, and attack the lungs, eyes, and skin [e.g., tabun, sarin, soman, VX][12]

Of these five categories of chemical weapons, nerve agents—like those deployed in the Tokyo subway attack—are among the most potent, lethal, rapid-acting, persistent, and, not surprisingly, feared. The Nerve agents are not quite as simple to manufacture as, for example, blistering agents like mustard gas (the manufacturing process for which has been thoroughly understood for over a century). Nevertheless, the techniques for manufacturing nerve agents such as tabun, soman, and sarin have been available in open scientific literature for over half a century. Many of the ingredients necessary in order to manufacture nerve agents are widely available. The ingredients for making sarin, for instance, are readily available from supply-house catalogs. All that is typically required in order to obtain these ingredients is the submission of a check and a written request on "official" letterhead stationary. Moreover, two of sarin's main ingredients, ordinary rubbing (isopropyl) alcohol and methyl alcohol, may be purchased at any drugstore.[13]

Supreme Harbinger

The March 20, 1995, sarin nerve gas attack against the Tokyo subway system by Aum Shinrikyo, or "Supreme Truth," marks the first and only successful use of nonconventional WMD by any terrorist organization, transnational organization, or, for that matter, nonstate actor. As such, this act and the bizarre organization which brought it to fruition merit close attention.

In order to fully comprehend Aum Shinrikyo, it is essential to examine its supreme, highly autocratic leader, or "guru," Shoko Asahara. Born Chizuo Matsumoto in 1955, Shoko Asahara is a native of southern Japan. Totally sightless in his left eye and only partially sighted in his right eye, the young Asahara habitually bullied and intimidated his fully sightless fellow students during his years at a boarding school for the blind. The frustrated, and eternally ambitious, Asahara then went on to pursue a life of chronic fraud, theft, and manipulation, which led ultimately to his formation of the Aum Shinrikyo religious cult in 1987. Asahara's teachings were a bizarre blend of yoga, Hindu and Buddhist mysticism, and the Christian notion of apocalypse. In creating Aum Shinrikyo, Asahara was fully aware of the fact that Japanese religious organizations had enjoyed nearly complete freedom since the end of the Second World War.[14]

By the early 1990s, Aum Shinrikyo had become far more than a simple religious cult. By this juncture, Aum Shinrikyo was something of an astonishing cross between a huge transnational religious cult with tens of thousands of members in at least six nations, a prosperous transnational corporation, and, most ominously, a powerful transnational terrorist organization. Asahara's combined transnational organization, which by some credible estimates held total assets in excess of one billion dollars, had corporate subsidiaries (in fact, front companies) in Japan, Russia, Australia, Sri Lanka, Germany, Yugoslavia, Taiwan, and the United States.

Asahara's extravagant prophesies of renewed, final warfare between Japan and the United States, of the resulting destruction of global society, and of Aum Shinrikyo's rise to supreme global power, came at the very time that the organization was making plans to deploy CBRN weapons against the Japanese and American power establishments. Which nonconventional weapons of mass destruction most intrigued Asahara and his top disciples? Although Asahara had a particular fascination with chemical weapons, it is of no small significance that Aum Shinrikyo had also acquired serious biological and nuclear weapons expertise, if not actual weapons, from Russia and numerous other sources.[15]

Given the relative—and, in the case of Aum Shinrikyo, proven—technical difficulties of successfully acquiring, yet alone deploying, biological, radiological, or nuclear weapons on a grand scale, Asahara opted to utilize deadly sarin nerve gas against a mass target, the Tokyo subway system. In June 1994, Asahara ordered a trial run of a crude yet highly lethal sarin concoction against an apartment complex in Matsumoto. A large container of liquefied sarin was dripped onto a powerful electric heater, and the resulting vapors were then fan-blown out of a window inside a refrigerated truck. The Matsumoto sarin deployment led to eight deaths and over two hundred injuries.[16]

Following the success of the Matsumoto attack, Asahara felt emboldened to approve the Tokyo subway operation. That event was carried out by five Aum Shinrikyo members: Kenichi Hirose, Masato Yokoyama, Toru Toyoda, Ikuo Hayashi, and Yasuo Hayashi. Each of these five men was a highly educated scientist or medical doctor. Hirose and Yokoyama were applied physicists. Toyoda was a particle physics graduate student. Ikuo Hayashi was a cardiovascular surgeon. Yasuo Hayashi was an electronics engineer. Each was also a high-ranking "official" of Aum Shinrikyo's Ministry of Science and Technology, a "cabinet ministry" in the organization's shadow government. And each had been given PAM, an antidote to sarin nerve gas.[17]

Kaplan and Marshall set the stage for the Tokyo subway attack:

Tokyo, March 20, 1995. For nearly 400 miles the Tokyo subway system sprawls beneath this vast metropolis, a maze of concrete and steel tunneling into the night like a giant ant farm. It is the world's busiest underground railway, used by 9 million passengers each day. It is also an ideal site for mass murder. . . . At 7:45 A.M., five members of the Aum Supreme Truth cult blend into this massive press of humanity. The cultists board five trains at different ends of the subway system. They know the exact times and locations for each train at each station. They also know that by 8:15, all five trains will converge upon Kasumigaseki, the center of power in Japan, being home to the bureaucracies that rule over 125 million Japanese. . . . Now aboard the trains, it is all for real: each bag holds a chemical solution that is 30 percent sarin, a nerve gas invented by the Nazis. Sarin is colorless, odorless and deadly. In minutes, perhaps seconds, it can destroy the nervous system of every living being within 100 feet. . . . At the prescribed moment, [the five Aum Shinrikyo members] will place their bags on the floor beneath their seats, puncture them [with plastic umbrellas], and let the sarin evaporate into a lethal gas.[18]

As a result of the sarin gas release, twelve people died either immediately or after the slow, agonizing symptoms of nerve gas exposure. It is estimated that as many as six thousand people were sickened by this operation. In the frantic weeks following the attack, various Aum Shinrikyo leaders were apprehended by Japanese security forces. Asahara himself was arrested on May 16, 1995, almost two months after the Tokyo attack.[19]

Police raids of Aum Shinrikyo facilities yielded grim confirmation of the organization's obsession with chemical weapons. Police seized as evidence huge quantities of sarin, VX, tabun, soman, pure mustard (a precursor, or key ingredient, to sulfur mustard gas), the precursors to a variety of nerve agents, such as sodium fluoride, phosphorous trichloride, and isopropyl alcohol, and the precursors to hydrogen cyanide, such as sodium cyanide and sulfuric acid. One Japanese newspaper, *Mainichi Shimbun*, reported that Aum Shinrikyo had stockpiled enough chemical weapons to kill ten million people. Reliable sources also reported that Aum Shinrikyo had planned to launch sarin attacks within the United States.[20]

Aum Shinrikyo's deployment of sarin nerve gas in the Tokyo and

Matsumoto attacks is exceedingly instructive. First, these events demonstrate that terrorist organizations—even the most financially and technologically well endowed—are, at least presently, more likely to resort to chemical than to biological, radiological, or nuclear attacks. Aum Shinrikyo actually deployed biological WMD on several occasions, without resulting casualties, and, despite its mightiest efforts (including the probable payment of substantial bribes), the organization seems to have been unable to secure radiological or nuclear materials from either Russia or other sources. Moreover, it is ominous to consider that, but for lack of a more effective delivery system, the Tokyo subway attack might have been far deadlier:

> The importance of aerosolizing the chemical agent was demonstrated by the Aum Shinrikyo subway attack. The fact that the sarin was allowed to evaporate rather than be delivered as an aerosol was one of the key factors in limiting casualties. Had Aum been able to develop an effective aerosolization mechanism—which they tried to do—the number of casualties would likely have been much higher.[21]

Second, Aum Shinrikyo exemplifies one of the types of transnational terrorist organizations which many terrorism analysts predict are most likely to turn to CBRN attacks. One is the theoterrorist organization. For example, al-Qaeda has attempted to acquire, and may have indeed actually acquired, certain CBRN capabilities. The other is the apocalyptic cult. These latter groups, as the title of Robert Jay Lifton's book implies, really do intend to "destroy the world in order to save it." For fanatical theoterrorist groups (such as al-Qaeda), or cults that also function as terrorist organizations, there is scant regard for global opinion and the relatively limited goals which seem to have restricted most left-wing and ethnoterrorist organizations from pursuing nonconventional WMD.[22]

Third, Aum Shinrikyo's acquisition of chemical (as well as biological) weapons was greatly facilitated by the organization's contacts with various Russian politicians and scientists. These included Asahara's meeting with Russian vice president Aleksandr Rutskoi and various national legislators, such as Russian parliament member Ruslan Khasbulatov. More critically, it has been fairly well established that Aum Shinrikyo recruited several members at Russia's Mendeleyev Chemical Institute, where, as Kaplan and Marshall observe, "every chemistry graduate had the know-how and materials to synthesize World War II nerve gases." Cameron is even more explicit in his point that

... Aum received the instructions for a sarin nerve gas plant and the recipe for the agent itself from a Russian source, possibly Oleg Lobov, an allegation that [Lobov] vehemently denies, but which was made by Yoshihiro Inoue, Aum's head of intelligence, at his trial in May 1997. ... The accusation of a Russian connection is further supported by the method Aum used in their sarin-making. There are at least six different main methods for producing the nerve agent but, of the various states possessing chemical weapons, only the Russian military uses Aum's formula, utilizing phosphorous trichloride rather than phosphorous pentachloride. This further supports the suggestion that Lobov was the source of the "recipe." [23]

These points offer strong indications that Russia and other former Soviet republics may actually be more likely sources for chemical—as well as for biological and radiological—materials and expertise than for nuclear weapons.

Fourth, Aum Shinrikyo's choice of the Tokyo subway system certainly reinforces the argument that increasing urbanization greatly expands the range of targets which are highly vulnerable to CBRN terrorist attacks. Examples of urban targets which are particularly vulnerable to superterrorist attacks are major airports, lengthy transportation tunnels, huge domed stadiums and indoor arenas, large shopping malls and theaters, key financial centers, major embassies, large places of religious worship, major resorts, famous landmarks, and significant office and residential buildings. In point of fact, any infrastructure accommodating over one thousand people, particularly in an indoor setting, is an extremely attractive setting for a superterrorist attack.

Finally, the fact that Aum Shinrikyo's status as a religious organization shielded it from investigation by Japanese authorities illustrates the point that democratic respect for civil liberties makes it more difficult (although not impossible) to counter religious organizations which seek to acquire nonconventional—or conventional—WMD. This is also an issue in the United States, where precious constitutional guarantees of religious freedom shield organizations which, like Aum Shinrikyo, may not merely pursue innocent religious practices. Precisely where to draw the line between religious cults, corporations, and terrorist organizations (transnational or otherwise) is a difficult matter. It must certainly be granted, however, that when the activities of religious organizations present such a blatant threat to public safety as those of Aum Shinrikyo, then those activities, at minimum, demand the closest scrutiny by authorities.

Lethal Yet Living

The gloomy menace of chemical terrorist attacks is far overshadowed by the prospective terrorist employment of biological weapons of mass destruction. For one thing, as Jessica Stern astutely observes, "[p]lagues and diseases can be even more frightening than toxic chemicals." Second, many once-commonplace and dreaded diseases, such as small-pox, were only recently declared to be eradicated. Indeed, just prior to the current specter of superterrorism, even passing reference to these scourges seemed to have disappeared from common public discourse. It is therefore natural for revived, and serious, discussion of these seem-ingly vanquished public health threats to create deep anxiety.[24]

There are many other terrifying dimensions of biological terrorism. Most people, as Stern so keenly points out, "tend to fear unusual dis-eases," such as those typically contemplated by such terrorists, even "more than well-known killers," such as cancer or heart disease. It is also difficult to determine whether outbreaks of newly emerging dis-eases, such as the West Nile virus which has swept much of the United States, the current spate of livestock diseases (like Britain's "mad cow" disease), or the recent Severe Acute Respiratory Syndrome (SARS) epi-demic, are truly naturally occurring, or, perhaps, terrorist-induced phe-nomena. Lastly, and in the words of a retired U.S. Army general involved in both chemical and biological weapons programs, "chemical agents will cover only tens of square miles, whereas biological agents can blan-ket hundreds of thousands of square miles."[25]

There are few publicly confirmed instances of fatalities resulting from the terrorist use of biological weapons of mass destruction. Neverthe-less, influential government officials—particularly U.S. policymakers—have warned that biological terrorism may represent the single most sig-nificant national security threat of the twenty-first century. Conversely, a number of government officials and terrorism analysts might still se-cretly wish to paraphrase Winston Churchill's oft-quoted words of hom-age to England's Royal Air Force pilots that "never was so much owed by so many to so few." For these cynics, it might rather appear that "never was so much made by so many about so little." What is the na-ture of, and what are the prospects for, biological terrorism?[26]

Biological terrorism is the terrorist deployment of either (1) naturally existing bacteria, viruses, or biotoxins, or (2) artificially engineered vi-ruses or combinations of viruses (recombinant viruses, or chimeras) against human targets. These agents enter the body through inhalation or ingestion, causing illness and, all too frequently, death. The major distinction between bacteria and viruses is that bacteria are fully intact, living organisms which may reproduce themselves outside of a biological host, whereas viruses are merely combinations of genes (the smallest "building blocks" of life) which may reproduce only within a biological host. Bacteria and viruses all contain the tiny ribbon-shaped genetic material known as deoxyribonucleic acid (DNA) or ribonucleic acid (RNA). Biotoxins most frequently result from, for example, the combination of bacteria and parasitic molds.[27]

According to Jessica Stern, the major threats—and limitations—of biological agents are:

(1) *Toxicity:* Tiny amounts of biological agents can kill.

(2) *Speed of action:* Live biological agents act slowly. The agent must multiply in the victim before the victim will exhibit symptoms, a process that can take from several hours to several weeks.

(3) *Specificity:* Biological agents are specific: most affect either plants, humans, or other animals exclusively.

(4) *Controllability:* The effects of biological agents are highly dependent on difficult-to-control variables such as meteorological conditions and terrain.

(5) *Residual effects:* Most biological agents will not survive long in the atmosphere.[28]

It will be important to keep these characteristics in mind when considering both naturally occurring and genetically altered biological agents.

One of the most deadly, and readily available, forms of natural bacteria is *Bacillus anthracis,* commonly known as anthrax. Schweitzer accurately predicted in 1998 that anthrax was a "likely bioagent of choice by future terrorists":

Unfortunately, the bacteria are relatively easy to obtain from infected cattle or sheep or from other sources. They can be made to multiply rapidly in small biological laboratories. The spores remain stable for a period sufficiently long enough to allow their dissemination onto distant targets.[29]

Steven M. Block, however, stresses the problems associated with the deployment of anthrax—which must be delivered, through airborne means, over a mass target—as a true terrorist WMD:

Anthrax is by no means the perfect bioweapon, however, for several excellent but unrelated reasons. First and foremost, it is nontrivial to target a ground population with any airborne agent, due to the many difficulties of dissemination, that is, producing just the right aerosol, adjusting for the vagaries of wind and weather, and so forth. Second, prolonged exposure to sunlight kills most anthrax spores after release. Third, the minimal lethal dose for inhalation (reported to be 5,000 to 10,000 spores) is high compared with some other biological agents. Fourth, if diagnosed and treated early, anthrax may be cured with sufficient doses of penicillin-type antibiotics. Fifth, specific vaccines can be prepared that prevent infection by known strains of anthrax.[30]

Perhaps most significant, anthrax is not contagious on a human-to-human basis.

Although easy to acquire and cultivate, anthrax is relatively difficult to deliver as a genuine weapon of mass destruction. This is demonstrated by Aum Shinrikyo's failure to infect Tokyo inhabitants with anthrax spores sprayed from an eight-story Aum facility in June 1993. The post–September 11, 2001, U.S. anthrax attacks are another illustration of the poor candidate that anthrax makes for a true WMD. In those attacks, the delivery of a particularly potent, weapons-grade form of anthrax through the U.S. mail service ultimately led to the inhalation anthrax deaths of a Florida newspaper photo editor, two Washington, D.C., postal workers, a New York City hospital worker, and an elderly Connecticut woman. Despite these deaths, the infection of dozens of others, the preventive treatment of hundreds more, and the spread of intense fear among tens of millions of already panicky Americans, anthrax-related casualties remained far below the threshold of true mass destruction.[31]

Another form of deadly natural bacteria is *Yersinia pestis,* also known as bubonic plague, or simply plague. Plague bacteria are typically spread to humans by fleas originally hosted by infected rodents. Bubonic plague, then referred to as the "Black Death," wiped out as much as one-third of Europe's human population from 1348 to 1350. Like anthrax, plague is relatively easy to acquire and cultivate. Its ease of delivery as a terrorist WMD was demonstrated by the devastating Japanese attack over Changteh, China, during the Second World War. As indicated by Japan's experiences, however, the issue of how perpetrators may handle *Yersinia pestis* without infecting themselves is an extremely difficult one.

Ominously, terrorists already bent on suicide missions would not be deterred by such constraints.[32]

Viruses are another form of biological WMD which may be employed by terrorist organizations. Although quite contagious, most viruses, such as rhinoviruses, which cause the common cold, are generally not lethal. Certain strains or subtypes of influenza (commonly referred to as the flu) may, however, be highly lethal, as was the case during the influenza pandemic of 1918–1919. In point of fact, that pandemic actually led to more American fatalities than all of the combined wars fought by the United States during the twentieth century. Examples of naturally existing viruses identified as leading candidates for use as terrorist biological WMD include *Poxvirus variolae* (commonly known as smallpox) and *Filoviridae* (the Ebola virus). The contraction of these viruses leads to gruesome and agonizing symptoms. Both smallpox and Ebola are also highly lethal. Aum Shinrikyo's failed 1992 attempt to acquire Ebola cultures in Zaire is certainly an indication of that newly emerging disease's desirability as a biological weapon, if not an effective WMD.[33]

Smallpox, the more contagious of the two viruses, is a far more attractive bioterrorist weapon. Given the possible terrorist deployment of smallpox, American and foreign officials have debated whether potential target populations, which have not been immunized against the virus for decades, should be vaccinated. Even those vaccinated against smallpox prior to the announced eradication of the disease would have to be revaccinated, since earlier vaccinations no longer provide sufficient immunity to smallpox. Enough stockpiles of vaccine now exist, for example, to inoculate the entire population of the United States. Even if a target population were vaccinated against smallpox, however, certain other complications would almost certainly arise. For example, a tiny percentage of any treated population will die from the vaccine itself. It is also highly likely that any administered smallpox vaccine would not protect a target population from certain strains of smallpox. In 1971, for example, Soviet open-air field testing of a weaponized, and particularly potent, smallpox strain led to three accidental deaths and the sickening of seven people who had actually received vaccinations against the virus.[34]

Biotoxins are chemicals produced by various organisms. Biotoxins cannot reproduce, nor are their effects contagious. The most deadly of all biotoxins is *Clostridium botulinum,* commonly known as botulinum toxin. In 1980, a sizable amount of botulinum toxin was discovered in a West German Red Army Faction safe house in Paris. Aum Shinrikyo actually deployed botulinum toxin, without success, on two occasions in June 1993. The organization's targets were the Japanese Diet (national legislature) and the Crown Prince's wedding. Ricin, a byproduct of castor beans, is also highly lethal. Extraordinarily tiny amounts—less than a millionth of the size of the period at the end of this sentence—of either botulinum toxin or ricin are extremely deadly. The question of how to deliver these biotoxins as true weapons of mass destruction, however, has probably yet to be answered; one hopes it never will be.[35]

The Engineering of Doom

Artificially engineered combinations of viruses (recombinant viruses, or chimeras) are the most bewildering, frightening, and likely pathways toward the terrorist use of biological weapons of mass destruction. Named after the mythological chimera—a horrifying monstrosity with a lion's head, a goat's body, and a serpent's tail—a recombinant virus is a combination of the genetic material of two or more viral, or nonviral, organisms.[36]

Recombinant viruses are an unfortunate by-product of the biotechnological revolution. One of the crowning achievements of that revolution is the complete mapping of the human genome. This scientific achievement actually enables genetic therapists to alter human genes in order to prevent, or cure, genetically induced diseases. This process is based on the use of delivery vehicles, known as vectors, to deliver therapeutic genes to disease-causing cells within human DNA. These projects are based on extremely well-established and easy-to-master methods of genetic manipulation. For example, even high school biology students are now being taught how to (1) remove DNA from living organisms, (2) alter bacteria by placing genes into them, and (3) isolate DNA materials from the transformed bacteria.[37]

Profound concern has been raised in the policymaking, government research, and academic communities regarding the use of these simple, widely available, and extremely inexpensive technologies by terrorists seeking the perfect biological weapon of mass destruction. Block puts the matter very articulately:

Modern bioscience has led to the development of many powerful tools for manipulating genes. Such tools hold the key to revolutionary medical advances, among them gene therapy and the eventual

abolition of fatal diseases such as cancer. But they make equally possible the creation of entirely new WMD, endowed with unprecedented power to destroy. It seems likely that such weapons will eventually come to exist, simply because of the lamentable ease with
which they may be constructed. In contrast to nuclear weapons, [re-
combinant viral weapons] do not require rare materials, such as enriched uranium and plutonium. They do not require rare finances:
development and production are relatively inexpensive. They do not
require rare knowledge: most of the techniques involved are straightforward, well documented, and in the public domain. Today, thousands of biologists worldwide possess the requisite skills, and more
are trained every day (most often at U.S. universities). Finally, they do
not require rare infrastructure: some [recombinant viral weapons]
can be produced by small terrorist groups almost as easily as through
national biological warfare programs. Inevitably, someone, somewhere, sometime seems bound to try something. So, for better or
worse, genomics will change our world. It would be tragic if it took
the biological equivalent of Hiroshima to muster our response. Like
it or not, we need to begin certain preparations now.[38]

Block, a Stanford University–based molecular biologist, actually
thinks like a genetic terrorist when he speculates how recombinant viruses might be employed for the most diabolical purposes. These may
include:

(1) *Safer handling and deployment.* Biological warfare agents pose
direct threats to those who use them and many deaths appear to have
resulted from accidental releases of agents, not from their use as
weapons. What if this "boomerang problem" could be alleviated?

(2) *Easier propagation and/or distribution.* What if one could produce a better aerosol? Better yet, what if one didn't need an aerosol
at all, but relied on a different mechanism for distribution?

(3) *Improved ability to target the host.* What if an agent could
be developed that specifically targeted one or another population
group? Or, what if some group could be protected against infection
in advance?

(4) *Greater transmissivity, infectivity.* What if one could engineer
a viral disease with the lethality of (say) Ebola, but with the commu-
nicability of measles?

(5) *More difficulty in detection.* What if the disease was hard to diagnose? Or had never even been encountered before? Or had a long latency? Or behaved in a cryptic way?

(6) *Greater toxicity, more difficulty in combating.* What if the disease had [an] unusually high [susceptibility] or mortality [rate]? What if it was resistant to all known antibacterial or antiviral agents? Or defeated all existing vaccines?

(7) *More (self-limiting, self-enhancing . . .).* What if some pathogen could produce a localized outbreak but then render itself harmless? Conversely, what if a pathogen could continually alter itself in such a way as to evade treatment? [39]

Block further warns that biotechnology might actually enable genetic terrorists to create: (1) binary biological weapons (which are perfectly safe to handle until their two components are combined), (2) "designer genes and life forms," (3) "gene therapy as a weapon," (4) "stealth viruses," (5) "host-swapping diseases," or (6) "designer diseases." These are all very chilling prospects.[40]

The entire world now knows that the former Soviet Union, in complete violation of the 1972 Convention on the Prohibition of the Development, Production, and Stockpiling of Bacteriological and Toxin Weapons and on Their Destruction, had developed a huge, well-financed, and highly sophisticated offensive biological weapons program known as Biopreparat. Former Russian president Boris Yeltsin admitted that a 1979 anthrax outbreak in Sverdlovsk (now Yekaterinburg), Russia, which led to more than one hundred fatalities, was in fact due to an accidental release of anthrax spores cultivated by Soviet scientists. Ken Alibek, the first deputy chief of the Biopreparat program, defected to the United States in 1992. Alibek's fine book, *Biohazard,* provides unnerving details of the Soviet biological offensive weapons program, which developed both natural and genetically altered biological weapons. Alibek discusses a particularly disturbing episode involving a research colleague, Nikolai Ustinov, who was accidentally injected with the deadly and highly contagious Marburg virus in April 1988. During his agonizing, nearly three-week bout with the virus, Ustinov kept a careful chronicle of its symptoms. Throughout this ordeal, Alibek and all other Biopreparat scientists were ordered to continue their work. After Ustinov's death, genetically altered samples of the Marburg virus were actually harvested from his body for further development. The new virus was named "Marburg Variant U" (for Ustinov). According to Alibek, Soviet (and later Russian) scientists were developing the most highly advanced genetic WMD program in the world. Not surprisingly, Aum Shinrikyo's own scientists also conducted extensive research into genetic WMD during the early 1990s.[41]

Food for Thought

Given the wide range of possible biological weapons, terrorists are very likely to target a nation's food supply. Seed, soil, crops, and livestock are all inviting and utterly vulnerable targets for future agroterrorists. Indeed, agriculture, and the food industry in general, may be the softest of all potential transnational terrorist targets. Farms, ranches, food processing plants, food warehouses, and supermarkets are safeguarded by few (if any) measures. Yet a skillful and coordinated agroterrorist attack would deal a devastating blow to those billions of people dependent upon others for their food supply.[42]

The use of biological weapons against agricultural targets was seriously researched by Britain during the Second World War and by the Soviet Union throughout its decades-long development of an offensive biological weapons program. The British government considered, but did not develop, anti-crop and anti-livestock weapons for use against Nazi Germany and her allies. According to Alibek, anti-agricultural weapons were in fact successfully developed by the Soviet Union:

> One of the most successful programs was created by the Ministry of Agriculture. A special division was established to research and manufacture anti-livestock and anti-crop weapons. The division was given the uninspired title of Main Directorate for Scientific and Production Enterprises. The biowarfare program was code-named "Ecology." Scientists at the agriculture ministry developed variants of foot-and-mouth disease and rinderpest for use against cows, African swine fever for pigs, and ornithosis and psittacosis to strike down chickens. Like anti-personnel biological weapons, these agents were designed to be sprayed from tanks attached to Ilyushin bombers and flown low over a target area along a straight line for hundreds of miles. This "line source" method of dissemination could cover large stretches of farmland. Even if only a few animals were successfully infected, the contagious nature of the organisms ensured that the disease would wipe out agricultural activity over a wide area in a matter of months.[43]

Thus far, there have been few documented instances of agroterrorism. The most successful example came in February 1978, when a limited number of Israeli oranges were contaminated by liquid mercury. As a result of these relatively low-level attacks, Israel was forced to reduce her orange exports by nearly half. The Israeli citrus industry was devastated by these events.[44]

Although no known terrorist attack against U.S. agriculture has yet taken place, the likelihood of such an attack remains highly disturbing. The agriculture industry is one of the largest employers in the United States, and agricultural products represent about two-thirds of all U.S. exports. Moreover, as Joseph W. Foxell, Jr., points out, U.S. agriculture is particularly vulnerable since the livestock industry is concentrated in a very few geographically isolated areas; the vast bulk of the nation's seed supply derives from a very limited number of locales; "agribusiness" farms are extremely large, highly centralized, and lacking in crop diversity; and herbicides, pesticides, and antibiotics are being overused, thus leading to new vulnerabilities. Should terrorist organizations target the American food supply, public loss of confidence in U.S. agricultural products might lead to widespread panic, hunger, and devastating economic losses.[45]

Prospects for Bioterrorism

Given current circumstances, terrorists are very likely to acquire and use biological WMD in the near future. It is still far too easy to acquire these weapons. There are over fifteen hundred microbe supply houses, such as the huge American Type Culture Collection, throughout the world. Too few restrictions are still placed on the national or international purchase of even the most lethal biological agents. There have also been reports of thousands of unpaid or unemployed former Biopreparat scientists willing to sell their expertise to the highest bidder. Given the realities of the situation, the specter of biological and genetic terrorism is grim.

Potential scenarios for the terrorist use of biological WMD are not difficult to imagine. Schweitzer states, for example, that

> ... the most likely use of biological agents on a significant scale in the United States appears to be the release of a cloud of infected air, a biological aerosol, into a heating or air conditioning system or into a confined space bristling with people. Once released, it will be difficult to find the perpetrator.[46]

Another likely scenario would be the dropping of lightbulb-like objects containing bacteria onto subway station tracks just prior to the arrival of an approaching train. The wheels of the train would then spread bacteria over the entire subway route. This tactic was actually employed by American biological weapons scientists who conducted experiments in New York City subway stations during the cold war.[47]

The situation, nevertheless, is not a hopeless one. For one thing, the successful terrorist deployment of natural biological WMD is not nearly as simple a matter as some observers have speculated. Second, the United States has begun to take the threat of superterrorism very seriously. On November 14, 1994, former U.S. president Bill Clinton issued Executive Order 12938, which made it a federal felony offense to have any involvement in the potential or actual use of CBRN weapons. Clinton, in stating that CBRN weapons were "an unusual and extraordinary threat to the national security, foreign policy, and economy of the United States," also placed the United States in a state of emergency. Few Americans are aware of the fact that that executive order has been renewed each year since 1994. In addition, new programs and interagency networking arrangements have been established to deal with the problem of CBRN weapons. The operational effectiveness of these multi-agency arrangements, or of the new U.S. Department of Homeland Security, is a matter of considerable debate. (A far more practical response would be the creation of a single agency to deal with the entire highly complex issue of terrorism.) The United States has also created a program to provide work for unemployed or underemployed Biopreparat scientists, which may, in effect, keep them off the open market, and potentially provide the United States with additional defensive biological weapons expertise.[48]

Although biological and (particularly) genetic terrorism is a daunting problem, there are practical, although not perfect, means of defense. It has been fairly well established that the use of vaccines is an extremely limited, impractical, and in all likelihood useless response to the complex range of biological or genetic WMD. As Alibek argues, however, "boosting our nonspecific immune system[s] may offer at least temporary protection from pathogenic agents" in the event of a biological or even genetic terrorist attack. One such technique is the stimulation of what are known as cytokines, natural bodily defenses which may "prompt the growth and activation of a host of essential immune cells," thus "helping to destroy pathogenic bacteria and cells invaded by viruses." Perhaps the most well-known—albeit expensive—example of a cytokine is interferon. Last, and most critical, although genetic engineering may provide terrorists with what appears to be the perfect doomsday weapon, it is also true that that same technology might enable scientists to quickly determine the genetic makeup of a particular agent and devise some genetic means of defense, or even attack, against it. Neither countermeasure is a perfect solution. There are bound to be mass casualties in any well-planned, well-orchestrated biological or genetic terrorist attack. But to either surrender to the problem, or to ridicule it, is an unacceptable response to this very real national security threat.[49]

It has long been maintained that terrorists want a lot of people watching, not a lot of people dead. In the case of biological terrorism, would it be enough to make a lot of people sick? This is a question which has yet to be definitively answered.[50]

Dirty Weapons

Government policymakers, scientists, and academicians once clustered the threats of radiological and nuclear terrorism together under a single category, nuclear terrorism. For many years, a general (although not universal) assumption was that radioactive materials stolen or otherwise acquired from military or civilian nuclear sites were, after all, intended for use in the fashioning of nuclear devices. It is now widely recognized that radiological and nuclear terrorism are distinctly different forms of superterrorism.[51]

Radiological terrorism is the terrorist dispersal of deadly radioactive materials. One such material is highly enriched uranium (HEU), a chemical substance which contains more than 20 percent uranium-235 (tiny amounts of which are found in raw uranium, otherwise known as uranium-238). Another is plutonium-239 (typically referred to simply as plutonium), an artificial element produced from the abundant isotope of uranium called uranium-238. When HEU or plutonium is paired with a low-intensity dispersal device (a relatively weak explosive), the combination is commonly referred to as a "dirty bomb." HEU or plutonium may also be released as a result of the sabotage of civilian nuclear research or power facilities, or deployed through other means. If so dispersed, HEU and plutonium can cause radiation sickness and, ultimately, cancer and leukemia. Additional radioactive materials which may be fashioned into a dirty bomb include cesium, strontium, cobalt, and other substances. There are various sources for such radioactive materials, such as U.S. and foreign hospitals, universities, and industrial complexes. Radioactive materials suitable for use in a dirty bomb are also reportedly available within former Soviet republics such as Kyrgyzstan, Kazakhstan, and Tajikistan. It was to these nations that alleged al-Qaeda associate Ibrahim al-Muhajir (born José Padilla) traveled in his own quest for a dirty bomb.[52]

Nuclear terrorism is the terrorist deployment of either (1) stolen, intact, or (2) self-manufactured nuclear weapons against mass human and other physical targets. There are two basic types of nuclear weapons. Fission weapons are designed to cause uranium-235 or plutonium-239 atoms to split, leading to a runaway nuclear chain reaction, and, in an instant, an explosion leading to tremendous mass destruction. Fusion weapons utilize the effects of fission (splitting) to cause a fusion (uniting) of light chemical elements (such as hydrogen) to form heavier elements, which leads to even greater explosive effects than fission explosions. Nuclear weapons may contain either weapons-grade HEU, weapons-usable HEU, or plutonium. Weapons-grade uranium, which is that form of HEU most suitable for nuclear weapons use, has been enriched to a uranium-235 level of more than 90 percent. Weapons-usable uranium, or HEU enriched to a uranium-235 level of less than 90 percent, may also be employed in nuclear weapons. (In the latter case, however, the total amount of HEU which must be employed increases as the enrichment level decreases.) A second nuclear weapons ingredient is plutonium-239, an artificial element produced from uranium-238. Like HEU, plutonium is employed in both military and civilian nuclear programs. Plutonium, however, is far safer for terrorists to handle than HEU. In the case of nuclear terrorism, the relatively elaborate weapons used only *contain* deadly radioactive materials. In the case of radiological terrorism, on the other hand, these radioactive materials are themselves directly deployed against human targets.[53]

There are a number of reasons why radiological terrorism and nuclear terrorism are now regarded as separate issues:

(1) Radiological terrorism and nuclear terrorism are, as seen above, technically quite different in nature.

(2) The relatively unsophisticated dispersal of radioactive materials is a much simpler technical prospect than the deployment of either a stolen/intact or self-manufactured nuclear weapon. For this and other reasons, radiological terrorism is far more likely than nuclear terrorism.

(3) Chemical and biological terrorism, which already represent a kind of "poor man's atomic bomb," offer instructive lessons to those terror-

ists contemplating the far more expensive and technologically challenging feat of nuclear terrorism. The relative ease of lower-technology chemical and biological terrorist attacks may well encourage terrorists to contemplate the much more realistic radiological scenario.

(4) There has been at least one instance of radiological terrorism, whereas there has been no nuclear terrorist event.

(5) There have been numerous attempted—and perhaps successful—instances of plutonium or HEU smuggling, whereas there has been no single credibly confirmed instance involving an intact nuclear weapon.

(6) The simple fact is that the once seemingly probable, if not inevitable, prospect of intact nuclear weapons being smuggled from Russia, or other former Soviet republics, is now regarded as extremely, if not totally, unlikely. The prospect, on the other hand, of HEU or plutonium smuggling from those or many other sources, both Western and non-Western, is considerably higher.[54]

A considerable volume of literature on the former Soviet republics suggests that "loose" radioactive materials, and possibly even nuclear weapons, will "leak" into various hands. Some of these works also suggest that Russian, Chechen, or other transnational crime syndicates would be naturally instrumental in this radiological and nuclear trade. This literature tends to stress (1) poor Russian and other former Soviet republic control over both civilian and military nuclear-related facilities and materials, (2) the miserable economies of the former Soviet republics, and (3) the natural inclination of organized crime to do virtually anything for a profit. These are, quite simply, naive generalizations.[55]

Another, much more realistic, set of literature emphasizes that although there have been—and continue to be—opportunities for radiological, if not nuclear, leakage from the former Soviet republics, there are no serious links between Russian organized crime and the few isolated radiological thieves. Writing in 1998, for example, noted transnational organized crime analyst Rensselaer W. Lee III deprecated the notion of such links. Lee argues that it is neither profitable nor practical for Russian organized crime syndicates to become involved in the dangerous, tedious process of radiological enrichment and smuggling. It is also almost certainly true that Russian organized crime is generally pleased with the political and economic status quo and wishes to do nothing to upset that applecart. Lee does raise the strong possibility, nevertheless, that the Chechen mafiya "already have made forays into the nuclear black market." Writing in 1999, Stern notes that Chechen terrorists issued credible threats to attack Russian nuclear plants. One wonders whether these activities may have played a role in Russia's brutal reinvasion of Chechnya very shortly after the publication of these two works.[56]

In reference to the prospect of nuclear terrorism, Bruce G. Blair, a highly respected nuclear weapons expert, provides perhaps the best argument against the potential smuggling of nuclear weapons out of Russia:

> The evident effectiveness of safeguards on nuclear weapons and their ingredients reflects the high priority of nuclear command and control in the Russian political and military culture. The Soviets went to extraordinary lengths to ensure strict central control over nuclear force deployments, and this obsession with control ran through the entire weapons cycle—from production and assembly to operational deployment to dismantlement. *The Russians show no signs of relaxing the traditional standards.*[57]

The disintegration of the former Soviet Union, therefore, probably makes the prospect of nuclear terrorism no more likely than had been the case prior to 1991.[58]

Blair recognizes, however, that "[l]ooser security within the non-weapon nuclear infrastructure" may allow the leakage of weapons-usable, if not weapons-capable, HEU or plutonium. Like Lee and others, Blair acknowledges that the Russian mafiya has no use for this type of criminal activity, and that those "small-time opportunists" attempting to sell these materials had no buyers for their wares. The disincentives for radiological smuggling are, therefore, not to be ignored.[59]

What, then, of the prospects for radiological terrorism? There appear to be two schools of thought on this matter. One is that radiological terrorism would be a fairly simple means for terrorists to employ nonconventional WMD. As Louis Rene Beres, a veteran analyst of nuclear terrorism, observes, "The forms such weapons might take include plutonium dispersal devices (only 3.5 ounces of plutonium could prove lethal to everyone within a large office building or factory)." Lee paints an even gloomier portrait when he warns:

> Even if traffic in weapons-grade or weapons-usable materials is successfully contained, widespread availability of toxic radioactive materials such as cesium-137, cobalt-60, and strontium-90 is in itself worrisome. Even ordinary [nuclear] reactor waste can be a weapon in

the hands of terrorists. . . . Certain powdered radioactive substances introduced into a ventilation system of an office building or hospital could cause massive fatalities.[60]

Other observers discount the prospect that radiological weapons in the hands of terrorists would serve as true weapons of mass destruction. Stern, for example, asserts that "radiological materials [are] unlikely to kill or injure many people." Mullen quite bluntly states, "The plutonium dispersal device is, simply, not a weapon of mass destruction."[61]

In sum, radiological—and to some extent nuclear—weapons are not particularly cost-effective as true WMD. At present, chemical WMD are far less expensive, more available, and less complex than either nuclear or radiological WMD. In time, biological WMD—particularly the genetically altered variety—may prove less expensive, more available, and less complex than even chemical WMD. What WMD analyst R. William Mengel, in a chapter on nuclear terrorism, had to say about the matter in 1978 is, if anything, even more true today: "Much easier to initiate are acts using chemical and biological agents and their related technologies."[62]

Superterrorism as a Transnational Threat

Despite all of the difficulties imposed by the acquisition, development, and deployment of nonconventional WMD, a number of factors make it extremely likely that transnational terrorist organizations will deploy superterrorist weapons. A growing range of terrorist organizations have developed abundant, albeit varying, capabilities of acquiring CBRN materials and of fashioning these substances into crude but functional weapons. This is particularly true of TTOs with the economic power and technological sophistication of Aum Shinrikyo. The financial resources, proven desire, ability to cause genuine mass destruction, and global reach of al-Qaeda imply that that TTO might also possess, or come to possess, certain CBRN capabilities. Other TTOs with similar arsenals are likely to emerge over the next few decades at most.

The evolving nature and motivations of today's terrorist organizations make the use of nonconventional WMD an increasingly attractive option. Transnational terrorist organizations such as Aum Shinrikyo and al-Qaeda have none of the concern for public opinion which distinguished most earlier intranational and international terrorist organizations. Indeed, in Aum Shinrikyo's case, members of that TTO were led to believe that CBRN attacks would be blamed not on their organization, but rather, on the United States! When questioned during a 1999 interview about whether al-Qaeda had acquired chemical and biological weapons, Osama bin Laden emphasized that God is the only audience who matters to him:

> Acquiring weapons for the defense of Muslims is a religious duty. If I have indeed acquired these [chemical and biological] weapons, then I thank God for enabling me to do so. And if I seek to acquire these weapons, I am carrying out a duty. It would be a sin for Muslims not to try to possess the weapons that would prevent the infidels from inflicting harm on Muslims.[63]

In another interview, bin Laden twice made veiled references to the U.S. nuclear attacks on Hiroshima and Nagasaki during the Second World War. Again, other TTOs, of similar nature to al-Qaeda and with equivalent motivations, may well emerge during the next several decades, if not sooner.[64]

Those who have questioned the likelihood of future CBRN attacks have argued, among other things, that the deployment of superterrorist weapons would lead to massive counterterrorist strikes by affected nation-states and their allies. This assumption is based, of course, on the ability of targeted nation-states to identify the perpetrators of those attacks. In the case of the 2001 U.S. anthrax attacks, to cite one example, no perpetrator has yet been identified. Transnational terrorist organizations rarely, if ever, claim responsibility for their actions. In addition, the increasing permeability of national boundaries, the democratic respect for freedom of movement, and the intrinsic transnationality of TTOs makes it quite easy for members of those organizations to plant a CBRN device and exit a targeted nation-state days or even weeks before the effects are noticed. This is particularly the case with biological agents. In the words of one U.S. government report:

> An advantage for the terrorists is that, in a well-planned and well-executed [biological] attack, there is less likelihood of apprehension than in case[s] where more conventional weapons are used—they may be thousands of miles away when the first casualties occur. Such attacks may leave no signature unless the participant terrorist group . . . claims credit. . . . [In addition, biological agents] could be sent in small amounts in valises, parcels, or trunks and, over a period

of months, stockpiled in major U.S. cities for later use. Since it is impossible, at present, to stop the arrival of relatively large amounts of drugs in the United States, it would similarly be impossible to prevent the arrival of much smaller quantities of living micro-organisms or toxins. Such shipments could even enter through normal shipping or airfreight routes. Alternatively, seed cultures could be smuggled into North America and the agents mass produced in clandestine laboratories in the United States or Canada.[65]

Consider, too, the case of radiological materials, which may take weeks, months, or even years to exhibit any noticeable effect.

The structure and behavior of many transnational terrorist organizations provide further incentives for TTOs to resort to superterrorist attacks. TTOs tend to have a relatively brief shelf-life and a fluid, amorphous, and unidentifiable membership of highly diverse individuals. Many TTOs are in fact ad hoc entities created for the purpose of conducting a single act of terrorism. Such TTOs are ideal for conducting bold CBRN assaults in that their fleeting organizational existence makes them difficult, if not impossible, to trace. In addition, many TTOs are characterized by ceaseless factionalism and multiple centers of decision-making. The desire of one particularly extreme subgroup or leader to overwhelm more moderate factions or decision-makers, or to present the latter with a fait accompli, makes superterrorism an irresistibly attractive and utilitarian option for certain transnational terrorists. These factors make it highly likely that tiny, more violent, and less risk-averse TTOs (i.e., radical religious fundamentalists, transnational religious cults, or perhaps, as suggested in certain literature, right-wing extremists) may embark upon future superterrorist attacks.[66]

The proper response to the prospect of superterrorism is neither rampant panic nor absurd ridicule of this very real threat. Superterrorism is a highly complex issue which must be dealt with in a sober and realistic manner. None of us can expect to live in a risk-free society. None of us can guarantee that events far more horrifying than the Tokyo subway, anthrax, or September 11 attacks will never take place. What we can and must do is to think seriously about the "unthinkable" in order to be properly prepared for these terrorist threats.[67]

CHAPTER SEVEN

After September 11:
Responding to Transnational Terrorism

Man is his own star, and the soul that can
Render an honest and a perfect man
Commands all light, all influence, all fate.
Nothing to him falls early, or too late.
Our acts our angels are, or good or ill,
Our fatal shadows that walk by us still.

JOHN FLETCHER ET AL., *THE HONEST MAN'S FORTUNE*

IT IS EXCRUCIATINGLY DIFFICULT to "conclude" a book about a global threat now unimaginably more ominous than when writing on that very book began. Yet that is the situation facing the author of the book which you now hold in your hands. As the new year of 2004 commences, the worldwide threat of transnational terrorism seems like the crest of an immense new wave of global disorder.

On September 11, 2001, the world's sole superpower experienced the horror of a vicious war waged against—and within—her own homeland. The final death toll—3,056 lives lost in New York City, Washington, and Pennsylvania—seems incomprehensible, almost surreal. Other figures, although far less significant, are equally staggering. In New York City alone, 3.1 million hours of labor were required to remove 1,642,698 tons of debris from the Ground Zero site. The September 11 attacks also resulted in the largest single insurance loss in history: approximately $50 billion. The U.S. economy, which has lost hundreds of billions of dollars, has yet to recover from the events of that single day. Hundreds of books have been written about September 11. Even new terms—like *ground zero* and *debris surge*—have been added to our popular language.[1]

In a very real sense, the new global disorder confronts us with an entirely new paradigm. When putting together the puzzle presented by the old global order, all of the pieces (i.e., issues, challenges, and threats) were ultimately made to fit, albeit at times clumsily. In essence, what nation-states were faced with during the old global order period was the threat not of shadowy transnational organizations, but rather, that of other, clearly identifiable nation-states. It is supremely ironic that the cold war now seems like a much safer, much more predictable time.

As Thomas S. Kuhn points out in his brilliant work *The Structure of Scientific Revolutions,* when certain pieces simply refuse to fit into the old, "normal" puzzle, that is probably because they are actually part of an entirely new puzzle. As Kuhn observes, this creates a period of crisis during which the outlines of the new puzzle begin to take shape. What we are witnessing today are the vague outlines of that new global puzzle. Some observers have already coined a term for it: They call it the new normal.[2]

Most Westerners, and Americans in particular, impatiently demand quick, painless, and above all practical solutions to the world's countless problems. The relatively recent challenge of transnational terrorism has received the same response. What seventeenth-century English political philosopher Thomas Hobbes emphasized in his major works is what we now accept as a given: that the most basic responsibility of any government is the physical—and by extension emotional—security of its citizens. Terrorism is above all a threat to our physical and emotional security. It is therefore natural for us to expect our national capitals to provide us with solutions to this scourge.[3]

It is a relatively simple matter for nondemocratic nation-states to respond to terrorist attacks. Their citizens enjoy few if any political or human rights, and their leaders generally care little for domestic or global opinion. What is particularly difficult is when nation-states which genuinely embrace democratic values and rights are confronted by major terrorist threats.

What does the recent historical record show? There are numerous illustrations of democratic governments whose struggles with terrorist organizations produced serious political fallout. In Spain, for example, so-called Anti-Terrorist Liberation Groups (GAL) killed at least twenty-seven members or supporters of the Basque ethnoterrorist organization ETA. GAL's four-year reign of terror, which took place between 1983 and 1987, targeted ETA enclaves in France's Basque region. A government investigation into GAL led to the conviction and imprisonment of a former Spanish interior minister and eleven other officials. Although exonerated of direct involvement in the killings, Spanish prime minister Felipe González was politically tarnished by the scandal. In 1978, two members of the Armed Revolutionary Movement, a Puerto Rican ethnoterrorist organization, were gunned down well after having been fully subdued by Puerto Rican police forces. Seven Puerto Rican police officials were convicted and sentenced for the killings, and former Puerto Rican governor Carlos Romero Barcelo was defeated in his quest for reelection. In Corsica, Henri Mazeres, the disgraced former head of that French island's military police, admitted that he ordered police officers to commit an arson attack against a restaurant frequented by members of the Corsican National Liberation Front. In Northern Ireland, a Protestant organization mysteriously known as the "Committee" is claimed to have systematically killed Irish Republican Army and Irish National Liberation Army members and sympathizers. In Spain, Germany, Italy, Britain, India, Colombia, and even the United States, stern new laws have been passed which allow for the use of secret courts, secret evidence, secret witnesses, warrantless arrests, arbitrary imprisonment, restrictions on legal representation in terrorism-related cases, and other measures. Since September 11, 2001, the United States has apprehended or killed hundreds of al-Qaeda members in Afghanistan and, in at least one case, in Yemen. Many of those transnational terrorists will probably face military tribunals which will decide their ultimate fate. Whether those U.S.-based al-Qaeda members who resist arrest will also be so targeted should certainly prove to be an extremely complex, difficult, and contentious issue.[4]

Despite these controversies, an increasing number of nation-states—and in particular the United States—have made significant strides in countering terrorism. Very encouragingly, many of these measures are of a financial or otherwise economic nature. Since September 11, 2001, budgets for counterterrorism programs have increased dramatically. The freezing of assets even remotely linked to transnational terrorist organizations has dried up some (but by no means all) TTO financial resources. The number of informants' tips on suspected transnational terrorist activities (many of which have come as a result of government rewards and other incentives for producing such reports) has increased dramatically. Explosives detection systems for airports, government buildings, and other "hard targets" have been substantially improved. High-technology intelligence-gathering programs are undergoing continuous development. National borders are now more vigilantly guarded. The most significant restructuring of the U.S. federal government in over fifty years has culminated in an enormous and entirely new cabinet-level Department of Homeland Security.

These measures have been reasonably productive. Scores of low-, medium-, and (in a few cases) high-profile terrorist suspects have been apprehended since September 11, 2001. Although President George W. Bush's "war on terrorism" neither has been won, nor ever (as Bush himself has admitted) will be, that war, for the first time in world history, is being fought, and seriously fought. But it will be up to tomorrow's historians to judge whether today's historic war on terrorism either was or was not an overall success.

Most important, international cooperation on counterterrorism has grown slowly, but steadily. By its very nature, transnational terrorism demands a broad international response. That international response is coming from (1) individual cooperation between nation-states, (2) intergovernmental organizations such as the United Nations, the North Atlantic Treaty Organization, the European Union (within which, due to the large-scale elimination of border checkpoints, transnational terrorism presents a particularly formidable threat), and Interpol (the international police organization), and (3) more informal contacts developed during, for example, the annual G-7 summit meetings, which are attended by the leaders of the United States, Canada, Britain, France, Germany, Italy, Japan, and Russia. In order for efforts at countering transnational terrorism to have any chance of success, nation-states must act to expedite deportation, extradition, and if necessary even the extraterritorial apprehension of transnational terrorists residing in foreign nations.[5]

It has been suggested that the Internet may become both a target for TTOs and a vehicle by means of which they might further pursue their respective agendas. To this point, what has been loosely dubbed *cyberterrorism* has in fact amounted to little more than aimless, albeit frightfully costly, high-technology vandalism. Whether the destruction or damage of computer files by lone actors with no discernible purpose other than highly sophisticated vandalism qualifies as terrorism—transnational or otherwise—is at best highly doubtful. In the future, of course, it is possible that such activities may become part of an organized transnational terrorist campaign against various governmental, business, academic, or other targets in order to advance some type of political, religious, social, or economic agenda. At present, however, this has simply not been the case.

In point of fact, transnational terrorists are most benefited not by damaging or destroying the Internet, but rather, by exploiting this extraordinary means of truly transnational, global communication. In 1995, Theodore Kaczynski, an intranational terrorist better known as the Unabomber, successfully demanded that his anti-industrial "manifesto" be published in major American newspapers. (Indeed, the publication of Kaczynski's manifesto, which did lead to his capture, was itself a highly controversial counterterrorist issue.) Transnational terrorists of the future may simply e-mail their manifestos to millions of Internet users.

TTOs and their members make heavy use not only of the Internet but also of encrypted or coded e-mail. Encryption is one of the most hotly contested issues in the campaign against transnational terrorists, and transnational criminals in general. The U.S. Federal Bureau of Investigation (FBI) has sought broad powers to decode encrypted e-mail messages. Unfortunately, legitimate transnational corporations, which also make heavy use of encrypted e-mail messages in order to convey proprietary information, feel threatened by the FBI's efforts. Whether this aspect of the war against terrorism may be pursued without unduly hampering legitimate transnational actors remains an open question.

The issue of chemical, biological, radiological, and nuclear terrorism is without a doubt the most difficult of all counterterrorist challenges. In reference to chemical and biological terrorism (particularly the latter), great emphasis has already been placed on the emergency medical response to such likely catastrophes. The extraordinary threat of genetic terrorism, and the need to develop genetically engineered and other immunological defenses from this horror, demands similar attention. Radiological and nuclear terrorist incidents, although relatively remote threats in light of the far greater prospect of chemical or biological terrorist scenarios, are by no means an impossibility. United States Nuclear Emergency Search Teams (NESTs), whose mission is to locate and remove radiological or nuclear weapons, have been in place for some years. Far greater priority should be placed on increasing NEST budgets than on nuclear missile defense appropriations. For years, America's National Rifle Association has preached that "guns don't kill; people kill." In this case, it might be observed that nuclear missiles don't kill thousands; nuclear warheads do. A transnational terrorist organization does not need a missile in order to trigger a radiological or nuclear scenario. Let us never lose sight of this vital fact.

Transnational terrorism is the most formidable, yet by the same token instructive, global threat of the twenty-first century. It is both part of the new global disorder and a key contributor to that disorder. In coming to grips with this new menace, we may yet bring a bit more order and security to a world in profound transition.

NOTES

1. What Is Terrorism?

1. For a more detailed discussion of this controversy, see for example Richard M. Pearlstein, *The Mind of the Political Terrorist*, 1–3, and Bruce Hoffman, *Inside Terrorism*, 13–44.

2. On the alleged impossibility of defining terrorism, see Walter Laqueur, *A History of Terrorism*, 7. For a more current work on this point, see Omar Malik, *Enough of the Definition of Terrorism*. On the often overlooked, and invaluable, distinction between terrorism and terror, see Frederick J. Hacker, *Crusaders, Criminals, Crazies*, x.

3. The term *organization* is defined as any functional structure with which one or more individuals are affiliated. It should also be noted that the different generations of terrorist organizations are not discrete entities; rather, each generation has gradually evolved into, or overlapped, each succeeding generation.

4. The term *active support* shall be defined as deliberate and intentional support beyond mere access to nation-state territory.

5. Four of the better works on second-generation, international terrorist organizations are Ovid Demaris, *Brothers in Blood;* Uri Ra'anan et al., eds., *Hydra of Carnage;* Claire Sterling, *The Terror Network;* and Robert D. Chapman and M. Lester Chapman, *The Crimson Web of Terror*. The financing of terrorist organizations by nation-states, intergovernmental organizations, and transnational organizations has been superbly addressed in James Adams, *The Financing of Terror*.

6. See for example "Premier Says Terrorist Group Dismantled," *Dallas Morning News*, September 9, 2002. For a fuller analysis of the November 17 terrorist organization, see George Kassimeris, *Europe's Last Red Terrorists*, and Andrew Corsun, "Group Profile: The Revolutionary Organization 17 November in Greece (1975–91)," in Yonah Alexander and Dennis A. Pluchinsky, eds., *European Terrorism*, 93–125.

7. On the Cuban sponsorship of Puerto Rican ethnoterrorist organizations, see for example U.S. Senate, Committee on the Judiciary, *Terrorist Activity* (94th Cong., 1st sess., 1975).

8. Increasing transnational communication between American and European right-wing terrorist organizations is a topic that is extremely well explored in Jeffrey Kaplan and Leonard B. Weinberg, *The Emergence of a Euro-American Radical Right*. Kaplan and Weinberg note that, whereas radical right-wing ideology was transmitted from Europe to the United States in the earlier part of the twentieth century, that ideology now originates in the United States and moves to Europe.

2. *The Rise of the New Global Disorder*

1. John T. Rourke, *International Politics on the World Stage*, 60–64. The term *global system* may be defined as an interacting group of world actors forming a unified whole.

2. Ibid., 61, 62–63.

3. During this period, a growing number of developing, or "third world," nation-states refused to formally align with either bloc. However, these nonaligned nation-states never organized any competing bloc of their own. Moreover, although many of the nonaligned nation-states, such as India, Egypt, and Indonesia, claimed formal neutrality during the cold war period, those same nation-states did indeed informally tilt toward one bloc or another at a given juncture.

4. Rourke, *International Politics on the World Stage*, 61.

5. Ibid.

6. Ibid., 61–62.

7. For an excellent overview of global politics during the last five centuries, see Karen A. Rasler and William R. Thompson, *The Great Powers and Global Struggle*. Diverging from the conventional view that the global system during the period between the First and Second World Wars (1918–1939) was multipolar in nature is Randall Schweller, *Deadly Imbalances*. Schweller argues that the interwar global system was tripolar, with the United States, the Soviet Union, and Germany serving as the dominant centers or poles. On the general issue of dynamic change among global systems, see Stuart J. Kaufman, "The Fragmentation and Consolidation of International Systems," *International Organization* 51 (1997): 755–776. See also Richard Falk, "In Search of a New World Model," *Current History* 23 (1993): 145–149.

8. Rourke, *International Politics on the World Stage*, 62–63.

9. For more on these points, see especially Hedley Bull, *The Anarchical Society*. Other significant works on the disintegration of the old global order include Zbigniew Brzezinski, *Out of Control*; Matthew James Connelly, *A Diplomatic Revolution*; Samuel P. Huntington, "The Clash of Civilizations," *Foreign Affairs* 72 (1993): 56–73; Huntington, *The Clash of Civilizations and the Remaking of World Order*; Stanley Hoffman, *World Disorders*; Robert D. Kaplan, *The Coming Anarchy*; James N. Rosenau, *Turbulence in World Politics*; and Winston A. van Horn, ed., *Global Convulsions*. For a divergent perspective on these points, see for example Yahya Sadowski, *The Myth of Global Chaos*, and Thomas J. Volgy and Lawrence E. Imwalle, "Hegemonic and Bipolar Perspective on the New World Order," *American Journal of Political Science* 39 (1995): 819–834. These general points are also explored in Birthe Hansen and Bertel Heurlin, *The New World Order*; David Jablonsky, *Paradigm Lost?*; Keith Philip Lepor, ed., *After the Cold War*; Matthew Polesetsky, ed., *The New World Order*; Joseph Wayne Smith, Graham Lyons, and Evonne Moore, *Global Anarchy in the Third Millennium?*; and Andrew Williams, *Failed Imagination?* The alternative concept of an emerging multipolar global system is explored in Charles W. Kegley, *A Multipolar Peace*.

10. The term *transnational organization* is being used in place of the customary, but more general, term *nonstate organization*. *Transnational organization* is the preferred term because these organizations are indeed nonstate, but also transcend both state borders and state interests. Strictly speaking, the term *nonstate organizations* might also encompass those organizations which function exclusively within the borders of single nation-states. The seminal work on transnational relations is Robert Keohane and Joseph Nye, *Transnational Relations and World Politics*. See

also Werner J. Feld, *International Relations,* and Thomas Risse-Kappen, *Bringing Transnational Relations Back In.*

11. For an excellent analysis, see Rachel Ehrenfeld, *Narco-terrorism.*

3. Transnational Terrorism and the New Global Disorder

1. The general concept of transnational terrorism was first suggested by Stephen Sloan in his *Anatomy of Non-Territorial Terrorism,* 3. In this work, Sloan introduced a new term, *non-territorial terrorism,* or NTT, defined as "a form of terror that is not confined to a clearly delineated geographical area."

2. Stephen Sloan, "Terrorism: How Vulnerable Is the United States?" in Stephen C. Pelletiere, ed., *Terrorism,* 63. The concept of "gray areas" within which legitimate nation-state authority has broken down and which provide convenient access to opportunistic TTOs, transnational crime syndicates, and other transnational organizations seems to have been introduced by Peter Lupsha in his "Gray Area Phenomenon: New Threats and Policy Dilemmas," a paper presented to the Conference on High Intensity Crime/Low Intensity Conflict, September 27–30, 1992, at Chicago, Illinois. This concept was further developed in Max G. Manwaring, ed., *Gray Area Phenomena,* and in Max G. Manwaring and William J. Olson, eds., *Managing Contemporary Conflict.* Manwaring states, for example, that "[p]robably the most insidious security problem facing the United States and the rest of the world now and for the future centers on the threats to a given nation-state's ability and willingness . . . to deal with transnational threats to the control of national territory. . . . The major players involved in these threats to the stability of targeted nation-states generally include non-state actors and non-governmental groups who may or may not be supported by other non-state entities or nation-states. This is the gray area phenomenon . . ." See Max G. Manwaring, "Beyond the Cold War," in Manwaring, ed., *Gray Area Phenomena,* 63. Scott B. MacDonald argues that "[a] key element of the disorder of nations is the 'gray area' where the jurisdiction of governments is ineffective in maintaining control over a particular geographic area or a type of activity" in MacDonald, "The New 'Bad Guys,'" in Manwaring, ed., *Gray Area Phenomena,* 34.

3. Nation-states which have in recent years endured such conflict and been subjected to varying degrees of transnational terrorist (and transnational criminal) infiltration include: Afghanistan, Albania, Algeria, Angola, Armenia, Azerbaijan, Bangladesh, Bolivia, Bosnia-Herzegovina, Bulgaria, Burundi, Colombia, Congo, Ecuador, Egypt, El Salvador, Eritrea, Ethiopia, Georgia, Guatemala, Guinea-Bissau, India, Indonesia, Iraq, Jordan, Kazakhstan, Kyrgyzstan, Lebanon, Liberia, Mexico, Myanmar, Pakistan, Panama, Peru, Philippines, Republic of Congo, Russia, Rwanda, Senegal, Sierra Leone, Somalia, South Africa, Sri Lanka, Sudan, Tajikistan, Turkey, Turkmenistan, Uganda, Ukraine, Uzbekistan, Venezuela, Yemen, and Yugoslavia. Although lengthy, the preceding is by no means an exhaustive list of the world's "gray areas."

4. For more on Aum Shinrikyo's Zaire visit, see Gavin Cameron, "Multi-track Microproliferation," *Studies in Conflict and Terrorism* 22 (1999): 295; David E. Kaplan and Andrew Marshall, *The Cult at the End of the World,* 97; and Robert Jay Lifton, *Destroying the World to Save It,* 186–187. In its quest for weapons of mass destruction, Aum Shinrikyo had in fact created a network of transnational front companies. For more on this point, see especially Kaplan and Marshall, *The Cult at the End of the World,* 90–92.

5. One might also speculate about whether the declining volume of Puerto Rican ethnonationalist terrorism by formerly Cuban-sponsored organizations such as the FALN, Los Macheteros, and the Armed Revolutionary Movement is linked to Cuba's increasing isolation, vulnerability, and economic decline since the collapse of her own patron-state, the Soviet Union. There also appears to have been a relative decrease in Syrian sponsorship of Palestinian terrorist organizations at least since Operation Desert Storm, an international conflict which placed Syria (at one time a major sponsor of various Palestinian terrorist organizations) and the United States within the same coalition. For a number of reasons, sponsorship of international terrorism by nation-states such as Libya, North Korea, and South Yemen also appears to be declining. It might be noted that King Hussein's expulsion of Palestinian terrorist organizations from Jordan in September 1970 inspired the formation of the Black September international terrorist organization. Black September, itself an offshoot of the Palestine Liberation Organization, claimed responsibility for the 1972 Munich Olympics attack, which resulted in the deaths of eleven Israeli athletes and coaches. Three of the best sources on Black September are John K. Cooley, *Green March, Black September;* Christopher Dobson, *Black September;* and George Jonas, *Vengeance.*

6. For more on the point that, although the number of terrorist incidents has been decreasing in recent years, the number of terrorist casualties is actually increasing, see, for example, Bruce Hoffman, "Terrorism Trends and Prospects," in Ian O. Lesser et al., eds., *Countering the New Terrorism, 7–38,* and Roger Medd and Frank Goldstein, "International Terrorism on the Eve of a New Millennium," *Studies in Conflict and Terrorism* 20 (1997): 286–287.

7. The issue of anonymous terrorism has been addressed by a number of observers. See especially Bruce Hoffman, "Why Terrorists Don't Claim Credit," *Terrorism and Political Violence* 9 (1997): 1–6; Dennis A. Pluchinsky, "The Terrorism Puzzle," *Terrorism and Political Violence* 9 (1997): 7–10; and David C. Rapoport, "To Claim or Not to Claim," *Terrorism and Political Violence* 9 (1997): 11–17. See also Bruce Hoffman, "Reply to Pluchinsky and Rapoport Comments," *Terrorism and Political Violence* 9 (1997): 18–19.

8. The relationship between the rise of the European Union, the tearing down of European border crossings, and security threats such as transnational terrorism is explored in Kjell Eliassen, ed., *Foreign and Security Policy in the European Union;* Stephen Iwan Griffiths, *Nationalism and Ethnic Conflict;* Fernando Reinares, ed., *European Democracies against Terrorism;* and Jenone Walker, *Security and Arms Control in Post-Confrontation Europe.*

9. How far counterterrorists may go in decoding encrypted communications has become the subject of an increasingly serious debate. On the general issue of how new information technologies have immensely strengthened the positions of transnational organizations relative to those of states, see especially Walter B. Wriston, *The Twilight of Sovereignty.*

4. Ethnoterrorism: Menace from Within and Without

1. Benjamin R. Barber, *Jihad vs. McWorld,* 3–4. Works which address the theme of a tribalistic reaction against globalization include Brzezinski, *Out of Control;* Bull, *The Anarchical Society;* Kenneth Christie, *Ethnic Conflict, Tribal Politics;* Carl Conn, *Culture Wars and the Global Village;* Stanley Hoffman, *World Disorders;* Huntington, *The Clash of Civilizations and the Remaking of World Order;* Michael W.

Hughey, *New Tribalisms;* Erik Melander, *Anarchy Within;* Daniel Patrick Moyni-han, *Pandaemonium;* Manning Nash, *The Cauldron of Ethnicity in the Modern World;* James N. Rosenau, *Turbulence in World Politics;* Robert C. Trundle, Jr., "Has Global Ethnic Conflict Superseded Cold War Ideology?" *Studies in Conflict and Terrorism* 19 (1996): 93–107; and Winston A. van Horne, ed., *Global Convulsions.* Globalization is also a central theme in Maryann K. Cusimano, ed., *Beyond Sovereignty;* Heidi H. Hobbs, ed., *Pondering Postinternationalism;* and Richard W. Mansbach and Edward Rhodes, eds., *Global Politics in a Changing World.*

2. Talcott Parsons, "Some Theoretical Considerations on the Nature and Trends of Change of Ethnicity," in Nathan Glazer and Daniel P. Moynihan, eds., *Ethnicity,* 56. (Emphasis in original.)

3. Ibid., 57. (Emphasis deleted.)

4. Parsons thus blurs some of the distinctions between what Lake and Rothchild classify as the "primordialist," the "instrumentalist," and the "constructivist" approaches toward ethnicity. Lake and Rothchild argue that the primordialist approach views ethnicity as a "fixed characteristic of individuals and communities . . . rooted in inherited biological traits or centuries of past practice now beyond the ability of individuals or groups to alter." They state that the instrumentalist approach "understands ethnicity as a tool used by individuals, groups, or elites to obtain some larger, typically material end." The constructivist approach accepts that ethnicity "is constructed from dense webs of social interactions. In the constructivist view, ethnicity is not an individual attribute but a social phenomenon. A person's identity remains beyond the choice or control of that individual." See David A. Lake and Donald Rothchild, "Spreading Fear," in Lake and Rothchild, eds., *The International Spread of Ethnic Conflict,* 5, 6.

5. Michael Ignatieff, *Blood and Belonging,* 6. The term *creed* may be defined as any set of basic or core beliefs.

6. Ibid., 7–8. Gurr also speaks of "ethnonationalists," or "[l]arge, regionally concentrated peoples with a history of organized political autonomy who have pursued separatist objectives." See Ted Robert Gurr, *Minorities at Risk,* 18. See also Gurr, *Peoples versus States,* and Rajat Ganguly and Raymond C. Taras, *Understanding Ethnic Conflict,* 23–24.

7. On the general topic of ethnic nationalism, see also Walker Connor, *Ethnonationalism.*

8. For example, the recently stated preference of many American citizens claiming African ancestry to be identified as "African-Americans," rather than as (previously used terms such as) *blacks, negroes,* or *coloreds,* may well derive from their desire to be considered as an ethnic, rather than as a racial, group. African-Americans thus join the ranks of such ethnic groups as, for example, Irish-Americans, Italian-Americans, Hispanic-Americans, and Native Americans. During the late 1960s and early 1970s, a similarly motivated preference was expressed for African-Americans to be identified as "Afro-Americans."

9. The seminal work on ethnic conflict is Donald L. Horowitz, *Ethnic Groups in Conflict.* For other well-done analyses of this important global dynamic, see for example Kathleen A. Cavanaugh, "Interpretations of Political Violence in Ethnically Divided Societies," *Terrorism and Political Violence* 9 (1997): 33–54; Charles P. Cozic, ed., *Ethnic Conflict;* S. A. Giannakos, ed., *Ethnic Conflict;* Ted Robert Gurr and Barbara Harff, *Ethnic Conflict and World Politics;* Human Rights Watch, *Slaughter among Neighbors;* Michael Ignatieff, *The Warrior's Honor;* Stuart J. Kaufman, *Mod-*

ern Hatreds; Charles King, "The Myth of Ethnic Warfare," *Foreign Affairs* 80 (2001): 165–170; Patrick A. McGuire, "The Roots of Ethnic Violence," in Myra H. Immel, ed., *Ethnic Violence,* 14–16; Richard Shultz and William Olson, *Ethnic and Religious Conflict;* Jay Stuller, "Nationalism Causes Ethnic Conflict," in Charles P. Cozic, ed., *Nationalism and Ethnic Conflict,* 163–167; Trent N. Thomas, "Global Assessment of Current and Future Trends in Ethnic and Religious Conflict," in Bernard Schecterman and Martin Slann, eds., *Violence and Terrorism,* 23–26; United Nations Research Institute for Social Development, "Four Categories of Ethnic Conflicts," in Immel, ed., *Ethnic Violence,* 17–22; and Robin Wright, "Ethnic Conflict," in Cozic, ed., *Nationalism and Ethnic Conflict,* 157–162.

10. On the relationship between political crises and ethnic conflict, see for example Stephen Ryan, "Political Crises Intensify Ethnic Conflict," in Cozic, ed., *Nationalism and Ethnic Conflict,* 191-193. On ethnic conflict in Russia, see especially Valery Tishkov, *Ethnicity, Nationalism, and Conflict in and after the Soviet Union.* On this latter point, see also Leokadia Drobizheva et al., eds., *Ethnic Conflict in the Post-Soviet World.* For an extremely insightful—and influential—historical account of ethnic conflict in the former Yugoslavia (and throughout the Balkans), see Robert D. Kaplan, *Balkan Ghosts.* See also V. P. Gagnon, "Ethnic Nationalism and International Conflict," in Michael E. Brown, Owen R. Cote, Jr., Sean M. Lynn-Jones, and Steven E. Miller, eds., *Nationalism and Ethnic Conflict,* 132–168; Michael T. Kaufman, "The Bitter Struggle between Serbs and Albanians," in Immel, ed., *Ethnic Violence,* 117–121; and Chuck Sudetic, "Bosnia," in Immel, ed., *Ethnic Violence,* 106–112.

11. The term *ethnic cleansing* is in fact a euphemism for genocide. For more on this disturbing topic, see for example Anna Simons, "Making Sense of Ethnic Cleansing," *Studies in Conflict and Terrorism* 22 (1999): 1–20. On the manipulation of long-standing ethnic hatreds by ultranationalistic political leaders, see Sonia Shah, "The Political Exploitation of Ethnicity Causes Ethnic Conflict," in Cozic, ed., *Nationalism and Ethnic Conflict,* 184–190. Ethnic conflict between minority Tamils and majority Sinhalese in Sri Lanka is, as Gamini Samaranayake puts it, "not a phenomenon of recent origin but could be traced back over the centuries in the historical annals." See Samaranayake, "Ethnic Conflict in Sri Lanka and Prospects of Management," in Schecterman and Slann, eds., *Violence and Terrorism,* 94. It is nevertheless true that the Official Language Act of 1956, which decreed that the Sinhala language would be Sri Lanka's official language, and the settlement of Sinhalese in traditionally and predominantly Tamil areas of Sri Lanka were events which have undoubtedly aggravated Sri Lanka's chronically violent ethnic conflict. See Samaranayake, "Ethnic Conflict in Sri Lanka," 95.

12. Timur Kuran, "Ethnic Dissimilation and Its International Diffusion," in Lake and Rothchild, eds., *The International Spread of Ethnic Conflict,* 38–39. (Emphasis deleted.)

13. On the interrelationship between religious conflict and ethnic conflict, see especially Mark Juergensmeyer, "Religious Radicalism Causes Ethnic Conflict," in Cozic, ed., *Nationalism and Ethnic Conflict,* 168–175.

14. Myra H. Immel, "Introduction," in Immel, ed., *Ethnic Violence,* 10.

15. Walker Connor lists only Denmark, Iceland, Japan, Luxembourg, the Netherlands, Norway, and Portugal as those ethnically homogeneous nations whose dominant ethnic group does not extend much beyond its own national boundaries. As Connor remarks, "These states would account for less than 4 percent of the world

population and, if we exclude Japan, for less than 1 percent." See Connor, *Ethnonationalism*, 155. On ethnic conflict as a transnational issue, see for example Thomas Ambrosio, *Irredentism;* Jan Angstrom, "The International Dimensions of Ethnic Conflict," *Studies in Conflict and Terrorism* 24 (2001): 59–69; Michael E. Brown, ed., *The International Dimensions of Internal Conflict;* David Carment and Patrick James, eds., *Wars in the Midst of Peace;* K. M. De Silva and R. J. May, *Internationalization of Ethnic Conflict;* Jack David Eller, *From Culture to Ethnicity to Conflict;* Manus I. Midlarsky, ed., *The Internationalization of Communal Strife;* David C. Rapoport, "The Role of External Forces in Supporting Ethno-Religious Conflict," in Schecterman and Slann, eds., *Violence and Terrorism,* 57–63; Stephen Ryan, *Ethnic Conflict and International Relations;* and Taras and Ganguly, *Understanding Ethnic Conflict.*

16. Milton J. Esman, "Ethnic Actors in International Politics," *Nationalism and Ethnic Politics* 1 (1995): 114. On the topic of diasporas, see for example Jonathan Boyarin and Daniel Boyarin, *Powers of Diaspora;* Robin Cohen, *Global Diasporas;* Karim H. Karim, ed., *Diaspora and Communication;* and Gabriel Sheffer, ed., *Modern Diasporas in International Politics.* For case studies of specific diasporas, see for example Loring M. Danforth, *The Macedonian Conflict,* 79–107; Michael S. Laguerre, *Diasporic Citizenship;* Michael Mandelbaum, ed., *The New European Diasporas;* Susanah Lily L. Mendoza, *Between the Homeland and the Diaspora;* Jonathan Y. Okamura, *Imagining the Filipino American Diaspora;* and Igor Zevelev, *Russia and Its New Diasporas.*

17. Esman, "Ethnic Actors," 122.

18. Gurr, *Minorities at Risk,* 133. The diffusion of transnational ethnic conflicts is also considered in Jonathan Friedman, "Transnationalization, Socio-political Disorder, and Ethnification," *International Political Science Review* 19 (1998): 233–250; Lake and Rothchild, "Spreading Fear," 23–29; Kuran, "Ethnic Dissimilation"; Stuart Hill, Donald Rothchild, and Colin Cameron, "Tactical Information and the Diffusion of Peaceful Protests," in Lake and Rothchild, eds., *The International Spread of Ethnic Conflict,* 61–88; and Edmond J. Keller, "Transnational Ethnic Conflict in Africa," in Lake and Rothchild, eds., *The International Spread of Ethnic Conflict,* 275–292.

19. Gurr, *Minorities at Risk,* 134.

20. This is by no means an exhaustive list of transnational ethnoterrorist organizations. For instance, on September 10, 1976, an organization calling itself "Fighters for Free Croatia" hijacked a Trans World Airlines jetliner from the United States to Canada, Iceland, and, finally, France. This dramatic act is discussed in detail in J. Bowyer Bell, *A Time of Terror,* 6–35. On the motivations of Zvonko Busic, the leader of Fighters for Free Croatia, see Jeanne N. Knutson, "Social and Psychodynamic Pressures toward a Negative Identity," in Yonah Alexander and John M. Gleason, eds., *Behavioral and Quantitative Perspectives on Terrorism,* 105–150; and Richard M. Pearlstein, "Lives of Disquieting Desperation," Ph.D. diss., University of North Carolina at Chapel Hill, 1986, 184–230. Although Croatia, like Armenia, has become an independent nation-state, the activities of the Armenian Secret Army for the Liberation of Armenia and the Justice Commandos of the Armenian Genocide are considered here because these groups' respective ethnoterrorist campaigns were obviously far more extensive, and lasted much longer, than the single act of Fighters for Free Croatia. Further instances of transnational terrorism have been provided by various Kashmiri ethnoterrorist organizations (e.g., Harakat ul-Ansar, Harakut ul-

Mujadeen, whose activities are alleged to have included the killing of an Indian diplomat in Birmingham, England, in February 1984 and the hijacking of an Indian Airlines jetliner from Nepal to Pakistan, India, Oman, the United Arab Emirates, and Afghanistan in December 1999. See, for example, "British Authorities Seek Killers of Indian Aide," *Boston Globe,* February 7, 1984, and Tarek al-Issawi, "Indian Jet Hijacked with 189 on Board," *Dallas Morning News,* December 25, 1999. There is also the case of the "Free South Moluccan Youth," an ethnoterrorist organization drawn from the South Moluccan diaspora in the Netherlands. This organization was responsible for the hijacking of two Dutch trains and the taking of hostages at a Dutch school and the Indonesian consulate in the Netherlands in 1975 and 1977. This short-lived organization, which sought independence for the South Moluccan Islands (also known as the Spice Islands) from Indonesia, is discussed in detail in Ralph Barker, *Not Here, But in Another Place.* For more on this topic, see Valentine Herman and Rob van der Laan Bouma, "Nationalists without a Nation," in Juliet Lodge, ed., *Terrorism,* 119–145; Carl H. Yaeger, "Menia Muria," *Terrorism* 13 (1990): 215–226; and Lee E. Dutter, "Ethno-Political Activity and the Psychology of Terrorism," *Terrorism* 10 (1987): 145-163.

21. For two excellent psychopolitical analyses of ethnoterrorism, see Vamik Volkan, *Blood Lines,* and Dutter, "Ethno-Political Activity."

22. It might be noted that the original IRA, which developed during the Easter Rising of 1916, was eventually "succeeded" by the present IRA, founded in 1970 and also known as the Provisional Irish Republican Army (PIRA). The best single work on the Irish Republican Army is J. Bowyer Bell, *The Secret Army.* Another fine work on the IRA is Tim Pat Coogan, *The IRA.*

23. For further details on IRA transnational terrorist activity, see for example "Three British Soldiers Killed in IRA Attacks in Netherlands," *Boston Globe,* May 2, 1988; "British Detonate Bomb Found in Car on Base in Germany," *Boston Globe,* May 4, 1988; and "IRA Bomb Suspects Captured in France," *Boston Globe,* July 18, 1989. See also Clifford E. Simonsen and Jeremy R. Spindlove, *Terrorism Today,* 81; J. A. Emerson Vermaat, "Terrorist Sympathizers in the Netherlands," *Terrorism* 10 (1987): 331; and *Terrorist Group Profiles,* 56–60. On the transnational terrorist activities of the Irish National Liberation Army, see for example "Four Suspects Held in French Drive on Terrorists," *Boston Globe,* August 31, 1982, and *Terrorist Group Profiles,* 50–52.

24. The best single work on the Kurds is John Bulloch and Harvey Morris, *No Friends but the Mountains.* Other excellent works on the Kurds include Henri J. Barkey and Graham E. Fuller, *Turkey's Kurdish Question;* Massoud Barzani, *Mustafa Barzani and the Kurdish Liberation Movement;* Gerard Chaliand and Philip Black, *The Kurdish Tragedy;* Gerard Chaliand et al., *A People without a Country;* Michael M. Gunter, *The Kurdish Predicament in Iraq;* George S. Harris, "Whither the Kurds?" in van Horne, ed., *Global Convulsions,* 205–223; Ferhard Ibrahim and Gulistan Gurbey, eds., *The Kurdish Conflict in Turkey;* Mehrdad R. Izady, *The Kurds;* Kemal Kirisci and Gareth M. Winrow, *The Kurdish Question and Turkey;* David McDowall, *A Modern History of the Kurds;* Edgar O'Ballance, *The Kurdish Struggle;* and Robert W. Olson, ed., *The Kurdish Nationalist Movement in the 1990s.*

25. On the PKK's terrorist campaign in Western Europe, see for example Bulloch and Morris, *No Friends but the Mountains,* 186. For more on the PKK, see for example Simonsen and Spindlove, *Terrorism Today,* 110–111.

26. On the Basques in general, see for example Yonah Alexander, Michael S. Swetnam, and Herbert M. Levine, *ETA,* and Marianne Heiberg, *The Making of the Basque Nation.* On ETA's relationship with France and the Irish Republican Army and other terrorist organizations, see for example Peter F. Janke, "Spanish Separatism," in William Gutteridge, ed., *Contemporary Terrorism,* 161–162. On the more general topic of the Basques and ETA, see particularly Robert P. Clark, *The Basque Insurgents;* Clark, *The Basques;* Clark, *Negotiating with ETA;* Clark, "Patterns in the Lives of ETA Members," *Terrorism* 6 (1983): 423–454; Miren Gutierrez, "Terror in the Pyrenees," in Thomas J. Badey, ed., *Violence and Terrorism,* 85–87; Cynthia Irvin, *Militant Nationalism;* James Edwin Jacob, "The Basques and Occitans of France," Ph.D. diss., Cornell University, 1979; Siamak Khatami, "Between Class and Nation," *Studies in Conflict and Terrorism* 20 (1997): 395–417; Francisco Letamendia, *Game of Mirrors;* Francisco Lliora, Joseph M. Mata, and Cynthia L. Irvin, "ETA," *Terrorism and Political Violence* 5 (1993): 106–134; Goldie A. Shabad and Francisco Jose Llera Ramo, "Basque Terrorism in Spain," paper presented to the Terrorism in Context Conference, June 8–10, 1989, at Middletown, Connecticut; Simonsen and Spindlove, *Terrorism Today,* 97–100; John Sullivan, *ETA and Basque Nationalism; Terrorist Group Profiles,* 35–40; Michel Wieviorka, *The Making of Terrorism,* 147–214; Paddy Woodworth, *Dirty War, Clean Hand;* and Cyrus E. Zirakzadeh, *A Rebellious People.*

27. During the 1970s and 1980s, the ASALA—for reasons that are not entirely clear—also targeted a Trans World Airlines office in Madrid, Spain, and an Air Canada office in Los Angeles. On Armenian ethnoterrorism, the Armenian Secret Army for the Liberation of Armenia, and the Justice Commandos of the Armenian Genocide, see for example Gerard Chaliand and Yves Ternon, *The Armenians;* Jacques Derogy, *Resistance and Revenge;* Michael Gunter, "The Armenian Terrorist Campaign against Turkey," *Orbis* 27 (1983): 447–477; Francis P. Hyland, *Armenian Terrorism;* Khacig Toloyan, "Terrorism and the Politics of the Armenian Diaspora," paper presented to the Joint Convention of the International Studies Association and the British International Studies Association, March 28–April 1, 1989, at London; Anat Kurz and Ariel Merari, *ASALA; Terrorist Group Profiles,* 32–35, 52–54; and Simonsen and Spindlove, *Terrorism Today,* 111. Like the PKK, the ASALA subscribed to Marxist-Leninist beliefs which may in part account for its targeting of American and Canadian interests. During the late 1980s, the JCAG also employed the name "Armenian Revolutionary Army."

28. On the general topic of Sri Lankan ethnic conflict, see for example Dennis Austin, *Democracy and Violence in India and Sri Lanka;* Lakshmanan Sabaratnam, *Ethnic Attachments in Sri Lanka;* and S. J. Tambiah, *Sri Lanka.* On the Tamils in general, see for example Alan J. Bullion, *India, Sri Lanka, and the Tamil Crisis;* William McGowan, *Only Man Is Vile;* and Samaranayake, "Ethnic Conflict in Sri Lanka and Prospects of Management," 94–99. On the Liberation Tigers of Tamil Eelam, see especially Manoj Joshi, "On the Razor's Edge," *Studies in Conflict and Terrorism* 19 (1996): 19–42. See also Raymond Bonner, "Tamil Guerrillas in Sri Lanka," in Schecterman and Slann, eds., *Violence and Terrorism,* 171–173; Robert C. Oberst, "Sri Lanka's Tamil Tigers," *Conflict* 8 (1988): 185–202; John D. Rogers, Jonathan Spencer, and Jayadeva Uyangoda, "Sri Lanka," *American Psychologist* 58 (1998): 771–777; Simonsen and Spindlove, *Terrorism Today,* 219–221; Daya Wijesekera, "The Cult of Suicide and the Liberation Tigers of Tamil Eelam," *Low Intensity Conflict and Law Enforcement* 5 (1996): 18–28; and Wijesekera, "The Liberation Tigers

of Tamil Eelam (LTTE)," *Low Intensity Conflict and Law Enforcement* 2 (1993): 308–317.

29. On the Sikhs in general, see for example Brian Keith Axel, *The Nation's Tortured Body;* V. D. Chopra et al., *Agony of Punjab;* Citizens for Democracy, *Oppression in Punjab;* Surjan Singh Gill, *Case for Republic of Khalistan;* Dipankar Gupta, *The Context of Ethnicity;* Robin Jeffery, *What's Happening to India?;* Mark Juergensmeyer, "The Logic of Religious Violence," *Contributions to Indian Sociology* 22 (1988): 65–88; Rajiv A. Kapur, *Sikh Separatism;* Murray J. Leaf, "The Punjab Crisis," *Asian Survey* 25 (1985): 475–498; Joyce Pettigrew, *The Sikhs of Punjab;* Shinder Purewal, *Sikh Ethnonationalism and the Political Economy of Punjab;* Puri Harish, Paramjit Singh Judge, and Jagrup Sekhon, *Terrorism in Punjab;* D. P. Sharma, *The Punjab Story;* Gurdev Singh, *Punjab Politics;* Gurharpal Singh, "The Punjab Crisis since 1984," *Ethnic and Racial Studies* 18 (1995): 476–493, and "Understanding the 'Punjab Problem,'" *Asian Survey* 27 (1987): 1268–1277; Satinder Singh, *Khalistan,* and "Terrorism in Punjab," *Guru Nanak Journal of Sociology* 18 (1997): 5–12; and Darshan Singh Tatla, *The Sikh Diaspora.* On Sikh ethnoterrorism, see for example Clark Blaise and Bharati Mukherjee, *The Sorrow and the Pity;* Jugdep S. Chima, "Back to the Future in 2002?" *Studies in Conflict and Terrorism* 25 (2002): 19–39; Chopra et al., *Agony of Punjab;* Darshan Lai Choudhary, *Violence in the Freedom Movement of Punjab;* Edward A. Gargan, "Violence, Like Punjab's Wheat, Finds Fertile Soil," in Schecterman and Slann, eds., *Violence and Terrorism,* 104–105; Salim Jiwa, *The Death of Air India Flight 182;* Balraj Madhok, *Punjab Problem;* Cynthia Keppley Mahmood, *Fighting for Faith and Nation;* Ian Mulgrew, *Unholy Terror;* Kuldip Nayar and Khushwant Singh, *Tragedy of Punjab;* Simonsen and Spindlove, *Terrorism Today,* 217–218; Stanley Jeyaraja Tambiah, *Buddhism Betrayed?;* Hamish Telford, "Counter-Insurgency in India," *Journal of Conflict Studies* 21 (2001): 73–100; Mark Tully and Satish Jacob, *Amritsar;* Carl H. Yaeger, "Sikh Terrorism in the Struggle for Khalistan," *Terrorism* 14 (1991): 221–231; and *Terrorist Group Profiles,* 124–127.

30. Quoted in Edward Walker, "No War, No Peace in the Caucasus," in Gary K. Bertsch, Cassady Craft, Scott A. Jones, and Michael Beck, eds., *Crossroads and Conflict,* 154. For more on the Chechen-Russian conflict, see for example John B. Dunlop, *Russia Confronts Chechnya;* Matthew Evangelista, *The Chechen Wars;* Ben Fowkes, ed., *Russia and Chechnia;* Carlotta Gall and Thomas de Waal, *Chechnya;* Anatol Lieven, *Chechnya;* Olga Oliker, *Russia's Chechen Wars;* and Sebastian Smith, *Allah's Mountains.*

31. Yeltsin's comments are quoted in "Security Beefed up after New Moscow Bombing," *Dallas Morning News,* July 13, 1996. For more on Chechen transnational terrorist attacks against Russia, see "Pro-Chechen Gunmen Hijack Plane with 109 on Board," *Dallas Morning News,* March 9, 1996, and "Russian Embassy Attacked in Beirut," *Dallas Morning News,* January 4, 2000. On the May 2002 bombing in Dagestan, see Sharon Lafraniere, "Bomb Strikes Parade in Russia, Killing 36," *Dallas Morning News,* May 10, 2002. On the October 2002 Moscow theater takeover, see Peter Baker and Susan B. Glasser, "Chechen Rebels Storm Theater," *Dallas Morning News,* October 24, 2002.

5. Holy Rage

1. On the general topic of religious fundamentalism, see especially Martin E. Marty and R. Scott Appleby, eds., *Fundamentalisms Observed* and *Fundamental-*

isms Comprehended. See also Marty and Appleby, eds., *Accounting for Fundamentalisms, Fundamentalisms and Society,* and *Fundamentalisms and the State;* Martin E. Marty, *The Glory and the Power;* R. Scott Appleby, *Religious Fundamentalisms and Global Conflict;* Appleby, *The Ambivalence of the Sacred;* and Karen Armstrong, *The Battle for God.* On Jewish fundamentalism in general, see Ehud Sprinzak, *The Ascendance of Israel's Radical Right;* Sprinzak, "From Messianic Pioneering to Vigilante Terrorism," in Rapoport, ed., *Inside Terrorist Organizations,* 194–216; Sprinzak, *Brother against Brother;* Sprinzak, *Fundamentalism, Terrorism, and Democracy;* and Sprinzak, "Extremism and Violence in Israeli Democracy," *Terrorism and Political Violence* 12 (2000): 209–236. See also Raphael Cohen-Almagor, "Vigilant Jewish Fundamentalism," *Terrorism and Political Violence* 4 (1992): 44–66; Gerald Cromer, "Jewish Underground," *Terrorism* 11 (1988): 350–354; Cromer, *Narratives of Violence;* Cromer, "'The Roots of Lawlessness,'" *Terrorism* 11 (1988): 43–51; Laurence S. Hanauer, "The Path to Redemption," *Studies in Conflict and Terrorism* 18 (1995): 245–270; Michael Karpin and Ina Friedman, *Murder in the Name of God;* Ian Lustick, *For the Land and the Lord;* Rafael Medoff, "Gush Emunim and the Question of Jewish Counterterror," *Middle East Review* 18 (1986): 17–23; David Newman, ed., *The Impact of Gush Emunim;* Samuel Peleg, "They Shoot Prime Ministers Too, Don't They?" *Studies in Conflict and Terrorism* 20 (1997): 227–247; Israel Shahak and Norton Mezvinsky, *Jewish Fundamentalism in Israel;* and David Weisburd, *Jewish Settler Violence.* On radical fundamentalist Christian abortion clinic violence in the United States, see for example Patricia Baird-Windle and Eleanor J. Bader, *Targets of Hatred;* Susan R. Sloan, *Act of God;* and Michele Wilson and John Lynxwiler, "Abortion Clinic Violence as Terrorism," *Terrorism* 11 (1988): 263–273. On the topic of Hindu fundamentalism, or revivalism, see for example Sikata Banerjee, *Warriors in Politics;* Christophe Jaffrelot, *The Hindu Nationalist Movement in India;* Lise McKean, *Divine Enterprise;* and Peter van der Veer, *Religious Nationalism.*

2. For a particularly succinct analysis of Islamic fundamentalism, see especially Johannes J. G. Jansen, *The Dual Nature of Islamic Fundamentalism.* On the differences between Islamic fundamentalism and fundamentalist sects in other religions, see Gabriel Ben-Dor, "The Uniqueness of Islamic Fundamentalism," *Terrorism and Political Violence* 8 (1996): 239–252. Some students of Islam substitute the terms *militant Islam, Islamic revivalism, radical Islam,* or simply *Islamic fundamentalism* in place of *radical Islamic fundamentalism.* Although the four terms are sometimes used interchangeably, the preferred term in this work is *radical Islamic fundamentalism.* This is due to the fact that not all Islamic fundamentalists agree on the use of terrorism, or of violence in general, in order to achieve their goals.

3. For an examination of radical Islamic fundamentalist terrorism within the United States, see Steven Emerson, *American Jihad;* Christopher Hewitt, *Understanding Terrorism in America;* and Daniel Pipes, *Militant Islam Reaches America.* The best single source on the 1993 World Trade Center bombing is Jim Dwyer, *Two Seconds under the World.* See also Peter Caram, *The 1993 World Trade Center Bombing;* Robert I. Friedman, *Sheik Abdel Rahman;* Carolyn Gard, *The Attacks on the World Trade Center;* Adrian Kerson, *Terror in the Towers;* Laurie Mylroie, *The War against America;* and Charles J. Shields, *The 1993 World Trade Center Bombing.*

4. Radical Islamic fundamentalist terrorist attacks in Argentina, Panama, Britain, France, Tunisia, and Kenya have included the massive 1994 bombing of a build-

ing in Buenos Aires housing two large Jewish organizations, the 1994 bombing of a commuter airliner over Panama carrying a dozen Jewish businessmen, the 1994 car bombing of the Israeli embassy in London, the 1995 bombing of a Jewish school near Lyons, France, the 2002 bombing of a synagogue in Djerba, Tunisia, and the 2003 bombing of an Israeli-owned hotel in Mombasa, Kenya.

5. On the longtime radical Islamic fundamentalist campaign in Egypt, see for example Walid Mahmoud Abdelnasser, *The Islamic Movement in Egypt;* Mahmud A. Faksh, *The Future of Islam in the Middle East;* Mohammed Heikal, *Autumn of Fury;* Gilles Kepel, *Muslim Extremism in Egypt;* Elie Podeh, "Egypt's Struggle against the Militant Islamic Groups," *Terrorism and Political Violence* 8 (1996): 43–61; Stanley Reed, "The Battle for Egypt," *Foreign Affairs* 72 (1993): 94–107; Barnett Rubin, *Islamic Fundamentalism in Egyptian Politics;* John Ruedy, ed., *Islamism and Secularism in North Africa;* Gabriel R. Warburg and Uri M. Kupferschmidt, eds., *Islam, Nationalism and Radicalism in Egypt and the Sudan;* and Mary Anne Weaver, *A Portrait of Egypt.* On the radical Islamic fundamentalist revolt against the Algerian military regime, see for example Kay Adamson, *Algeria;* Rabia Bekkar, "Taking up Space in Tlemcen," *Middle East Report* 22 (1992): 11–21; Camille Bonora-Waisman, *France and the Algerian Conflict;* James Ciment, *Algeria;* Faksh, *The Future of Islam;* Graham E. Fuller, *Algeria;* Shireen T. Hunter, *The Algerian Crisis;* Robert Malley, *The Call from Algeria;* Luis Martinez, *The Algerian Civil War;* Andrew J. Pierre and William B. Quandt, *The Algerian Crisis;* Pierre and Quandt, *Between Bullets and Ballots;* Ruedy, *Islamism and Secularism in North Africa;* Reza Shah-Kazemi, ed., *Algeria;* Martin Stone, *The Agony of Algeria;* Abdelaziz Testas, "The Roots of Algeria's Religious and Ethnic Violence," *Studies in Conflict and Terrorism* 25 (2002): 161–183; and Michael Willis, *The Islamist Challenge in Algeria.* On the radical Islamic fundamentalist campaign in Pakistan, see for example Robert D. Kaplan, *Soldiers of God;* Seyyed Vali Reza Nasr, *The Vanguard of the Islamic Revolution;* and Jessica Stern, "Pakistan's Jihad Culture," in Harvey W. Kushner, ed., *Essential Readings on Political Terrorism,* 119–129.

6. Jansen, *The Dual Nature of Islamic Fundamentalism,* 1, 11.

7. An extremely succinct discussion of basic Islamic beliefs may be found in David E. Long, "The Land and Peoples of the Middle East," in David E. Long and Bernard Reich, *The Government and Politics of the Middle East and North Africa,* 17–20. See also John L. Esposito, *Islam and Politics,* 1–29, and Judith Miller, "Even a Jihad Has Its Rules," in Schecterman and Slann, eds., *Violence and Terrorism,* 217–218.

8. See Jansen, *The Dual Nature of Islamic Fundamentalism,* 1, 11.

9. Ibid., 2, 3.

10. Ibid., 4 (emphasis in original). On the pathbreaking influence of the Muslim Brotherhood, see especially Ishaq Musa al-Husayni, *The Moslem Brethren,* and Richard P. Mitchell, *The Society of the Muslim Brothers.* See also Brynjar Lia, *The Society of the Muslim Brothers in Egypt.* The role of the Muslim Brotherhood in the Palestinian territories is explored in Ziad Abu-Amr, "Hamas," *Journal of Palestine Studies* 22 (1993): 5–19; and Abu-Amr, *Islamic Fundamentalism in the West Bank and Gaza.* On the meaning and importance of the Iranian revolution, see, for example, Ervand Abrahamian, *Khomeinism;* Abrahamian, *Radical Islam;* Said Amir Arjomand, *The Turban for the Crown;* Shaul Bakhash, *The Reign of the Ayatollahs;* Cheryl Benard and Zalmay Khalilzad, *"The Government of God": Iran's Islamic Republic;* Hamid Dabashi, *Theology of Discontent;* John L. Esposito, ed., *The Iranian*

Revolution; Dilip Hiro, *Iran under the Ayatollahs;* Shireen T. Hunter, *Iran after Khomeini;* Hunter, *Iran and the World;* Nikki R. Keddie and Eric Hooglund, eds., *The Iranian Revolution and the Islamic Republic;* David Menashri, ed., *The Iranian Revolution and the Muslim World;* R. K. Ramazani, *Revolutionary Iran;* R. K. Ramazani, ed., *Iran's Revolution;* Amir Taheri, *The Spirit of Allah;* Robin Wright, *The Last Great Revolution;* and Wright, *In the Name of God.* On the sponsorship of terrorism by Iran, see for example Ray S. Cline and Yonah Alexander, *Terrorism: The Iranian Connection;* Sean K. Anderson, "Iran," in Edwin G. Corr and Stephen Sloan, eds., *Low-Intensity Conflict,* 173–195; Jerrold Green, "Terrorism and Politics in the Islamic Republic of Iran," paper presented to the Terrorism in Context Conference, June 8–10, 1989, at Middletown, Connecticut; and Bruce Hoffman, *Recent Trends and Future Prospects of Iranian-Sponsored International Terrorism.*

11. Jansen, *The Dual Nature of Islamic Fundamentalism,* 10.

12. Ibid., 21.

13. Hamas is an acronym derived from Harakat al-Muqawama al-Islamiyya, or "Islamic Resistance Movement." This acronym may also be translated as "zeal." Hamas is the armed wing of the Muslim Brotherhood in Israel. On this point see, for example, Jansen, *The Dual Nature of Islamic Fundamentalism,* 69. On the general topic of Hamas, see Abu-Amr, "Hamas"; Khaled Hroub, *Hamas;* Samuel M. Katz, *The Hunt for the Engineer;* Anat Kurz and Tal Nahman, *Hamas;* Shaul Mishal and Avraham Sela, *Hamas;* Mishal and Sela, *The Palestinian Hamas;* Andrea Nusse, *Muslim Palestine;* Ilene R. Prusher, "Also Terrorism," in Schecterman and Slann, eds., *Violence and Terrorism,* 156–157; Aviva Shabi and Roni Shaked, *Hamas;* Paul Steinberg and Annmarie Oliver, *Rehearsals for a Happy Death;* N. T. Anders Strindberg, "Challenging the 'Received View,'" *Studies in Conflict and Terrorism* 25 (2002): 263–273; and Paul Wilkinson, "Hamas," *Jane's Intelligence Review* 5 (1993): 31–32. On the leadership of Hamas, see for example Herb Keinon, "Hamas's Sheikh Ahmed Yassin," in Schecterman and Slann, eds., *Violence and Terrorism,* 68–69. Hizbollah, which originated among the minority Shi'ite Muslim community of Lebanon, has been in existence since the early 1980s. On Hizbollah (the spelling varies), see for example Hala Jaber, *Hezbollah;* Martin Kramer, "The Moral Logic of Hizballah," in Walter Reich, ed., *Origins of Terrorism,* 131–157; Magnus Ranstorp, *Hizb'Allah in Lebanon;* Amal Saad-Ghorayeb, *Hizbu'llah;* Carl Anthony Wege, "Hizbollah Organization," *Studies in Conflict and Terrorism* 17 (1994): 151–164; and Eyal Zisser, "Hizballah in Lebanon," *Terrorism and Political Violence* 8 (1996): 90–100. On the leadership of Hizbollah, see for example Thomas O'Dwyer, "Hizbullah's Ruthless Realist," in Schecterman and Slann, eds., *Violence and Terrorism,* 70–71. Both Hizbollah and its armed wing, Islamic Jihad, have received considerable financial and other support from Iran and Syria. Differences between the majority Sunni and minority Shi'ite sects of Islam derive from a seventh-century struggle over who the Prophet Muhammad's caliph, or earthly successor, should be. The relatively small number of fighters led by Muhammad's grandson, Hussein, were defeated by the much larger forces of the Umayyad dynasty in 680. Those Muslims who supported Hussein, and came to glorify his martyrdom, grew into the Shi'ite Islamic minority. Those Muslims who rejected Hussein's claim to be caliph became the Sunni Islamic majority. The Sunni majority has historically accepted a more moderate, or mainstream, approach to Islam, whereas the Shi'ite minority has taken a more defiant, militant approach in its religious beliefs. The Shi'ite minority, which has been at the forefront of Islamic fundamentalism, has taken the

historical view that the minority Shi'ites have been not only religiously but also socially and economically persecuted by the majority Sunnis. The rise of Islamic fundamentalism among Sunnis is therefore particularly indicative of the extensive appeal of fundamentalism within the Muslim community. For very readable inquiries into the origins of the Shi'ite-Sunni conflict, see, for example, Robin Wright, *Sacred Rage*, 37–38, and Muhammad Hanif, "Islam," in William Spencer, ed., *The Middle East*, 170–175. Fadlallah's beliefs are outlined in Mohammed Hussein Fadlallah, *Islam and the Logic of Force*. For more on Fadlallah's views on radical Islamic fundamentalism and terrorism, see, for example, Kramer, "The Moral Logic of Hizballah." For more on Islamic Jihad's activities in the Palestinian territories, see Abu-Amr, *Islamic Fundamentalism in the West Bank and Gaza*. For Qutb's works, see Sayyid Qutb, *In the Shade of the Quran* and *Milestones*.

14. See Jansen, *The Dual Nature of Islamic Fundamentalism*, 69. For example, Faraj quotes a brief passage from Qutb's *In the Shade of the Quran* in Johannes J. G. Jansen, ed., *The Neglected Duty*, 226. For an excellent analysis of Qutb's early contributions to radical Islam, see especially Ahmad S. Moussalli, *Radical Islamic Fundamentalism*. See also Armstrong, *The Battle for God*, 239–244; John L. Esposito, *Unholy War*, 56–61; Mark Huband, *Warriors of the Prophet*, 87–90; and Malise Ruthven, *A Fury for God*, 72–98.

15. Adams's points are presented in Charles J. Adams, "Foreword," in Jansen, ed., *The Neglected Duty*, xv. Jansen's own points are made on 152. Faraj's work is also accorded much notice in Emmanuel Sivan, *Radical Islam*, and Kepel, *Muslim Extremism in Egypt*. It is interesting to note that Faraj was neither a member of the Islamic clergy nor a Muslim scholar; he was, rather, an electrician with no formal religious training. On this point, see David C. Rapoport, "Sacred Terror," in Reich, ed., *Origins of Terrorism*, 105. Rapoport observes that Faraj's background follows "a pattern common throughout Sunni Islamicist movements, which, unlike their Shia counterparts, are profoundly hostile to the [traditional] religious establishment." Another earlier, mid-twentieth-century example of this pattern is that of Abul Ala el-Mawdudi, the Pakistani founder of a similar organization, Jama'at-i-Islami.

16. Jansen, ed., *The Neglected Duty*, 160–161. The term *jihad* is also spelled *gihad* or *jihaad*.

17. Ibid., 205.

18. Ibid., 162.

19. Ibid., 165 (emphasis added).

20. Jansen, *The Dual Nature of Islamic Fundamentalism*, 22. Or, as Faraj puts it, "To fight an enemy who is near is more important than to fight an enemy who is far." See Jansen, ed., *The Neglected Duty*, 192.

21. Jansen, ed., *The Neglected Duty*, 169. On the conflict between the classical and more recent Sunni and Shi'ite views of how far jihad is to extend, see, for example, Rapoport, "Sacred Terror," 110–111.

22. Faraj is quoting from a fourteenth-century work on jihad by Ibn Taymiyah in Jansen, ed., *The Neglected Duty*, 181.

23. Ibid., 199, 198. See also Rapoport, "Sacred Terror," 110–111.

24. On the necessity of targeting volunteers and conscripts alike, see Jansen, ed., *The Neglected Duty*, 169.

25. Ibid., 210, 211, 217, 226–227. On the issue of suicide attacks, see, for example, Raphael Israeli, "Islamikaze and Their Significance," *Terrorism and Political Violence* 9 (1997): 96–121; Kramer, "Moral Logic of Hizballah," 141–149;

Harvey W. Kushner, "Suicide Bombers," *Studies in Conflict and Terrorism* 19 (1996): 329–337; and Ariel Merari, "The Readiness to Kill and Die," in Reich, ed., *Origins of Terrorism*, 192–207.

26. On these points, see for example David G. Kibble, "The Threat of Militant Islam," *Studies in Conflict and Terrorism* 19 (1996): 353–364. See also Clarence J. Bouchat, "A Fundamentalist Islamic Threat to the West," *Studies in Conflict and Terrorism* 19 (1996): 339–352.

27. For a practical exploration of this point, see, for example, Haggay Ram, "Exporting Iran's Islamic Revolution," *Terrorism and Political Violence* 8 (1996): 7–24.

28. The body of literature on Osama bin Laden and al-Qaeda is considerable. The best major recent works on these topics include Rohan Gunaratna, *Inside al Qaeda;* Peter L. Bergen, *Holy War, Inc.;* and Roland Jacquard, *In the Name of Osama bin Laden.* Two of the better earlier works on bin Laden and al-Qaeda are Yossef Bodansky, *Bin Laden,* and Simon Reeve, *The New Jackals.* Other sources include Yonah Alexander and Michael S. Swetnam, *Usama bin Laden's al-Qaida;* Jane Corbin, *Al-Qaeda;* John Miller and Michael Stone, *The Cell;* James S. Robbins, "Bin Laden's War," in Russell D. Howard and Reid L. Sawyer, eds., *Terrorism and Counterterrorism,* 354–366; Adam Robinson, *Bin Laden;* and Paul L. Williams, *Al Qaeda.* See also Anthony J. Dennis, *Osama bin Laden.* The term *global reach* was first popularized by Richard J. Barnet and Ronald E. Muller in their pioneering study of transnational corporations. See Barnet and Muller, *Global Reach.*

29. Recovered al-Qaeda documents include a multi-volume terrorist "encyclopedia" and the al-Qaeda training manual. For publicly available versions of this training manual and other materials, see Ben N. Venzke, ed., *The al-Qaeda Documents,* and Jerrold M. Post, ed., *Military Studies in the Jihad against the Tyrants.*

30. Quoted in Magnus Ranstorp, "Interpreting the Broader Context and Meaning of Bin Laden's Fatwa," *Studies in Conflict and Terrorism* 21 (1998): 329. Although at least three Western journalists have attempted to interview Osama bin Laden, these "interviews" are for the most part mere restatements of bin Laden's 1998 fatwa. This is in large degree due to the fact that bin Laden does not directly respond to interview questions or allow follow-up questions. For attempts to interview Osama bin Laden, see John Miller, "American Policies in the Middle East Justify Islamic Terrorism," in Laura K. Egendorf, ed., *Terrorism,* 123–130; Miller and Stone, *The Cell,* 186–191; Bergen, *Holy War, Inc.,* 19–23; and Robert Fisk, "My Days with Bin Laden," *Gentleman's Quarterly,* November 2001, 366ff.

31. See Gunaratna, *Inside al Qaeda,* 16.

32. Ibid., 19.

33. Bodansky, *Bin Laden,* 3; and Gunaratna, *Inside al Qaeda,* 17.

34. Quoted in Gunaratna, *Inside al Qaeda,* 4. On bin Laden's first encounters with Azzam, see Bodansky, *Bin Laden,* 11.

35. See Gunaratna, *Inside al Qaeda,* 21–23. See also "Militants' Money Man Warns U.S.," *Dallas Morning News,* May 11, 1997. For an excellent work on the relationship between bin Laden and U.S. support for the Afghan rebels, see John K. Cooley, *Unholy Wars.* See also Bodansky, *Bin Laden,* 15–24.

36. On bin Laden's 1991 exile from Saudi Arabia, see for example Bodansky, *Bin Laden,* 32–40; Reeve, *The New Jackals,* 172; Bergen, *Holy War, Inc.,* 78; and Williams, *Al Qaeda,* 83–95. On Islamic fundamentalism in Sudan, see T. Abdou Maliqalim Simone, *In Whose Image?* On bin Laden's move from Sudan to Afghanistan in 1996, see for example Bodansky, *Bin Laden,* 186; Reeve, *The New Jackals,* 186;

Bergen, *Holy War, Inc.*, 91–92; and Jacquard, *In the Name of Osama bin Laden*, 35. On Islamic fundamentalism in Afghanistan, and the Taliban regime which until recently ruled most of that nation-state, see especially M. J. Gohari, *Taliban*; Larry P. Goodson, *Afghanistan's Endless War*; Michael Griffin, *Reaping the Whirlwind*; Robert D. Kaplan, *Soldiers of God*; Neamatollah Nojumi, *The Rise of the Taliban in Afghanistan*; and Ahmed Rashid, *Taliban*. For somewhat earlier treatment of these topics, see Ralph H. Magnus and Eden Naby, *Afghanistan*; William Maley, ed., *Fundamentalism Reborn?*; Peter Marsden, *The Taliban*; Kamal Matinuddin, *The Taliban Phenomenon*; Asta Olesen, *Islam and Politics in Afghanistan*; Barnett Rubin, *The Fragmentation of Afghanistan* and *The Search for Peace in Afghanistan*.

37. Much of this information on al-Qaeda was gleaned from Paul Pillar's outstanding presentation to the Panel Discussion on Counterterrorism at the Second Annual Conference on Preparing America's Foreign Policy for the 21st Century, February 25, 1999, at Norman, Oklahoma. For an excellent analysis of the organizational structure underlying al-Qaeda, see Cameron, "Multi-track Microproliferation," 282–283. For more on the financial infrastructure of al-Qaeda, see Bodansky, *Bin Laden*, 313–319, and Vernon Loeb, "The Man Who Pulls the Terrorists' Strings," in Schecterman and Slann, eds., *Violence and Terrorism*, 92–95.

38. Gunaratna, *Inside al Qaeda*, 2.

39. See "Bin Laden Financing Muslim Militants in Bangladesh," *Dallas Morning News*, February 20, 1999.

40. See "Bin Laden Runs European Terrorist Network," *Dallas Morning News*, November 30, 1998. See also Lee Michael Katz, "Terrorism's Money Web," in Schecterman and Slann, eds., *Violence and Terrorism*, 187–190.

41. See "Businessmen Reportedly Gave bin Laden Millions," *Dallas Morning News*, July 7, 1999. (In an attempt to sow dissension within bin Laden's organization, the U.S. Central Intelligence Agency and National Security Agency are reported to have electronically transferred funds from bin Laden's own treasury to the accounts of his closest followers.) It is also suspected that al-Qaeda operatives invested heavily in the U.S. airline and insurance sectors—which were particularly hard hit by the September 11, 2001, terrorist attacks—and traded those holdings just days before the attacks.

42. On Mohammed Atef's reported death, see Richard Whittle, "Bin Laden Deputy Reportedly Killed," *Dallas Morning News*, November 17, 2001.

43. On the reaction to the August 20, 1998, U.S. raids against Sudan and Afghanistan, see for example Paul Richter, "U.S. Has Right to Kill Terrorists," *Dallas Morning News*, October 29, 1998. See also "U.S. Asserts Right to Attack Governments Hosting Terrorists," *Dallas Morning News*, February 8, 1999; "Bin Laden Reportedly Has New Afghan Base," *Dallas Morning News*, July 5, 1999; Edward G. Shirley, "The Etiquette of Killing bin Laden," in Schecterman and Slann, eds., *Violence and Terrorism*, 185–186; and Ryan C. Hendrickson, "American War Powers and Terrorists," *Studies in Conflict and Terrorism* 23 (2000): 161–174.

44. On the newly reconstituted al-Qaeda, see for example David Johnston, Don van Natta, Jr., and Judith Miller, "Surviving al-Qaeda Seen as Loosely Knit But Potent," *Dallas Morning News*, June 16, 2002. On al-Qaeda's emerging alliance with Jemaah Islamiyah, see for example "Malaysia Accuses Man of Terrorist Ties," *Dallas Morning News*, September 28, 2002; and "Singapore: Man Met with Moussaoui," *Dallas Morning News*, September 28, 2002.

45. Gunaratna, *Inside al Qaeda*, 10.

6. Superterrorism: What's in It for You?

1. Prior to the Tokyo subway attack, terrorists had used, or planned to use, chemical weapons on several occasions. For example, in 1972, a terrorist conspiracy to use chemical warfare agents against a U.S. nuclear storage site in Europe was successfully detected and thwarted by authorities. In February 1978, the Arab Revolutionary Army Palestinian Commandos terrorist organization accepted responsibility for injecting mercury and other harmful chemicals into Israeli citrus products. During the latter part of 1978 and the early part of 1979, four hundred kilograms of chemicals suitable for the manufacture of organophosphates, which are used as components for nerve gas, were detected in a terrorist safe-house in West Germany. On these three incidents, see Joseph D. Douglass, Jr., and Neil C. Livingstone, *America the Vulnerable,* 183–184. On organophosphates, see for example Leonard A. Cole, *The Eleventh Plague,* 152.

2. Preston's novel is actually one of the more thoroughly researched fiction—or, for that matter, nonfiction—treatments of the superterrorism theme. *The Cobra Event* has also become one of the most influential of these works. Former U.S. president Bill Clinton's reading of Preston's novel reportedly led Clinton to issue an executive order directing drastically increased funding for research on the threat of advanced biological terrorist weapons. See Richard Preston, *The Cobra Event.* On Clinton's alarmed reading of *The Cobra Event,* see for example "U.S. Still Unprepared for Biological Attack," *Dallas Morning News,* April 26, 1998.

3. The First World War was not the first major military conflict in which civilian targets served key roles. Most military historians regard the American Civil War (1861–1865, which predates the invention of conventional WMD by at least three decades) as the first truly "modern" war in that both military *and* civilian targets played key tactical and strategic roles. Unlike the First (and certainly the Second) World War, however, civilian targeting during the American Civil War primarily resulted in property, rather than human, losses. Note too that dynamite (a mixture of nitroglycerine—a highly unstable explosive first invented in 1846—wood pulp, and sodium nitrate), first devised in 1867, has for technical reasons never played a significant combat role. This is due to the fact that dynamite, although potent, lacks the explosive power to serve as an effective weapon of mass destruction. Dynamite was, however, fairly frequently employed by terrorists and assassins during the late nineteenth and early twentieth centuries. On the enthusiastic—and highly instructive—use of dynamite by these earlier terrorists, see David Ronfeldt and William Sater, "The Mindsets of High-Technology Terrorists," in Yonah Alexander and Charles K. Ebinger, eds., *Political Terrorism and Energy,* 15–38.

4. Among terrorism analysts, the term *chemical, biological, radiological, and nuclear (CBRN) terrorism* seems to have replaced earlier terms such as *nuclear, biological, and chemical (NBC) terrorism* and *chemical, biological, and nuclear (CBN) terrorism.* This new, more comprehensive term takes into account the critical, and often overlooked, fact that terrorists need not employ fully functioning nuclear weapons in order to create a nonconventional WMD. Indeed, radioactive materials themselves may be deployed either alone or with conventional explosives. For an excellent historical survey of the use of chemical and biological weapons, see John Cookson and Judith Nottingham, *A Survey of Chemical and Biological Warfare.* Perhaps the finest and most comprehensive work on chemical warfare during the First World War is L. F. Haber, *The Poisonous Cloud.* On the Japanese use of biological WMD in China, see for example George W. Christopher, Theodore J. Cieslak, Julie A. Pavlin,

and Edward M. Eitzen, Jr., "Biological Warfare," *Journal of the American Medical Association* 278 (1997): 413. Two of the best works on Japan's biological weapons development program prior to and during the Second World War are Sheldon H. Harris, *Factories of Death,* and Peter Williams and David Wallace, *Unit 731.* For an authoritative, and shocking, account of U.S. Army experimentation with biological agents on American citizens during the cold war, see Leonard A. Cole, *Clouds of Secrecy.* There is conclusive evidence of the Iraqi use of chemical WMD in a 1988 attack against the Iraqi city of Birjinni, which was home to tens of thousands of Kurds. For more on this topic, see for example Lois Ember, "Chemical Weapons," *Chemical and Engineering News,* May 3, 1993, and Alastair Hay and Gwynne Roberts, "The Use of Poison Gas against the Iraqi Kurds," *Journal of the American Medical Association* 263 (1990): 1065–1066.

5. On the point that terrorists may well continue to use more familiar weaponry, see for example Brian M. Jenkins, "Keynote Address," presented to Terrorism and Beyond: The 21st Century Conference, April 17–19, 2000, at Oklahoma City, Oklahoma. It is widely agreed that the first terrorist act to receive truly global attention during the second half of the twentieth century was the kidnapping and subsequent killing of eleven Israeli athletes and coaches at the 1972 Munich Olympics. This event, and similar acts which soon followed, sparked the first serious study of terrorism as a contemporary phenomenon. It is interesting to note that the first general study of superterrorism was published during that same year. See B. J. Berkowitz et al., *Superviolence.* Other early general studies of superterrorism include (in chronological order): Brian M. Jenkins, *High Technology Terrorism and Surrogate War;* R. William Mengel, "Terrorism and New Technologies of Destruction," in National Advisory Committee on Criminal Justice Standards and Goals, eds., *Disorders and Terrorism,* 443–473; Robert K. Mullen, "Mass Destruction and Terrorism," *Journal of International Affairs* 32 (1978): 63–89; Brian Clark, *Technological Terrorism;* Yonah Alexander, "Super-Terrorism," in Yonah Alexander and John M. Gleason, eds., *Behavioral and Quantitative Perspectives on Terrorism,* 343–361; and Ronfeldt and Sater, "The Mindsets of High-Technology Terrorists."

6. On Moodie's observation, see Michael L. Moodie, "The Chemical Weapons Threat," in Sidney D. Drell, Abraham D. Sofaer, and George D. Wilson, eds., *The New Terror,* 35. For Falkenrath, Newman, and Thayer's remarks, see Richard A. Falkenrath, Robert D. Newman, and Bradley A. Thayer, *America's Achilles' Heel,* 27.

7. Some of the better recent general works on the likely use of CBRN weapons by terrorists include Falkenrath, Newman, and Thayer, *America's Achilles' Heel,* 167–215; Sam Nunn, "Weapons of Mass Destruction Pose a Terrorist Threat," in Laura K. Egendorf, ed., *Terrorism,* 35–40; Bruce Hoffman, *Responding to Terrorism across the Technological Spectrum;* Hoffman, *Terrorism and Weapons of Mass Destruction;* Jessica Stern, *The Ultimate Terrorists,* 48–68; and Glenn E. Schweitzer, *Superterrorism.* See also Yonah Alexander and Milton M. Hoenig, eds., *Super Terrorism,* and James K. Campbell, *Weapons of Mass Destruction and Terrorism.* For a highly abridged version of Campbell's work, see James K. Campbell, "Excerpts from Research Study 'Weapons of Mass Destruction and Terrorism,'" *Terrorism and Political Violence* 9 (1997): 24–50. For somewhat earlier perspectives on the likely use of CBRN weapons by terrorists, see for example Neil C. Livingstone, *The War against Terrorism,* 109–122; Yonah Alexander, "Terrorism and High Technology Weapons," in Lawrence Zelic Freedman and Yonah Alexander, eds., *Perspectives on Terrorism,* 225–240; Neil C. Livingstone, "The Impact of Technological Innova-

tion," in Uri Ra'anan et al., eds., *Hydra of Carnage,* 139–153; and Robert H. Kupperman and Jeff Kamen, *Final Warning,* 87–115. For more on this topic, see Kathleen Bailey, *Doomsday Weapons in the Hands of Many;* Richard A. Falkenrath, "Confronting Nuclear, Biological, and Chemical Terrorism," *Survival* 40 (1998): 43–65; Bruce Hoffman, "The Debate over Future Terrorist Use of Chemical, Biological, Radiological and Nuclear Weapons," in Brad Roberts, ed., *Hype or Reality?* 207–224; Hoffman, *Inside Terrorism,* 196–213; Karl Heinz Kamp, Joseph Pilat, Jessica Stern, and Richard A. Falkenrath, "WMD Terrorism," *Survival* 40 (1998): 168–183; John F. Sopko, "The Changing Proliferation Threat," in Charles W. Kegley, Jr., and Eugene R. Wittkopf, eds., *The Global Agenda,* 78–88; Robert Wright, "Be Very Afraid," *New Republic,* May 1, 1995; Jerrold M. Post, "Superterrorism," *Terrorism* 13 (1990): 165–176; Pearlstein, *The Mind of the Political Terrorist,* 177–179; William B. Wark, "Managing the Consequences of Nuclear, Biological, and Chemical (NBC) Terrorism," *Low Intensity Conflict and Law Enforcement* 6 (1997): 179–184; and Paul Wilkinson, "Editor's Introduction," in Paul Wilkinson, ed., *Technology and Terrorism,* 1–11. See also Richard K. Betts, "The New Threat of Mass Destruction," *Foreign Affairs* 77 (1998): 26–41; Ashton Carter, John Deutch, and Philip Zelikow, "Catastrophic Terrorism," *Foreign Affairs* 77 (1998): 80–94; and Frank Barnaby, *Instruments of Terror.* One recent work warning of the likely terrorist acquisition and deployment of chemical and biological weapons is Vinod Jain and Bharati Dhruva, "Chemical and Biological Terrorism Is a Serious Threat," in Jennifer A. Hurley, ed., *Weapons of Mass Destruction,* 17–21. Two somewhat earlier works which focus upon the likely terrorist acquisition and deployment of chemical and biological weapons are Neil C. Livingstone and Joseph D. Douglass, Jr., *CBW,* and Douglass and Livingstone, *America the Vulnerable.* Two recent works which warn of the growing likelihood of both radiological and nuclear terrorism are Sharon Begley, "Nuclear Arms Increase the Threat of Terrorism," in A. E. Sadler and Paul A. Winters, eds., *Urban Terrorism,* 27–29; and Andrew Loehmer, "The Nuclear Dimension," in Wilkinson, ed., *Technology and Terrorism,* 48–69.

    8. For careful analyses of why future CBRN attacks may not materialize, at least on a large scale, see Falkenrath, Newman, and Thayer, *America's Achilles' Heel,* 45–62; and John V. Parachini, "Mass Casualty Terrorism," paper presented to Terrorism and Beyond: The 21st Century Conference, April 17–19, 2000, at Oklahoma City, Oklahoma. Two works which not only discount but outright ridicule the current political, scientific, and academic obsession with superterrorism are Ehud Sprinzak, "The Great Superterrorism Scare," in Glenn P. Hastedt, ed., *American Foreign Policy,* 186–193; and Hastedt, "Weapons of Mass Destruction Do Not Pose a Terrorist Threat," in Egendorf, ed., *Terrorism,* 41–44. For a challenge to the likelihood of chemical and biological terrorism, see Marie Isabelle Chevrier, "The Threat of Chemical and Biological Terrorism Is Exaggerated," in Hurley, ed., *Weapons of Mass Destruction,* 22–25.

    9. This definition of biological terrorism has been culled in part from U.S. Congress, Office of Technology Assessment, *Technology against Terrorism: Structuring Security,* 35.

    10. On the Matsumoto attack, see for example Kaplan and Marshall, *The Cult at the End of the World,* 140–146; Lifton, *Destroying the World to Save It,* 39–40; Stern, *The Ultimate Terrorists,* 63–64; and "Japanese Cult Member Admits 1994 Gas Attack," *Dallas Morning News,* January 24, 1996. On the 1984 Wasco County, Oregon, *Salmonilla typhosa* contamination, see especially Christopher, Cieslak, Pav-

lin, and Eitzen, "Biological Warfare," 416. Like Aum Shinrikyo, the transnational organization responsible for the Matsumoto and Tokyo assaults, the Rajneeshee group which perpetrated the Oregon biological attack combined the qualities of a transnational religious cult, a transnational corporation, and a transnational terrorist organization. On the Moscow radiation incident, see for example "Radioactive Container Found at Park in Moscow Not Dangerous, Officials Say," *Dallas Morning News,* November 25, 1995; "Chechen Rebel Threatens Radiation Attack," *Dallas Morning News,* December 23, 1995; and Steve D. Boilard, *Russia at the Twenty-First Century,* 165.

11. Moodie, "The Chemical Weapons Threat," 6, 7.

12. Ibid., 7–11.

13. On the potency, lethality and persistence of nerve agents, see ibid., 9–11. On the ease of manufacturing nerve agents such as sarin, see Cole, *The Eleventh Plague,* 158–159. On the general issue of chemical terrorism, see Yonah Alexander, "Will Terrorists Use Chemical Weapons?" in Schecterman and Slann, eds., *Violence and Terrorism,* 169; Kathleen A. Buck, "Superterrorism," *Terrorism* 12 (1989): 433–435; Falkenrath, Newman, and Thayer, *America's Achilles' Heel;* Elliot Hurwitz, "Terrorists and Chemical/Biological Weapons," *Naval War College Review* 35 (1982): 36–40; Harvey J. McGeorge II, "The Deadly Mixture," *Nuclear, Biological, and Chemical Defense and Technology* 1 (1986): 56–61; Wayman C. Mullins, "An Overview and Analysis of Nuclear, Biological, and Chemical Terrorism," *American Journal of Criminal Justice* 16 (1992): 95–119; Post, "Superterrorism"; Ron Purver, *Chemical and Biological Terrorism;* Brad Roberts, ed., *Terrorism with Chemical and Biological Weapons;* Schweitzer, *Superterrorism,* 83–108; Frederick R. Sidell, "Chemical Agent Terrorism," *Annals of Emergency Medicine* 28 (1996): 223–224; Stern, *The Ultimate Terrorists,* 38–40; Stern, "Will Terrorists Turn to Poison?" *Orbis* 37 (1993): 393–410; Eric R. Taylor, *Lethal Mists;* Jonathan B. Tucker, "Chemical/Biological Terrorism," *Politics and the Life Sciences* 15 (1996): 167–183; Jonathan B. Tucker, ed., *Toxic Terror;* and U.S. Congress, Office of Technology Assessment, *Technology against Terrorism: The Federal Effort,* 32, 51–54. On the public availability of information on how to produce VX nerve gas, see for example Nicholas Wade, "Going Public with VX Formula," *Science* 187 (1975): 414.

14. On Asahara's early life and the formation of Aum Shinrikyo, see Kaplan and Marshall, *The Cult at the End of the World,* 8–15, and Lifton, *Destroying the World to Save It,* 14–25. For more on Aum Shinrikyo, see also D. W. Brackett, *Holy Terror;* Eric Croddy, "Urban Terrorism," *Jane's Intelligence Review* 7 (1995): 520–523; Helen Hardacre, *Aum Shinrikyo and the Japanese Media;* Japan Times, *Special Report: Terror in the Heart of Japan;* David E. Kaplan, "Aum Shinrikyo (1995)," in Tucker, ed., *Toxic Terror,* 207–226; Kiyoyasu Kitabatake, "Aum Shinrikyo," *Japan Quarterly* 42 (1995): 376–383; Daniel A. Metraux, *Aum Shinrikyo and Japanese Youth;* Metraux, *Aum Shinrikyo's Impact on Japanese Society;* Haruki Murakami, *Underground;* Ron Purver, *Chemical Terrorism in Japan;* Ian Reader, *A Poisonous Cocktail?;* and Reader, *Religious Violence in Contemporary Japan.*

15. On Aum Shinrikyo's attempts to acquire biological, radiological, and nuclear weapons from Russia and other sources, see especially Cameron, "Multi-track Microproliferation," 285–290, 293–296. See also Kaplan and Marshall, *The Cult at the End of the World,* 70–76, 190–198; Lifton, *Destroying the World to Save It,* 179–201; and William Rosenau, "Aum Shinrikyo's Biological Weapons Program," *Studies in Conflict and Terrorism* 24 (2001): 289–301.

16. The apartment complex was inhabited by three judges who were deciding a land dispute involving Aum Shinrikyo. Although incapacitated, all three judges survived the attack. Aum Shinrikyo had therefore accomplished two of its goals: (1) to field-test sarin nerve gas, and (2) to disrupt the land dispute trial. On the Matsumoto attack, see especially Kaplan and Marshall, *The Cult at the End of the World*, 140–146. See also Lifton, *Destroying the World to Save It*, 39–40; Stern, *The Ultimate Terrorists*, 63–64; and "Japanese Cult Member Admits 1994 Gas Attack." It might be noted that Asahara also had a fascination with laser weapons. On this point, see for example Kaplan and Marshall, *The Cult at the End of the World*, 207–208; and Lifton, *Destroying the World to Save It*, 61, 69, 189–191, 194.

17. On these five key members of Aum Shinrikyo, see Kaplan and Marshall, *The Cult at the End of the World*, 2, 244–246.

18. Ibid., 1, 2.

19. On Asahara's arrest, see ibid., 280–282, and Lifton, *Destroying the World to Save It*, 173. On the medical treatment of Tokyo subway victims, see for example Tetsu Okumura et al., "Report on 640 Victims of the Tokyo Subway Sarin Attack," *Annals of Emergency Medicine* 28 (1996): 129–135. On the general topic of emergency response to chemical or biological terrorist attacks, see for example Frank J. Cilluffo and Jack Thomas Tomarchio, "Emergency Response Teams Can Mitigate the Effects of a Chemical or Biological Attack," in Hurley, ed., *Weapons of Mass Destruction*, 94–103, and David R. Franz et al., "Clinical Recognition and Management of Patients Exposed to Biological Warfare Agents," *Journal of the American Medical Association* 278 (1997): 399–411.

20. On the police raids, see Lifton, *Destroying the World to Save It*, 183; Kaplan and Marshall, *The Cult at the End of the World*, 257; and Cameron, "Multi-track Microproliferation," 293. On the *Mainichi Shimbun* estimate, see for example T. R. Reid, "Cult Leader: The U.S. Did It," *New Orleans Times-Picayune*, March 25, 1995. On Aum Shinrikyo's plans for operations against the United States, see for example Nicholas Kristof, "Japanese Cult Said to Have Planned Nerve-Gas Attacks in U.S.," *New York Times*, March 23, 1997.

21. Moodie, "The Chemical Weapons Threat," 15. On the point that terrorists are more likely to utilize chemical than other forms of nonconventional WMD, see for example Brian M. Jenkins, "Understanding the Link between Motives and Methods," in Roberts, ed., *Terrorism with Chemical and Biological Weapons*, 51. On Aum Shinrikyo's repeatedly unsuccessful deployment of biological agents, see for example Kaplan and Marshall, *The Cult at the End of the World*, 93–94; Lifton, *Destroying the World to Save It*, 186–188; and Ken Alibek, *Biohazard*, 278.

22. The probable planting of plutonium by Chechen terrorists in 1995 may be a notable—albeit never confirmed—exception to the point that ethnoterrorists at least appear to be totally averse to the deployment of nonconventional WMD. See "Radioactive Container in Moscow Park Not Dangerous, Officials Say," and "Chechen Rebel Threatens Radiation Attack." The confirmed attempted development of biological weapons by the left-wing Red Army Faction is another example. Right-wing terrorists, who have scant regard for public opinion and share many of the same apocalyptic views, have also been identified as likely candidates for the terrorist use of nonconventional WMD. On this point, see Lifton, *Destroying the World to Save It*, 271–340, and Kaplan and Marshall, *The Cult at the End of the World*, 289–295. On the interrelated phenomena of apocalyptic cults and terrorism, see especially Bradley C. Whitsel, "Catastrophic New Age Groups and Public Order," *Studies in*

Conflict and Terrorism 23 (2000): 21–36; James T. Richardson, "Minority Religions and the Context of Violence," *Terrorism and Political Violence* 13 (2001): 103–133; and Jean-François Mayer, "Cults, Violence and Religious Terrorism at the Dawn of the 21st Century," paper presented to Terrorism and Beyond: The 21st Century Conference, April 17–19, 2000, at Oklahoma City, Oklahoma. On al-Qaeda's pursuit of CBRN capabilities, see for example Cameron, "Multi-track Microproliferation," 290–293. On Aum Shinrikyo's attempts to acquire biological weapons, see William Rosenau, "Aum Shinrikyo's Biological Weapons Program," 289–301.

23. Rosenau, "Aum Shinrikyo's Biological Weapons Program," 294. For Kaplan and Marshall's statement on Aum Shinrikyo's recruitment of members at the Mendeleyev Chemical Institute, see *The Cult at the End of the World,* 76. See also Lifton, *Destroying the World to Save It,* 182. On Asahara's contacts with high-ranking Russian officials, see Kaplan and Marshall, *The Cult at the End of the World,* 70. Aum Shinrikyo was also able to acquire many of its chemical materials through overt contacts made by its many front companies with firms in the United States and other nations.

24. Stern, *The Ultimate Terrorists,* 41.

25. Ibid., 41. On the drastically increased field of exposure of biological agents, see J. H. Rothchild, *Tomorrow's Weapons,* 22.

26. Some of the better recent sources on bioterrorism include Wendy Barnaby, *The Plague Makers;* Bill Frist, *When Every Moment Counts;* Steven Kuhr and Jerome M. Hauer, "The Threat of Biological Terrorism in the New Millennium," in Harvey W. Kushner, ed., *Essential Readings on Political Terrorism,* 386–395; Matthew Meselman, "Bioterror," in Robert B. Silvers and Barbara Epstein, eds., *Striking Terror,* 257–276; and Raymond A. Zilinskas, "Rethinking Bioterrorism," in Helen E. Purkitt, ed., *World Politics,* 64–68. On the general topic of bioterrorism, see also Alibek, *Biohazard,* 278–292; Buck, "Superterrorism"; W. Seth Carus, *Bio-terrorism, Biocrimes, and Bioassassination;* Carus, *The Threat of Bioterrorism;* Carus, "Unlawful Acquisition and Use of Biological Agents," in Joshua Lederberg, ed., *Biological Weapons,* 211–231; Christopher F. Chyba, *Biological Terrorism, Emerging Infectious Diseases, and National Security;* Cole, *The Eleventh Plague,* 151–171; Lois Ember, "Bioterrorism," *Chemical and Engineering News,* July 5, 1999; Falkenrath, Newman, and Thayer, *America's Achilles' Heel;* Janet Heinrich, *Bioterrorism;* Arnie Heller, "Uncovering Bioterrorism," *Science and Technology Review,* May 2000; Hurwitz, "Terrorists and Chemical/Biological Weapons"; Karl Lowe, "Analyzing Technical Constraints on Bio-Terrorism," in Roberts, ed., *Terrorism with Chemical and Biological Weapons,* 53–64; Gary E. McCuen, ed., *Biological Terrorism and Weapons of Mass Destruction;* McGeorge, "The Deadly Mixture"; Mullins, "An Overview and Analysis of Nuclear, Biological, and Chemical Terrorism"; Michael T. Osterholm and John Schwartz, *Living Terrors;* John V. Parachini, *Combating Terrorism;* Post, "Superterrorism"; Potomac Institute for Policy Studies, *Conference on Countering Biological Terrorism, Countering Biological Terrorism in the United States,* and *Seminar on Emerging Threats of Biological Terrorism;* Purver, *Chemical and Biological Terrorism;* Roberts, ed., *Terrorism with Chemical and Biological Weapons;* Schweitzer, *Superterrorism,* 109–136; Jeffrey D. Simon, "Biological Terrorism," *Journal of the American Medical Association* 278 (1997): 428–430; Simon, *Terrorists and the Potential Use of Biological Weapons;* Ralph Eugene Stephens, "Cyber-Biotech Terrorism," in Harvey W. Kushner, ed., *The Future of Terrorism,* 203–205; Stern, *The Ultimate Terrorists,* 41–43; Taylor, *Lethal Mists;* Tucker, "Bio-

terrorism," 211–231; Tucker, ed., *Toxic Terror;* U.S. Congress, Office of Technology Assessment, *Technology against Terrorism: The Federal Effort,* 32, 51–54, and *Technology against Terrorism: Structuring Security,* 35–44; Pamela Weintraub, *Bioterrorism;* Stanley L. Wiener, "Terrorist Use of Biological Weapons," *Terrorism* 14 (1991): 129–133; and Raymond A. Zilinskas, "Terrorism and Biological Weapons," *Perspectives in Biology and Medicine* 34 (1990): 44–72.

27. For a highly readable discussion of the various categories of biological warfare agents, see Stern, *The Ultimate Terrorists,* 22–23.

28. Ibid., 21.

29. Schweitzer, *Superterrorism,* 114. On the ease of anthrax production, see also Cole, *The Eleventh Plague,* 159–160.

30. Steven M. Block, "Living Nightmares," in Drell, Sofaer, and Wilson, eds., *The New Terror,* 45.

31. On Aum's anthrax deployment, see for example Kaplan and Marshall, *The Cult at the End of the World,* 94–96, and Lifton, *Destroying the World to Save It,* 188. On the five 2001 U.S. inhalation anthrax deaths, see for example "Florida Man Dies of Anthrax," *Dallas Morning News,* October 6, 2001; David Jackson and Alfredo Corchado, "Anthrax Likely in 2 DC Deaths," *Dallas Morning News,* October 23, 2001; Michelle Mittelstadt, "Anthrax Victim's Last Days Retraced," *Dallas Morning News,* November 1, 2001; and "Latest Anthrax Baffles Officials," *Dallas Morning News,* November 22, 2001. See also Robert Harris and Jeremy Paxman, *A Higher Form of Killing,* 251–252; Frist, *When Every Moment Counts,* 1–19; and Barnaby, *The Plague Makers,* 2–4. For more on anthrax, see especially Jeanne Guillemin, *Anthrax.* See also Phillip Hanna, Nicholas Duesbery, George Vande Woude, and Stephen Leppla, "How Anthrax Kills," *Science,* June 12, 1998, and Thomas S. Heemstra, *Anthrax.* On the medical response to potential anthrax terrorist attacks, see for example Thomas V. Inglesby et al., "Anthrax as a Biological Weapon," *Journal of the American Medical Association* 281 (1999): 1735–1745.

32. For a discussion of this topic, see for example Cole, *The Eleventh Plague,* 65–66. On the number of Black Death fatalities in Europe, see for example Wallace K. Ferguson and Geoffrey Bruun, *A Survey of European Civilization,* 297. It might be added that bubonic plague, which affects the lymph glands, is an altogether different disease than pneumonic plague, which attacks the lungs.

33. On the Ebola virus, see for example Stern, *The Ultimate Terrorists,* 22, 164. On Aum Shinrikyo's failed attempts to acquire Ebola cultures, see for example Kaplan and Marshall, *The Cult at the End of the World,* 96–97; and Lifton, *Destroying the World to Save It,* 186–187.

34. For a discussion of smallpox as a bioterrorist weapon, see especially Jonathan B. Tucker, *Scourge.* See also, for example, D. A. Henderson et al., "Smallpox as a Biological Weapon," *Journal of the American Medical Association* 281 (1999): 2127–2137; Schweitzer, *Superterrorism,* 134–135; and Frist, *When Every Moment Counts,* 77. On the 1971 Soviet smallpox outbreak, see for example William J. Broad and Judith Miller, "Report: Soviet Smallpox Killed 3," *Dallas Morning News,* June 15, 2002.

35. On biotoxins, see for example Cole, *The Eleventh Plague,* 85, and Stern, *The Ultimate Terrorists,* 23. On the Red Army Faction's production of botulinum toxin, see for example Douglass and Livingstone, *America the Vulnerable,* 185. On Aum Shinrikyo's unsuccessful deployment of botulinum toxin, see for example Kaplan and Marshall, *The Cult at the End of the World,* 93–94, and Lifton, *Destroying the*

World to Save It, 186–188. Cameron notes that al-Qaeda also attempted to acquire, and may have indeed acquired, anthrax and other biological agents. See Cameron, "Multi-track Microproliferation," 290–293. Two Algerian men alleged to have ties to al-Qaeda and arrested in Manchester, England, in January 2003 were in possession of a substantial quantity of ricin. On this incident, see for example "Algerian Terrorists Linked to Poison Plot," *Dallas Morning News,* January 17, 2003. On the medical response to terrorist attacks involving botulinum toxin, see for example Roger L. Shapiro, Charles Hatheway, John Becher, and David L. Swerdlow, "Botulism Surveillance and Emergency Response," *Journal of the American Medical Association* 278 (1997): 433–435.

36. On the use of the term *chimera,* see for example Alibek, *Biohazard,* 259. This particular use of genetic engineering is sometimes referred to as "black biology."

37. Some of the better recent works on the genetic/biotechnological revolution, the Human Genome Project, and the controversies surrounding these issues include Susan Aldridge, *The Thread of Life;* Charles R. Cantor, Cassandra L. Smith, and the Human Genome Project, *Genomics;* Robert Cook-Deegan, *The Gene Wars;* Kevin Kelly, *Out of Control;* Maxwell J. Mehlman and Jeffrey R. Botkin, *Access to the Genome;* Charles Piller and Keith R. Yamamoto, *Gene Wars;* Matt Ridley, *Genome;* Jeremy Rifkin, *The Biotech Century;* and Enzo Russo and David Cove, *Genetic Engineering.* On the issue of genetic WMD, see for example Malcolm Dando, *Biological Warfare in the 21st Century;* Dando, *The New Biological Weapons;* James B. Engel, *Defense against the Military Use of Genetic Engineering;* Macha Levinson, "Custom-Made Biological Weapons," *International Defense Review* 19 (1986): 1611–1615; National Consortium for Genomic Resources Management and Services, *The 1997 GenCom Conference on Improving U.S. Capabilities for Defense from Bioterrorism;* Stephen Rose, "Biotechnology at War," *New Scientist* 113 (1987): 33–37; Jonathan B. Tucker, "Gene Wars," *Foreign Policy* 57 (1985): 58–79; U.S. Department of Defense, *Advances in Biotechnology and Genetic Engineering;* Susan Wright and Robert L. Sinsheimer, "Recombinant DNA and Biological Warfare," *Bulletin of the Atomic Scientists* 39 (1983): 20–26; and U.S. Congress, Office of Technology Assessment, *Technology against Terrorism: Structuring Security,* 39.

38. Block, "Living Nightmares," 42.

39. Ibid., 46–47.

40. Ibid., 52–71. Alibek notes: "There are two principal challenges in altering the genetic makeup of disease-producing bacteria. The first is to find the right mechanism for transporting genes into the DNA of another microorganism. The second is to achieve the transfer without reducing the bacteria's virulence." See Alibek, *Biohazard,* 160.

41. On the Sverdlovsk accident, see Alibek, *Biohazard,* 70–86. On the Ustinov episode, see ibid., 124–132. On Soviet (and charges of later Russian) development of a genetic WMD program, see ibid., 160–167, 259–260. On Aum Shinrikyo's genetic WMD research, see Kaplan and Marshall, *The Cult at the End of the World,* 233. Concern has also been expressed that terrorists might attempt to further develop and deploy emerging viruses such as Ebola and Marburg.

42. On the issue of agroterrorism, see especially Alibek, *Biohazard,* 37–38; Joseph W. Foxell, Jr., "Current Trends in Agroterrorism," *Studies in Conflict and Terrorism* 24 (2001): 107–129; Peter Chalk, *Terrorism, Infrastructure Protection and the U.S. Food and Agricultural Sector;* Thomas W. Frazier and Drew C. Richardson, eds., *Food and Agricultural Security;* Jason Pate and Gavin Cameron, *Covert Biolog-*

ical Weapons Attacks against Agricultural Targets; and Simon M. Whitby, *Biological Warfare against Crops.* See also Alexander, "Super-Terrorism," 346; Eric Croddy, *Chemical and Biological Warfare;* Frist, *When Every Moment Counts,* 146–152; Harris and Paxman, *A Higher Form of Killing,* 88–89; and Dean A. Wilkening, "BCW Attack Scenarios," in Drell, Sofaer, and Wilson, eds., *The New Terror,* 8–82.

43. Alibek, *Biohazard,* 37–38.

44. See Alexander, "Super-Terrorism," 346. On Britain's agricultural weapons program, see for example Harris and Paxman, *A Higher Form of Killing,* 88–90.

45. See Foxell, "Current Trends in Agroterrorism," 111–113, and Chalk, *Terrorism, Infrastructure Protection, and the U.S. Food and Agricultural Sector,* 2–3.

46. Schweitzer, *Superterrorism,* 136.

47. Cole, *The Eleventh Plague,* 160.

48. Clinton's remarks are quoted in Alibek, *Biohazard,* 281. On U.S. funding assistance to Biopreparat scientists, see for example "U.S. Funding Biological Research in Russia," *Dallas Morning News,* August 10, 1997.

49. For Alibek's remarks, see Alibek, *Biohazard,* 290, 289. Stern discusses means by which genetic engineering may provide "detection techniques" to warn a population to seek specific treatment. See Stern, *The Ultimate Terrorists,* 146–147. For more on defense against biological terrorism, see Arnold D. Kaufman, Martin I. Meltzer, and George P. Schmid, "The Economic Impact of a Bioterrorist Attack," *Emerging Infectious Diseases* 3 (1997): 1–12; Schweitzer, *Superterrorism,* 131–132; and Wiener, "Terrorist Use of Biological Weapons."

50. This very question was posed by Brian M. Jenkins in Jenkins, "Keynote Address."

51. Among the earlier literature on nuclear terrorism, one work which clearly recognizes the distinctions between radiological terrorism and nuclear terrorism is Louis Rene Beres, *Terrorism and Global Security,* 46–47. For other excellent examinations of nuclear facility sabotage, see Daniel Hirsch, "The Truck Bomb and Insider Threats to Nuclear Facilities," in Paul Leventhal and Yonah Alexander, eds., *Preventing Nuclear Terrorism,* 207–222; and Craig W. Kirkwood and Stephen M. Pollack, *Methodology for Characterizing Potential Adversaries of Nuclear Safeguard Systems.*

52. On the lack of security among radiation facility workers in the United States, see for example Robert Schlesinger, "Markey Decries Lack of Security Checks on Radiation Facility Staff," *Boston Globe,* July 31, 2002. On the availability of radioactive materials in the former Soviet republics of central Asia, see for example Charles J. Hanley, "New States Trading in Radioactive Materials," *New Orleans Times-Picayune,* June 15, 2002. On the Ibrahim al-Muhajir case, see for example "'Dirty Bomb' Suspect Found Islam while Living in Florida," *Dallas Morning News,* June 16, 2002. For a technical discussion of HEU and plutonium, see for example David Albright, Frans Berkhout, and William Walker, *World Inventory of Plutonium and Highly Enriched Uranium 1992,* 9–11, 14–16.

53. Much of the recent literature on radiological terrorism and nuclear terrorism does indeed deal with these two issues as separate threats. On this point, see for example Begley, "Nuclear Arms Increase the Threat of Terrorism"; Louis Rene Beres, "Responding to the Threat of Nuclear Terrorism," in Charles W. Kegley, Jr., ed., *International Terrorism,* 228–240; Gavin Cameron, "Nuclear Terrorism," *Jane's Intelligence Review,* September 1996; Cameron, *Nuclear Terrorism;* Steven Friedman, "Nuclear Terrorism," in Marc Genest, ed., *World Politics,* 74–76; Stanley S. Jacobs,

"The Nuclear Threat as a Terrorist Option," *Terrorism and Political Violence* 10 (1998): 149–163; Jenkins, "The Threat of Nuclear Terrorism Is Minimal"; John Liefer, "The Risk of Nuclear Terrorism Is High," in Hurley, ed., *Weapons of Mass Destruction*, 26–33; Loehmer, "The Nuclear Dimension," 48–69; Robert W. Marrs, *Nuclear Terrorism*; William C. Potter, *Less Well-Known Cases of Nuclear Terrorism and Nuclear Diversions in the Former Soviet Union*; Stern, *The Ultimate Terrorists*, esp. 54–60; and Paul N. Woesnner, "Chronology of Radioactive and Nuclear Materials Smuggling Incidents," *Transnational Organized Crime* 3 (1997): 114–209.

54. The term *poor man's atomic bomb* was first suggested in Livingstone and Douglas, *CBW*.

55. This literature includes, for example, Graham T. Allison, Owen R. Cote, Jr., Richard A. Falkenrath, and Steven E. Miller, *Avoiding Nuclear Anarchy*, esp. 46–47; Boilard, *Russia at the Twenty-First Century*, 165–166; Oleg Bukharin and William Potter, "Potatoes Were Guarded Better," in George A. Lopez and Nancy J. Myers, eds., *Peace and Security*, 76–79; Andrew Cockburn and Leslie Cockburn, *One Point Safe*; Friedman, "Nuclear Terrorism"; Stephen Handleman, *Comrade Criminal*, 224–228, 236–241, 263–264; David Hoffman, "A Shrunken and Rusty 'Nuclear Stick,'" in Richard W. Mansbach and Edward Rhodes, eds., *Global Politics in a Changing World*, 241–243; National Research Council, *Proliferation Concerns*; Liefer, "The Risk of Nuclear Terrorism Is High," 29–31; Valentin Tikhonov, *Russia's Nuclear and Missile Complex*; Christopher J. Ulrich and Timo A. Kivimaki, *Uncertain Security*; and Center for Strategic and International Studies, *The Nuclear Black Market*.

56. On the involvement of Chechen elements in radiological terrorism, see Rensselaer W. Lee III, *Smuggling Armageddon*, 65, and Stern, *The Ultimate Terrorists*, 99–100. For more on the unlikelihood of organized crime involvement in either nuclear or radiological smuggling, see especially Lee, *Smuggling Armageddon*, 61–65; Mark Galeotti, *The Age of Anxiety*, 184–187; and Vladimir A. Orlov, "Export Controls and Nuclear Smuggling in Russia," in Gary K. Bertsch and William C. Potter, eds., *Dangerous Weapons, Desperate States*, 172–175, 178–179, 184–186. See also Rensselaer W. Lee III, "Smuggling Update," *Bulletin of the Atomic Scientists* 53 (1997): 52–56; Rensselaer W. Lee III and James L. Ford, "Nuclear Smuggling," in Maryann K. Cusimano, ed., *Beyond Sovereignty*, 70–92; and Rensselaer W. Lee III, "Transnational Organized Crime," in Tom Farer, ed., *Transnational Crime in the Americas*, 19–22. For a less optimistic view of Russian organized crime's involvement in this form of smuggling, see Stern, *The Ultimate Terrorists*, 89, 102, 105, 106. Stern examines both sides of the debate. On the transnationality of radiological smuggling, Stern notes for example that "[o]rganized crime is taking advantage of permeable borders between Russia and the Baltic states to smuggle . . . radioactive materials" (see 102).

57. Bruce G. Blair, "Russian Control of Nuclear Weapons," in George Quester, ed., *The Nuclear Challenge in Russia and the New States of Eurasia*, 71. (Emphasis added.)

58. Cameron notes that both Aum Shinrikyo and al-Qaeda have made unsuccessful attempts to purchase nuclear weapons in Russia and the predominantly Muslim former Soviet republic of Kazakhstan, respectively. Cameron also observes ominously that but for lack of proper technical direction, Aum Shinrikyo—which had successfully mined an undetermined quantity of uranium on land it purchased in Australia—might have enjoyed better results in its haphazard endeavors to build a

nuclear device. See Cameron, "Multi-track Microproliferation," 285–289. On Aum Shinrikyo's interest in nuclear weapons, see Lifton, *Destroying the World to Save It*, 193–201. On Aum Shinrikyo's interest in Australian uranium mining, see Kaplan and Marshall, *The Cult at the End of the World*, 127.

59. Blair, "Russian Control of Nuclear Weapons," 71, 72.

60. Lee, "Transnational Crime," 21–22. Nevertheless, gamma emitters such as cobalt-60 and the barium-137m product in cesium-137 would be very difficult to employ effectively.

61. Stern, *The Ultimate Terrorists*, 55, and Mullen, "Mass Destruction and Terrorism," 83. On the ineffectiveness of radiological materials as true weapons of mass destruction, see also Jacobs, "The Nuclear Threat as a Terrorist Option," 153–155; and Loehmer, "The Nuclear Dimension," 56–57.

62. R. William Mengel, "The Impact of Nuclear Terrorism on the Military's Role in Society," in Marius H. Livingston, ed., *International Terrorism in the Contemporary World*, 408.

63. Rahimullah Yusufzai, "Conversation with Terror," *Time*, January 11, 1999.

64. Bin Laden's remarks are quoted in an interview by John Miller with al-Qaeda's leader. The interview is included in John Miller, "American Policies in the Middle East Justify Islamic Terrorism," in Egendorf, ed., *Terrorism*, 123–130. On bin Laden's specific comments, see 125, 127–128.

65. U.S. Congress, Office of Technology Assessment, *Technology against Terrorism: Structuring Security*, 37.

66. Al-Qaeda is an excellent illustration of these points. Aum Shinrikyo, on the other hand, was a rigidly centralized organization directed by a single supreme leader, Shoko Asahara, who was himself Aum Shinrikyo's staunchest advocate of superterrorist attacks. On the differing organizational structures of Aum Shinrikyo and al-Qaeda, see Cameron, "Multi-track Microproliferation," 282–284.

67. The point that we cannot "expect to live in a risk-free society" was made by Brian M. Jenkins in Jenkins, "Keynote Address."

7. After September 11

1. On these points, see "Totaling up the Devastation," *Dallas Morning News*, May 31, 2002; Joseph Treaster, "The Race to Predict Terror's Costs," *New York Times*, September 1, 2002; Michiko Kakutani, "The Information Age Processes a Tragedy," *New York Times*, August 28, 2002; and Janny Scott, "From 'Ground Zero,' a 'Debris Surge' of '9/11' Terms," *Dallas Morning News*, February 24, 2002.

2. See Thomas S. Kuhn, *The Structure of Scientific Revolutions*. The newly emerging global politics paradigm is a topic which receives serious attention in a number of excellent recent anthologies. These include Council on Foreign Relations, ed., *The New Shape of World Politics*; Cusimano, ed., *Beyond Sovereignty*; Hobbs, ed., *Pondering Postinternationalism*; Lepor, ed., *After the Cold War*; Mansbach and Rhodes, eds., *Global Politics in a Changing World*; and Rudra Sil and Eileen M. Doherty, eds., *Beyond Boundaries?*

3. See Thomas Hobbes, *Leviathan*.

4. On the GAL scandal, see for example Woodworth, *Dirty War, Clean Hand*, and "Spain Official, 11 Others Convicted of Kidnapping," *Dallas Morning News*, August 30, 1998. On the Puerto Rican incident, see for example "Sending Police to Jail," *Time*, June 3, 1985. On the Corsican arson case, see for example "Corsican Commander Admits He Ordered Separatist Hangout Burned," *Dallas Morning*

News, May 8, 1999. The charge that the Committee served as a Protestant death squad is made in Sean McPhilemy, *The Committee.* For a piercing critique of Mc-Philemy's claims, see Steve Bruce, "Loyalist Assassinations and Police Collusion in Northern Ireland," *Studies in Conflict and Terrorism* 23 (2000): 61–80. Strong opposition to the use of antiterrorist death squads is raised in Brian M. Jenkins, *Should Our Arsenal against Terrorism Include Assassination?* On the passage of stringent counterterrorism laws, see for example Bradley Graham, "Colombia Decrees Anti-terrorism Laws," *Washington Post,* January 28, 1988; Molly Moore, "India's Infamous Anti-Terrorism Law under Attack," *New Orleans Times-Picayune,* December 11, 1994; "Panel Hears Testimony on Secret-Evidence Law," *Dallas Morning News,* May 24, 2000; "Secretive Court to Rule on Prosecutor's Powers," *Dallas Morning News,* September 2, 2002; and James Risen and David Johnston, "CIA Authorized to Kill Top Terrorism Suspects," *Dallas Morning News,* December 15, 2002. On the purportedly counterproductive nature of extreme counterterrorism measures, see for example Jerrold M. Post, "Rewarding Fire with Fire?" in Anat Kurz, ed., *Contemporary Trends in World Terrorism,* 103–115. See also Nancy Chang et al., eds., *Silencing Political Dissent;* James X. Dempsey and David Cole, *Terrorism and the Constitution;* and Charles T. Eppright, "'Counterterrorism' and Conventional Military Force," *Studies in Conflict and Terrorism* 20 (1997): 333–344.

5. For an excellent anthology of essays on the international cooperative responses to various forms of terrorism, see Martha Crenshaw, ed., *Terrorism and International Cooperation.* See also Richard Allan, *Terrorism.* For an example of cooperation between individual nation-states on transnational terrorist threats, see Kathy Lewis, "U.S., Israel Sign Anti-Terrorism Accord," *Dallas Morning News,* May 1, 1996. On the involvement of the United Nations in the struggle against international and transnational terrorism, see for example Walter Enders, Todd Sandler, and Jon Cauley, "U.N. Conventions, Technology and Retaliation in the Fight against Terrorism," *Terrorism and Political Violence* 2 (1990): 83–105; Seymour Maxwell Finger, "The United Nations and International Terrorism," in Charles W. Kegley, Jr., ed., *International Terrorism,* 259–261; and "U.N. Renews Anti-Terrorism Stance," *Dallas Morning News,* October 20, 1999. On the similar involvement of the North Atlantic Treaty Organization, see for example Philip C. Wilcox, Jr., "The Western Alliance and the Challenge of Combating Terrorism," *Terrorism and Political Violence* 9 (1997): 1–7. On the European Community's role in thwarting transnational terrorism, see for example Peter Chalk, *West European Terrorism and Counter-Terrorism;* Trine Flockhart, ed., *From Vision to Reality;* Heinz Gartner, Adrian Hyde-Price, and Erich Reiter, eds., *Europe's New Security Challenges;* F. E. C. Gregory, "Police Cooperation and Integration in the European Community," *Terrorism* 14 (1991): 145–155; Reinares, ed., *European Democracies against Terrorism;* and Ken Robertson, "Terrorism," *Terrorism* 14 (1991): 105–110. On the attempts of G-7 leaders to coordinate their efforts against transnational terrorism, see for example Kathy Lewis, "Nations Back Anti-Terror Moves," *Dallas Morning News,* June 29, 1996. For an excellent essay on the proper international legal response to international terrorism, see Richard J. Erickson, "What International Law Approach Should Be Taken toward International Terrorism?" *Terrorism* 11 (1988): 113–137.

BIBLIOGRAPHY

Abdelnasser, Walid Mahmoud. *The Islamic Movement in Egypt: Perceptions of International Relations, 1967–81.* London: Kegan Paul, 1994.

Abdo, Geneive. *No God but God: Egypt and the Triumph of Islam.* Oxford: Oxford University Press, 2000.

Abraham, A. J. Khomeini. *Islamic Fundamentalism and the Warriors of God: An Islamic Reader.* Bristol, Ind.: Wyndham Hall, 2000.

Abrahamian, Ervand. *Khomeinism: Essays on the Islamic Republic.* Berkeley: University of California Press, 1993.

———. *Radical Islam: The Iranian Mojahedin.* London: I. B. Tauris, 1989.

Abu-Amr, Ziad. "Hamas: A Historical and Political Background." *Journal of Palestine Studies* 22 (1993): 5–19.

———. *Islamic Fundamentalism in the West Bank and Gaza: Muslim Brotherhood and Islamic Jihad.* Bloomington: Indiana University Press, 1994.

Abu-Rabi, Ibrahim M., and Mahmoud Ayoub. *Intellectual Origins of Islamic Resurgence in the Modern Arab World.* Albany: State University of New York Press, 1995.

Aburish, Said K. *The Rise, Corruption and Coming Fall of the House of Saud.* New York: St. Martin's, 1994.

Achcar, Gilbert. *The Clash of Barbarisms: September 11 and the Making of the New World Disorder.* New York: Monthly Review Press, 2002.

Adams, Charles J. "Foreword." In *The Neglected Duty: The Creed of Sadat's Assassins and Islamic Resurgence in the Middle East.* Edited by Johannes J. G. Jansen. New York: Macmillan, 1986.

Adams, James. *The Financing of Terror: How the Groups That Are Terrorizing the World Get the Money to Do It.* New York: Simon and Schuster, 1986.

Adamson, Kay. *Algeria: A Study in Competing Ideologies.* London: Cassell, 1997.

Adem, Seifudein. *Anarchy, Order and Power in World Politics: A Comparative Analysis.* Burlington, Vt.: Ashgate, 2001.

Ajami, Fouad. *Arab Predicament.* Cambridge: Cambridge University Press, 1992.

———. *The Dream Palace of the Arabs.* New York: Vintage, 1998.

———. *The Vanished Imam: Musa al Sadr and the Shia of Lebanon.* Ithaca, N.Y.: Cornell University Press, 1986.

Akbar, M. J. *India: The Siege Within.* New York: Penguin, 1985.

———. *The Shade of Swords: Jihad and the Conflict between Islam and Christianity.* New York: Routledge, 2002.

Albert, Mathias, David Jacobson, and Yosef Lapid, eds. *Identities, Borders, Orders: Rethinking International Relations Theory.* Minneapolis: University of Minnesota Press, 2001.

Albright, David, Frans Berkhout, and William Walker. *World Inventory of Plutonium and Highly Enriched Uranium 1992*. New York: Oxford University Press, 1993.

Aldridge, Susan. *The Thread of Life: The Story of Genes and Genetic Engineering*. Cambridge: Cambridge University Press, 1996.

Alexander, Yonah. *Middle Eastern Terrorism: Current Trends and Future Prospects*. New York: G. K. Hall, 1994.

———. "Super-Terrorism." In *Behavioral and Quantitative Perspectives on Terrorism*. Edited by Yonah Alexander and John M. Gleason. New York: Pergamon, 1981.

———. "Terrorism and High Technology Weapons." In *Perspectives on Terrorism*. Edited by Lawrence Zelic Freedman and Yonah Alexander. Wilmington, Del.: Scholarly Resources, 1983.

———. "Will Terrorists Use Chemical Weapons?" In *Violence and Terrorism*. Edited by Bernard Schecterman and Martin Slann. Guilford, Conn.: Dushkin, 1993.

Alexander, Yonah, and Charles K. Ebinger, eds. *Political Terrorism and Energy: The Threat and the Response*. New York: Praeger, 1982.

Alexander, Yonah, and Milton M. Hoenig, eds. *Super Terrorism: Biological, Chemical, and Nuclear*. Irvington-on-Hudson, N.Y.: Transnational, 2001.

Alexander, Yonah, and Michael S. Swetnam. *Usama bin Laden's al-Qaida: Profile of a Terrorist Network*. Irvington-on-Hudson, N.Y.: Transnational, 2001.

Alexander, Yonah, Michael S. Swetnam, and Herbert M. Levine. *ETA: Profile of a Terrorist Group*. Ardsley, N.Y.: Transnational, 2001.

Algar, Hamid. *Wahhabism: A Critical Essay*. Oneonta, N.Y.: Islamic Publications, 2002.

Algar, Hamid, ed. *Islam and Revolution: Writings and Declarations of Imam Khomeini*. Berkeley, Calif.: Mizan, 1981.

"Algerian Terrorists Linked to Poison Plot." *Dallas Morning News,* January 17, 2003.

Al-Hamad, Jawad, and Eyad al-Bargothi, eds. *A Study in the Political Ideology of the Islamic Resistance Movement (HAMAS): 1987–1996*. Amman: Dar El-Bashir, 1997.

Al-Husayni, Ishaq Musa. *The Moslem Brethren: The Greatest of Modern Islamic Movements*. Beirut: Khayat, 1956.

Ali, Tariq. *The Clash of Fundamentalisms: Crusades, Jihad and Modernity*. London: Verso, 2002.

Alibek, Ken. *Biohazard: The Chilling True Story of the Largest Covert Biological Weapons Program in the World*. New York: Random House, 1999.

Al-Issawi, Tarek. "Indian Jet Hijacked with 189 on Board." *Dallas Morning News,* December 25, 1999.

Allan, Richard. *Terrorism: Pragmatic International Deterrence and Cooperation*. Boulder, Colo.: Westview, 1990.

Allison, Graham T., Owen R. Cote, Jr., Richard A. Falkenrath, and Steven E. Miller. *Avoiding Nuclear Anarchy: Containing the Threat of Loose Russian Nuclear Weapons and Fissile Material*. Cambridge, Mass.: MIT Press, 1996.

AlSayyad, Nezar, and Manuel Castells, eds. *Muslim Europe or Euro-Islam: Politics, Culture, and Citizenship in the Age of Globalization*. Lanham, Md.: Rowman and Littlefield, 2002.

Ambrosio, Thomas. *Irredentism: Ethnic Conflict and International Politics*. Westport, Conn.: Greenwood, 2001.

Amon, Moshe. "Religion and Terrorism—A Romantic Model of Secular Gnosticism." In *The Rationalization of Terrorism*. Edited by David C. Rapoport and Yonah Alexander. Frederick, Md.: University Press of America, 1982.

"Analysts Point to Saudi Exile." *Dallas Morning News,* August 9, 1998.

Anderson, Benedict. *Imagined Communities: Reflections on the Origins and Spread of Nationalism.* Westport, Conn.: Greenwood, 2001.

Anderson, Sean K. "Iran: Terrorism and Islamic Fundamentalism." In *Low-Intensity Conflict: Old Threats in a New World.* Edited by Edwin G. Corr and Stephen Sloan. Oxford: Westview, 1992.

———. "Warnings versus Alarms: Terrorist Threat Analysis Applied to the Iranian State-Run Media." *Studies in Conflict and Terrorism* 21 (1998): 277–303.

Angstrom, Jan. "The International Dimensions of Ethnic Conflict." *Studies in Conflict and Terrorism* 24 (2001): 59–69.

Antoun, Richard T., and Mary Hegland, eds. *Religious Resurgence: Contemporary Cases in Islam, Christianity, and Judaism.* Syracuse, N.Y.: Syracuse University Press, 1987.

Appleby, R. Scott. *The Ambivalence of the Sacred: Religion, Violence, and Reconciliation.* Lanham, Md.: Rowman and Littlefield, 1999.

———. *Religious Fundamentalisms and Global Conflict.* New York: Foreign Policy Association, 1994.

Appleby, R. Scott, ed. *Spokesman for the Despised: Fundamentalist Leaders of the Middle East.* Chicago: University of Chicago Press, 1997.

Aran, Gideon. "From Religious Zionism to Zionist Religion: The Roots of Gush Emunim." In *Studies in Contemporary Jewry.* Edited by Peter Medding. New York: Oxford University Press, 1986.

———. "Jewish Zionist Fundamentalism: The Bloc of the Faithful in Israel (Gush Emunim)." In *Fundamentalisms Observed.* Edited by Martin E. Marty and R. Scott Appleby. Chicago: University of Chicago Press, 1991.

Ariel, Yaakov. "Doomsday in Jerusalem? Christian Messianic Groups and the Rebuilding of the Temple." *Terrorism and Political Violence* 13 (2001): 1–14.

Arjomand, Said Amir. *The Turban for the Crown: The Islamic Revolution in Iran.* New York: Oxford University Press, 1988.

Arjomand, Said Amir, ed. *From Nationalism to Revolutionary Islam.* Albany: State University of New York Press, 1984.

Armstrong, Karen. *The Battle for God: Fundamentalism in Judaism, Christianity, and Islam.* New York: Knopf, 2000.

Austin, Dennis. *Democracy and Violence in India and Sri Lanka.* London: Pinter, 1994.

Axel, Brian Keith. *The Nation's Tortured Body: Violence, Representation, and the Formation of a Sikh "Diaspora."* Durham, N.C.: Duke University Press, 2001.

Ayres, Russell W. "Policing Plutonium: The Civil Liberties Fallout." *Harvard Civil Rights–Civil Liberties Law Review* 10 (1975): 369–403.

Ayubi, Nazih. *Political Islam: Religion and Politics in the Arab World.* New York: Routledge, 1994.

Badey, Thomas J., ed. *Violence and Terrorism.* Guilford, Conn.: McGraw-Hill/ Dushkin, 2003.

Badolato, Edward V. "Terrorism and the U.S. Energy Infrastructure." *Terrorism* 13 (1990): 159–163.

Bailey, Kathleen. *Doomsday Weapons in the Hands of Many.* Urbana: University of Illinois Press, 1991.

Baird-Windle, Patricia, and Eleanor J. Bader. *Targets of Hatred: Anti-Abortion Terrorism*. New York: Palgrave-Macmillan, 2001.

Baker, Howard, and Lloyd Cutler, eds. *A Report Card on the Department of Energy's Nonproliferation Programs with Russia*. Washington: U.S. Department of Energy, 2001.

Baker, Peter, and Susan B. Glasser. "Chechen Rebels Storm Theater, Holding Hundreds Hostage." *Dallas Morning News,* October 24, 2002.

Bakhash, Shaul. *The Reign of the Ayatollahs: Iran and the Islamic Revolution*. New York: Basic Books, 1984.

Balzer, Marjorie Mandelstam. "From Ethnicity to Nationalism: Turmoil in the Russian Mini-Empire." In *The Social Legacy of Communism*. Edited by James R. Millar and Sharon L. Wolchak. Cambridge: Cambridge University Press, 1994.

Banerjee, Sikata. *Warriors in Politics: Hindu Nationalism, Violence and the Shiv Sena in India*. Boulder, Colo.: Westview, 1999.

Barber, Benjamin R. *Jihad vs. McWorld: How Globalism and Tribalism Are Reshaping the World*. New York: Ballantine, 1996.

Barker, Ralph. *Not Here, But in Another Place*. New York: St. Martin's, 1980.

Barkey, Henri J., and Graham E. Fuller. *Turkey's Kurdish Question*. Lanham, Md.: Rowman and Littlefield, 1998.

Barkun, Michael. *Religion and the Racist Right: The Origins of the Christian Identity Movement*. Chapel Hill: University of North Carolina Press, 1997.

Barnaby, Frank. *Instruments of Terror: Mass Destruction Has Never Been So Easy . . .* London: Vision, 1996.

Barnaby, Wendy. *The Plague Makers: The Secret World of Biological Warfare*. New York: Continuum, 2002.

Barnet, Richard J., and Ronald E. Muller. *Global Reach: The Power of the Multinational Corporations*. New York: Simon and Schuster, 1974.

Barzani, Massoud. *Mustafa Barzani and the Kurdish Liberation Movement*. New York: Palgrave, 2002.

Bass, Gail, et al. *The Appeal of Nuclear Crimes to the Spectrum of Potential Adversaries*. Santa Monica, Calif.: Rand, 1982.

———. *Motivations and Possible Actions of Potential Criminal Adversaries of U.S. Nuclear Programs*. Santa Monica, Calif.: Rand, 1980.

Beardsley, Tim. "The U.S. Gears Up to Deal with Biological Terrorism." *Scientific American,* April, 1999.

Beck, Aaron T. *Prisoners of Hate*. New York: Harper Trade, 2000.

Beck, Robert J., and Thomas Ambrosio, eds. *International Law and the Rise of Nations: The State System and the Challenge of Ethnic Groups*. New York: Chatham House, 2002.

Beckman, Robert L. "International Terrorism: The Nuclear Dimension." *Terrorism* 8 (1986): 351–378.

Begley, Sharon. "Nuclear Arms Increase the Threat of Terrorism." In *Urban Terrorism*. Edited by A. E. Sadler and Paul A. Winters. San Diego: Greenhaven, 1996.

Beinin, Joel, and Joe Stork. *Political Islam: Essays from Middle East Report*. Berkeley: University of California Press, 1996.

Bekkar, Rabia. "Taking up Space in Tlemcen: The Islamist Occupation of Urban Algeria." *Middle East Report* 22 (1992): 11–21.

Bell, J. Bowyer. *Murder on the Nile: The World Trade Center and Global Terror*. San Francisco: Encounter, 2003.

————. *The Secret Army: The IRA.* Somerset, N.J.: Transaction, 1997.

————. *A Time of Terror: How Democratic Societies Respond to Revolutionary Violence.* New York: Basic Books, 1978.

————. *Transnational Terror.* Washington: American Enterprise Institute for Public Policy Research, 1975.

Benard, Cheryl, and Zalmay Khalilzad. *"The Government of God": Iran's Islamic Republic.* New York: Columbia University Press, 1986.

Ben-Dor, Gabriel. "The Uniqueness of Islamic Fundamentalism." *Terrorism and Political Violence* 8 (1996): 239–252.

Benjamin, Daniel, and Steven Simon. *The Age of Sacred Terror.* New York: Random House, 2002.

Bereciartu, Gurutz Jauregui. *Decline of the Nation-State.* Reno: University of Nevada Press, 1994.

Beres, Louis Rene. "Countering Nuclear Terrorism." *Hastings International and Comparative Law Review* 14 (1990): 129–154.

————. "Israel, the 'Peace Process,' and Nuclear Terrorism: Recognizing the Linkages." *Studies in Conflict and Terrorism* 21 (1998): 59–86.

————. "Responding to the Threat of Nuclear Terrorism." In *International Terrorism: Characteristics, Causes, Controls.* Edited by Charles W. Kegley, Jr. New York: St. Martin's, 1990.

————. *Terrorism and Global Security: The Nuclear Threat.* Boulder, Colo.: Westview, 1979.

Bergen, Peter L. "The Bin Laden Trial: What Did We Learn?" *Studies in Conflict and Terrorism* 24 (2001): 429–434.

————. *Holy War, Inc.: Inside the Secret World of Osama Bin Laden.* New York: Free Press, 2001.

Berkowitz, B. J., et al. *Superviolence: The Civil Threat of Mass Destruction Weapons.* Santa Monica, Calif.: Advanced Concepts Research, 1972.

Bernstein, Richard, et al. *Out of the Blue: The Story of September 11, 2001, from Jihad to Ground Zero.* New York: Times Books, 2003.

Bertsch, Gary K., and William C. Potter, eds. *Dangerous Weapons, Desperate States: Russia, Belarus, Kazakhstan, and Ukraine.* New York: Routledge, 1999.

Bertsch, Gary K., Suzette Grillot, and Sam Nunn, eds. *Arms on the Market: Reducing the Risk of Proliferation in the Former Soviet Union.* New York: Routledge, 1998.

Betts, Richard K. "The New Threat of Mass Destruction." *Foreign Affairs* 77 (1998): 26–41.

Binder, Leonard, ed. *Ethnic Conflict and International Politics in the Middle East.* Gainesville: University Press of Florida, 1999.

"Bin Laden Calls for Holy War on U.S. on Arab TV." *Dallas Morning News,* June 11, 1999.

"Bin Laden Financing Muslim Militants in Bangladesh, Officials Say." *Dallas Morning News,* February 20, 1999.

"Bin Laden Reportedly Has New Afghan Base." *Dallas Morning News,* July 5, 1999.

"Bin Laden Runs European Terrorist Network, Paper Says." *Dallas Morning News,* November 30, 1998.

Black, Anthony. *The History of Islamic Political Thought.* New York: Routledge, 2001.

Blair, Bruce G. "Russian Control of Nuclear Weapons." In *The Nuclear Challenge in Russia and the New States of Eurasia.* Edited by George Quester. Armonk, N.Y.: M. E. Sharpe, 1995.

Blaise, Clark, and Bharati Mukherjee. *The Sorrow and the Pity: The Haunting Legacy of the Air India Tragedy.* New York: Viking, 1987.

Block, Steven M. "Living Nightmares: Biological Threats Enabled by Molecular Biology." In *The New Terror: Facing the Threat of Biological and Chemical Weapons.* Edited by Sidney D. Drell, Abraham D. Sofaer, and George D. Wilson. Stanford, Calif.: Hoover Institution Press, 1999.

Bodansky, Yossef. *Bin Laden: The Man Who Declared War on America.* Rocklin, Calif.: Forum, 1999.

Boilard, Steve D. *Russia at the Twenty-First Century.* Fort Worth, Tex.: Harcourt Brace, 1998.

Bonner, Raymond. "Tamil Guerrillas in Sri Lanka: How They Build Their Arsenal." In *Violence and Terrorism.* Edited by Bernard Schecterman and Martin Slann. Guilford, Conn.: Dushkin/McGraw-Hill, 1999.

Bonora-Waisman, Camille. *France and the Algerian Conflict: Issues in Democracy and Political Stability, 1988–1995.* Burlington, Vt.: Ashgate, 2002.

Booth, Ken, and Tim Dunne, eds. *Worlds in Collision: Terror and the Future of Global Order.* New York: Palgrave, 2002.

Bouchat, Clarence J. "A Fundamentalist Islamic Threat to the West." *Studies in Conflict and Terrorism* 19 (1996): 339–352.

Bowers, Stephen R., and Kimberly R. Keys. "Technology and Terrorism: The New Threat for the Millennium." *Conflict Studies* 309 (1998): 1–24.

Bowman, Stephen. *When the Eagle Screams: America's Vulnerability to Terrorism.* New York: Birch Lane, 1994.

Boyarin, Jonathan, and Daniel Boyarin. *Powers of Diaspora: Two Essays on the Relevance of Jewish Culture.* Minneapolis: University of Minnesota Press, 2002.

Brackett, D. W. *Holy Terror: Armageddon in Tokyo.* New York: Weatherhill, 1996.

Bremer, L. Paul, III. "Conference on Middle East Fundamentalism and Terrorism, the Carnegie Endowment for International Peace, April 21, 1988." *Terrorism* 11 (1988): 345–347.

"British Authorities Seek Killers of Indian Aide." *Boston Globe,* February 7, 1984.

"British Detonate Bomb Found in Car on Base in Germany." *Boston Globe,* May 4, 1988.

British Medical Association. *Biotechnology, Weapons and Humanity.* Amsterdam: Harwood Academic, 1999.

Broad, William J., and Judith Miller. "Report: Soviet Smallpox Killed 3." *Dallas Morning News,* June 15, 2002.

Brown, L. Carl. *Religion and State: The Muslim Approach to Politics.* New York: Columbia University Press, 2000.

Brown, Michael E. *Ethnic Conflict and International Security.* Princeton: Princeton University Press, 1993.

———. "Ethnic and Internal Conflicts: Causes and Implications." In *Turbulent Peace: The Challenges of Managing International Conflict.* Edited by Chester A. Crocker, Fen Osler Hampson, and Pamela Aall. Herndon, Va.: United States Institute of Peace Press, 2001.

Brown, Michael E., ed. *The International Dimensions of Internal Conflict.* Cambridge, Mass.: MIT Press, 1996.

Brown, Michael E., Owen R. Cote, Jr., Sean M. Lynn-Jones, and Steven E. Miller, eds. *Nationalism and Ethnic Conflict: An International Security Reader.* Cambridge, Mass.: MIT Press, 1997.

Brown, Michael E., Sean Lynn-Jones, and Steven Miller, eds. *The Perils of Anarchy: Contemporary Realism and International Security.* Cambridge, Mass.: MIT Press, 1995.

Brown, Robert McAfee. *Religion and Violence.* Philadelphia: Westminster, 1987.

Bruce, Steve. "Loyalist Assassinations and Police Collusion in Northern Ireland." *Studies in Conflict and Terrorism* 23 (2000): 61–80.

Brzezinski, Zbigniew. *Out of Control: Global Turmoil on the Eve of the Twenty-First Century.* New York: Scribner's, 1993.

Buck, Kathleen A. "Superterrorism: Biological, Chemical, and Nuclear." *Terrorism* 12 (1989): 433–435.

Builta, Jeffrey A. "Harakat al-Muqawama al-Islamiya (Hamas)." In *Extremist Groups.* Edited by John Murray and Richard H. Ward. Urbana: University of Illinois Press, 1996.

Bukharin, Oleg. *The Threat of Nuclear Terrorism and the Physical Security of Nuclear Installations and Materials in the Former Soviet Union.* Monterey, Calif.: Monterey Institute of International Studies, 1992.

Bukharin, Oleg, and William Potter. "Potatoes Were Guarded Better." In *Peace and Security: The Next Generation.* Edited by George A. Lopez and Nancy J. Myers. Lanham, Md.: Rowman and Littlefield, 1997.

Bull, Hedley. *The Anarchical Society: A Study of Order in World Politics.* New York: Columbia University Press, 1995.

Bulliet, Richard W. "The Future of the Islamic Movement." *Foreign Affairs* 72 (1993): 38–44.

Bullion, Alan J. *India, Sri Lanka, and the Tamil Crisis, 1976–1994: An International Perspective.* London: Pinter, 1995.

Bulloch, John, and Harvey Morris. *No Friends but the Mountains: The Tragic History of the Kurds.* New York: Oxford University Press, 1992.

Bunn, Matthew. *The Next Wave: Urgently Needed Steps to Control Warheads and Fissile Material.* Washington: Carnegie Endowment for Peace and Harvard Project on Managing the Atom, 2000.

Burgat, François, and William Dowell. *The Islamic Movement in North Africa.* Austin, Tex.: Center for Middle Eastern Studies, 1993.

Burrows, William E., and Robert Windrem. *Critical Mass: The Dangerous Race for Superweapons in a Fragmenting World.* New York: Simon and Schuster, 1994.

"Businessmen Reportedly Gave bin Laden Millions." *Dallas Morning News,* July 7, 1999.

Byman, Daniel L. "The Logic of Ethnic Terrorism." *Studies in Conflict and Terrorism* 21 (1998): 149–169.

Camarota, Steven A. *The Golden Door: How Militant Islamic Terrorists Entered the United States, 1993–2001.* Washington: Center for Immigration Studies, 2002.

Cameron, Gavin. "Lone Actors as Perpetrators of Incidents with CBRN Weapons." Paper presented to Terrorism and Beyond: The 21st Century Conference, April 17–19, 2000, at Oklahoma City, Oklahoma.

———. "Multi-track Microproliferation: Lessons from Aum Shinrikyo and al Qaida." *Studies in Conflict and Terrorism* 22 (1999): 277–309.

————. "Nuclear Terrorism: A Real Threat?" *Jane's Intelligence Review,* September 1996.

————. *Nuclear Terrorism: A Threat Assessment for the 21st Century.* New York: St. Martin's, 1999.

————. "WMD Terrorism in the United States: The Threat and Possible Countermeasures." *Nonproliferation Review* 7 (2000): 162–179.

Camilleri, Joseph A. "Rethinking Sovereignty in a Shrinking, Fragmented World." In *Contending Sovereignties: Redefining Political Community.* Edited by R. B. J. Walker and Saul H. Mendlovitz. Boulder, Colo.: Lynne Rienner, 1990.

Camilleri, Joseph A., and Richard A. Falk. *The End of Sovereignty: The Politics of a Shrinking and Fragmenting World.* Cheltenham, UK: Edward Elgar, 1993.

Campbell, James K. "Chemical and Biological Weapons Threats to America: Are We Prepared?" In *World Politics.* Edited by John T. Rourke. Guilford, Conn.: McGraw-Hill/Dushkin, 2002.

————. "Excerpts from Research Study 'Weapons of Mass Destruction and Terrorism: Proliferation by Non-State Actors.'" *Terrorism and Political Violence* 9 (1997): 24–50.

————. *Weapons of Mass Destruction and Terrorism.* Seminole, Fla.: Inter-Pact, 1997.

Caner, Ergun Mehmet, and Emir Fethi Caner. *Unveiling Islam: An Insider's Look at Muslim Life and Beliefs.* Grand Rapids, Mich.: Kregel, 2002.

Cantor, Charles R., Cassandra L. Smith, and the Human Genome Project. *Genomics: The Science and Technology behind the Human Genome Project.* New York: John Wiley, 1999.

Caplan, Lionel, ed. *Studies in Religious Fundamentalism.* Albany: State University of New York Press, 1987.

Caram, Peter. *The 1993 World Trade Center Bombing: Foresight and Warning.* Concord, Mass.: Janus, 2001.

Carment, David, and Patrick James, eds. *Wars in the Midst of Peace: The International Politics of Ethnic Conflict.* Pittsburgh: University of Pittsburgh Press, 1997.

Carter, Ashton, John Deutch, and Philip Zelikow. "Catastrophic Terrorism: Tackling the New Danger." *Foreign Affairs* 77 (1998): 80–94.

Carter, Gradon B. *Porton Down: 75 Years of Chemical and Biological Research.* London: HMSO, 1992.

Carus, W. Seth. "Biohazard." *New Republic,* August 2, 1999.

————. *Bio-terrorism, Bio-crimes, and Bioassassination: Case Studies.* Washington: National Defense University, 1998.

————. *The Threat of Bioterrorism.* Washington: National Defense University, 1997.

————. "Unlawful Acquisition and Use of Biological Agents." In *Biological Weapons: Limiting the Threat.* Edited by Joshua Lederberg. Cambridge, Mass.: MIT Press, 1999.

Cavanaugh, Kathleen A. "Interpretations of Political Violence in Ethnically Divided Societies." *Terrorism and Political Violence* 9 (1997): 33–54.

Center for Strategic and International Studies. *Combating Chemical, Biological, Radiological, and Nuclear Terrorism: A Comprehensive Strategy.* Washington: Center for Strategic and International Studies, 2001.

————. *The Nuclear Black Market.* Washington: Center for Strategic and International Studies, 1996.

Cetron, Marvin. *Terror 2000: The Future Face of Terrorism.* Washington: U.S. Department of Defense, 1995.

Chadda, Maya. *Ethnicity, Security, and Separatism in India.* New York: Columbia University Press, 1997.

Chadwick, Elizabeth. *Self-Determination, Terrorism, and the International Humanitarian Law of Armed Conflict.* Boston: M. Nijhoff, 1996.

Chaliand, Gerard, and Philip Black. *The Kurdish Tragedy.* Atlantic Highland, N.J.: Zed, 1994.

Chaliand, Gerard, and Yves Ternon. *The Armenians: From Genocide to Resistance.* London: Zed, 1983.

Chaliand, Gerard, et al. *A People without a Country: The Kurds and Kurdistan.* Northampton, Mass.: Interlink, 1993.

Chalk, Peter. *Non-Military Security and Global Order: The Impact of Extremism, Violence and Chaos on National and International Security.* New York: Palgrave, 2000.

———. *Terrorism, Infrastructure Protection and the U.S. Food and Agricultural Sector.* Santa Monica, Calif.: Rand, 2001.

———. *West European Terrorism and Counter-Terrorism: The Evolving Dynamic.* Houndsmill, UK: Macmillan, 1996.

Chandler, Robert W., and John R. Backschies. *The New Face of War: Weapons of Mass Destruction and the Revitalization of America's Transoceanic Strategy.* McLean, Va.: Amcoda, 1998.

Chang, Nancy, et al., eds. *Silencing Political Dissent.* New York: Seven Stories, 2002.

Chapman, Robert D., and M. Lester Chapman. *The Crimson Web of Terror.* Boulder, Colo.: Paladin, 1980.

Chasdi, Richard J. *Serenade of Suffering: A Portrait of Middle East Terrorism, 1968–1993.* Lanham, Md.: Rowman and Littlefield, 1999.

———. *Tapestry of Terror: A Portrait of Middle East Terrorism, 1994–1999.* Lanham, Md.: Rowman and Littlefield, 2002.

"Chechen Rebel Threatens Radiation Attack." *Dallas Morning News,* December 23, 1995.

Chevrier, Marie Isabelle. "The Threat of Chemical and Biological Terrorism Is Exaggerated." In *Weapons of Mass Destruction.* Edited by Jennifer A. Hurley. San Diego: Greenhaven, 1999.

Chima, Jugdep S. "Back to the Future in 2002? A Model of Sikh Separatism in Punjab." *Studies in Conflict and Terrorism* 25 (2002): 19–39.

Chopra, V. D., et al. *Agony of Punjab.* New Delhi: Patriot, 1984.

Choudhary, Darshan Lai. *Violence in the Freedom Movement of Punjab.* New Delhi: B. R. Publishing, 1986.

Choueiri, Youssef. *Islamic Fundamentalism.* Boston: Twayne, 1990.

Christie, Kenneth. *Ethnic Conflict, Tribal Politics: A Global Perspective.* Honolulu: Curzon, 1999.

Christopher, George W., Theodore J. Cieslak, Julie A. Pavlin, and Edward M. Eitzen, Jr. "Biological Warfare: A Historical Perspective." *Journal of the American Medical Association* 278 (1997): 412–417.

Chua, Amy. *World on Fire: How Exporting Free Market Democracy Breeds Ethnic Hatred and Global Instability.* New York: Doubleday, 2003.

Chyba, Christopher F. *Biological Terrorism, Emerging Infectious Diseases, and National Security.* New York: Project on World Security, 1998.

Cilluffo, Frank J., and Jack Thomas Tomarchio. "Emergency Response Teams Can Mitigate the Effects of a Chemical or Biological Attack." In *Weapons of Mass Destruction.* Edited by Jennifer A. Hurley. San Diego: Greenhaven, 1999.

Ciment, James. *Algeria: The Fundamentalist Challenge.* New York: Facts on File, 1997.

Citizens for Democracy. *Oppression in Punjab.* Columbus, Ohio: Sikh Religious and Educational Trust, 1986.

Claridge, David. "Exploding the Myths of Superterrorism." In *The Future of Terrorism.* Edited by Maxwell Taylor and John Horgan. London: Frank Cass, 2000.

Clark, Brian. *Technological Terrorism.* Old Greenwich, Conn.: Devin-Adair, 1980.

Clark, Robert P. *The Basque Insurgents: ETA, 1952–1980.* Madison: University of Wisconsin Press, 1984.

———. *The Basques: The Franco Years and Beyond.* Reno: University of Nevada Press, 1979.

———. *Negotiating with ETA: Obstacles to Peace in the Basque Country, 1975–1988.* Reno: University of Nevada Press, 1990.

———. "Patterns in the Lives of ETA Members." *Terrorism* 6 (1983): 423–454.

Cline, Ray S., and Yonah Alexander. *Terrorism: The Iranian Connection.* New York: Taylor and Francis, 1988.

Cockburn, Andrew, and Leslie Cockburn. *One Point Safe: A True Story.* New York: Doubleday, 1997.

Cohen, Bernard L. "The Potentialities of Terrorism." *Bulletin of the Atomic Scientists* 32 (1976): 34–35.

Cohen, Robin. *Global Diasporas: An Introduction.* Seattle: University of Washington Press, 1997.

Cohen-Almagor, Raphael. "Vigilante Jewish Fundamentalism: From the JDL to Kach (or 'Shalom Jews, Shalom Dogs')." *Terrorism and Political Violence* 4 (1992): 44–66.

Cohm, Haim. "Holy Terror." *Violence, Aggression, and Terrorism* 1 (1987): 1–12.

Cole, Leonard A. *Clouds of Secrecy: The Army's Germ Warfare Tests over Populated Areas.* Savage, Md.: Rowman and Littlefield, 1990.

———. *The Eleventh Plague: The Politics of Biological and Chemical Warfare.* New York: W. H. Freeman, 1997.

Collins, Aukai. *My Jihad: The True Story of an American Mujahid's Amazing Journey from Usama Bin Laden's Training Camps to Counterterrorism with the FBI and the CIA.* Guilford, Conn.: Lyons, 2002.

Combs, Cindy C. *Terrorism in the Twenty-First Century.* Upper Saddle River, N.J.: Prentice Hall, 2003.

Conn, Carl. *Culture Wars and the Global Village: A Diplomat's Perspective.* Amherst, N.Y.: Prometheus, 2000.

Connelly, Matthew James. *A Diplomatic Revolution: Algeria's Fight for Independence and the Origins of the Post–Cold War Era.* New York: Oxford University Press, 2002.

Connor, Walker. *Ethnonationalism: The Quest for Understanding.* Princeton: Princeton University Press, 1994.

Conversi, Daniele, ed. *Ethnonationalism in the Contemporary World: Walker Connor and the Study of Nationalism.* New York: Routledge, 2002.

Coogan, Tim Pat. *The IRA.* Glasgow, UK: Fontana, 1988.

Cook-Deegan, Robert. *The Gene Wars: Science, Politics, and the Human Genome.* New York: W. W. Norton, 1996.

Cookson, John, and Judith Nottingham. *A Survey of Chemical and Biological Warfare.* New York: Monthly Review Press, 1969.

Cooley, John K. *Green March, Black September: The Story of the Palestinian Arabs.* London: Frank Cass, 1973.

———. *Unholy Wars: Afghanistan, America and International Terrorism.* London: Pluto, 1999.

Cooper, Robert. "The Post-Modern State and the World Order." In *Global Issues.* Edited by Robert I. Jackson. Guilford, Conn.: Dushkin/McGraw-Hill, 1999.

Copeland, Thomas. "Is the 'New Terrorism' Really New? An Analysis of the New Paradigm for Terrorism." *Journal of Conflict Studies* 21 (2001): 7–27.

Corbin, Jane. *Al-Qaeda: The Terror Network That Threatens the World.* New York: Thunder's Mouth, 2002.

Cordesman, Anthony H. *Terrorism, Asymmetric Warfare, and Weapons of Mass Destruction.* Westport, Conn.: Greenwood, 2001.

Cornell, Svante E. *Small Nations and Great Powers: A Study of Ethnopolitical Conflict in the Caucasus.* Honolulu: Curzon, 2001.

Corrado, Raymond R. "Ethnic and Ideological Terrorism in Western Europe." In *The Politics of Terrorism.* Edited by Michael Stohl. New York: Dekker, 1988.

"Corsican Commander Admits He Ordered Separatist Hangout Burned." *Dallas Morning News,* May 8, 1999.

Corsun, Andrew. "Group Profile: The Revolutionary Organization 17 November in Greece (1975–91)." In *European Terrorism: Today and Tomorrow.* Edited by Yonah Alexander and Dennis A. Pluchinsky. Washington: Brassey's, 1992.

———. *Research Papers on Terrorism: Armenian Terrorism, 1975–1980.* Washington: U.S. Department of State, 1982.

Council on Foreign Relations, ed. *The New Shape of World Politics: Contending Paradigms in International Relations.* New York: W. W. Norton, 1999.

———. *Samuel P. Huntington's* THE CLASH OF CIVILIZATIONS?: *The Debate.* New York: W. W. Norton, 1996.

Cozic, Charles P., ed. *Ethnic Conflict.* San Diego: Greenhaven, 1995.

———. *Nationalism and Ethnic Conflict.* San Diego: Greenhaven, 1994.

Crenshaw, Martha. "Defining Future Threats: Terrorists and Nuclear Proliferation." In *Terrorism: Interdisciplinary Perspectives.* Edited by Yonah Alexander and Seymour Maxwell Finger. New York: John Jay, 1977.

Crenshaw, Martha, ed. *Terrorism and International Cooperation.* Boulder, Colo.: Westview, 1989.

Crenshaw, Martha, and Maryann Cusimano Love. "Networked Terror." In *Beyond Sovereignty: Issues for a Global Agenda.* Edited by Maryann Cusimano Love. Belmont, Calif.: Thomson/Wadsworth, 2003.

Criss, Nur Bilge. "The Nature of PKK Terrorism in Turkey." *Studies in Conflict and Terrorism* 18 (1995): 17–38.

Crockatt, Richard. *America Embattled: 9/11, Anti-Americanism and the Global Order.* New York: Routledge, 2003.

Crocker, Chester, Fen Osler Hampson, and Pamela Aall, eds. *Herding Cats: Multiparty Mediation in a Complex World.* Herndon, Va.: United States Institute of Peace Press, 1999.

Croddy, Eric. *Chemical and Biological Warfare: A Comprehensive Survey for the Concerned Citizen.* New York: Copernicus, 2002.

———. "Urban Terrorism—Chemical Warfare in Japan." *Jane's Intelligence Review* 7 (1995): 520–523.

Cromer, Gerald. "Jewish Underground: At the Center or on the Periphery of Israeli Society?" *Terrorism* 11 (1988): 350–354.

————. *Narratives of Violence.* Burlington, Vt.: Ashgate, 2001.

————. "'The Roots of Lawlessness': The Coverage of the Jewish Underground in the Israeli Press." *Terrorism* 11 (1988): 43–51.

Cronin, Isaac, ed. *Confronting Fear: A History of Terrorism.* New York: Thunder's Mouth, 2002.

Currie, Stephen. *Terrorists and Terrorist Groups.* Detroit: Lucent, 2002.

Cusimano, Maryann K., ed. *Beyond Sovereignty: Issues for a Global Agenda.* Boston: Bedford/St. Martin's, 2000.

Dabashi, Hamid. *Theology of Discontent: The Ideological Foundations of the Islamic Revolution in Iran.* New York: New York University Press, 1993.

Dalacourta, Katarina. "The Islamic Movement as Non-State Actor." In *Non-State Actors in World Politics.* Edited by William Wallace and Daphne Josselin. New York: Palgrave, 2002.

Dando, Malcolm. *Biological Warfare in the 21st Century: Biotechnology and the Proliferation of Biological Weapons.* New York: Macmillan, 1994.

————. *The New Biological Weapons: Threat, Proliferation, and Control.* Boulder, Colo.: Lynne Rienner, 2001.

Danforth, Loring M. *The Macedonian Conflict: Ethnic Nationalism in a Transnational World.* Princeton: Princeton University Press, 1997.

Danspeckgruber, Wolfgang, ed. *The Self-Determination of Peoples: Community, Nation, and State in an Interdependent World.* Boulder, Colo.: Lynne Rienner, 2002.

Danzig, Richard. "Why Should We Be Concerned about Biological Warfare?" *Journal of the American Medical Association* 278 (1997): 431–432.

Davidson, Lawrence. *Islamic Fundamentalism.* Westport, Conn.: Greenwood, 1993.

Davies, Thomas D. "What Nuclear Means and Targets Might Terrorists Find Attractive?" In *Nuclear Terrorism: Defining the Threat.* Edited by Paul Leventhal and Yonah Alexander. Washington: Pergamon-Brassey's, 1986.

Davis, Joyce M. *Between Jihaad and Salaam: Profiles in Islam.* New York: St. Martin's, 1999.

De Andreis, Marco, and Francesco Calogero. *The Soviet Nuclear Weapon Legacy.* Oxford: Oxford University Press, 1995.

Defense Science Board 1997 Summer Study Task Force. *DoD Responses to Transnational Threats.* Washington: Office of the Undersecretary of Defense for Acquisition and Technology, 1997.

Dekmejian, Hrair R. *Islam in Revolution: Fundamentalism in the Arab World.* Syracuse, N.Y.: Syracuse University Press, 1985.

————. "The Rise of Political Islam in Saudi Arabia." *Middle East Journal* 48 (1994): 627–643.

DeLeon, Peter, and Bruce Hoffman. *The Threat of Nuclear Terrorism: A Reexamination.* Santa Monica, Calif.: Rand, 1988.

Demaris, Ovid. *Brothers in Blood: The International Terrorist Network.* New York: Scribner's, 1977.

Dempsey, James X., and David Cole. *Terrorism and the Constitution: Sacrificing Civil Liberties in the Name of National Security.* Los Angeles: First Amendment Foundation, 1999.

Dennis, Anthony J. *Osama bin Laden.* Bristol, Ind.: Wyndham Hall, 2002.

Derogy, Jacques. *Resistance and Revenge: The Armenian Assassination of Turkish Leaders Responsible for the 1915 Massacres and Deportations.* New Brunswick, N.J.: Transaction, 1990.

Dershowitz, Alan M. *Why Terrorism Works: Understanding the Threat, Responding to the Challenge.* New Haven: Yale University Press, 2002.

Der Spiegel Magazine, eds. *Inside 9/11: What Really Happened.* New York: St. Martin's, 2001.

De Silva, K. M., and R. J. May. *Internationalization of Ethnic Conflict.* London: Pinter, 1991.

DeVito, Donald A., and Lucy Suiter. "Emergency Management and the Nuclear Terrorism Threat." In *Preventing Nuclear Terrorism: The Report and Papers of the International Task Force on Prevention of Nuclear Terrorism.* Edited by Paul Leventhal and Yonah Alexander. Lexington, Mass.: Lexington, 1987.

Diamond, Larry, and Marc Plattner, eds. *Nationalism, Ethnic Conflict, and Democracy.* Baltimore: Johns Hopkins University Press, 1994.

Dietl, Wilhelm. *Holy War.* New York: Macmillan, 1984.

"'Dirty Bomb' Suspect Found Islam while Living in Florida." *Dallas Morning News,* June 16, 2002.

Dishman, Chris. "Understanding Perspectives on WMD and Why They Are Important." *Studies in Conflict and Terrorism* 24 (2001): 303–313.

Dobson, Christopher. *Black September: Its Short, Violent History.* New York: Macmillan, 1974.

Do Ceu Pinto, Maria. *Political Islam and the United States: A Study of U.S. Policy towards Islamic Movements in the Middle East.* Reading, UK: Garnet, 1999.

———. "Some U.S. Concerns Regarding Islamist and Middle Eastern Terrorism." *Terrorism and Political Violence* 11 (1999): 72–96.

Douglass, Joseph D., Jr., and Neil C. Livingstone. *America the Vulnerable: The Threat of Chemical and Biological Warfare.* Lexington, Mass.: Lexington, 1987.

Drake, C. J. M. *Terrorists' Target Selection.* New York: St. Martin's, 1998.

Drell, Sidney D., Abraham D. Sofaer, and George D. Wilson, eds. *The New Terror: Facing the Threat of Biological and Chemical Weapons.* Stanford, Calif.: Hoover Institution Press, 1999.

Drobizheva, Leokadia, Rose Gottemoeller, Catherine McArdle Kelleher, and Lee Walker, eds. *Ethnic Conflict in the Post-Soviet World: Case Studies and Analysis.* Armonk, N.Y.: M. E. Sharpe, 1996.

Dunlop, John B. *Russia Confronts Chechnya: Roots of a Separatist Conflict.* New York: Cambridge University Press, 1998.

Durfee, Mary. "Constituting Complexity: Order and Turbulence in World Politics." In *Pondering Postinternationalism: A Paradigm for the Twenty-first Century?* Edited by Heidi H. Hobbs. Albany: State University of New York Press, 2000.

Dutter, Lee E. "Ethno-Political Activity and the Psychology of Terrorism." *Terrorism* 10 (1987): 145–163.

Dwyer, Jim. *Two Seconds under the World.* New York: Crown, 1994.

Eckholm, Eric. "America Gives China Good News: Rebels on Terror List." *New York Times,* August 27, 2002.

———. "China Muslim Group Planned Terror, U.S. Says." *New York Times,* August 31, 2002.

Edelhertz, Herbert, and Marilyn Walsh. *The White-Collar Challenge to Nuclear Safeguards.* Lexington, Mass.: Lexington, 1978.

Edwards, David B. *Before Taliban: Genealogies of the Afghan Jihad.* Berkeley: University of California Press, 2002.

Egendorf, Laura K., ed. *Terrorism.* San Diego: Greenhaven, 2000.

Ehrenfeld, Rachel. *Narco-terrorism.* New York: HarperCollins, 1990.

Eickelman, Dale F. "Trans-state Islam and Security." In *Transnational Religion and Fading States.* Edited by Hoeber Rudolph, Susanne Piscatori, and James Piscatori. Boulder, Colo.: Westview, 1996.

Eickelman, Dale F., and James Piscatori. *Muslim Politics.* Princeton: Princeton University Press, 1996.

El-Affendi, Abdelwahab. *Who Needs an Islamic State?* London: Grey Seal, 1991.

El Fadl, Khaled Abou. *Rebellion and Violence in Islamic Law.* New York: Cambridge University Press, 2002.

Eliassen, Kjell, ed. *Foreign and Security Policy in the European Union.* Thousand Oaks, Calif.: Sage, 1998.

Eller, Jack David. *From Culture to Ethnicity to Conflict: An Anthropological Perspective on International Ethnic Conflict.* Ann Arbor: University of Michigan Press, 1999.

Ember, Lois. "Bioterrorism: Combating the Threat." *Chemical and Engineering News,* July 5, 1999.

———. "Chemical Weapons: Residues Verify Iraqi Use on Kurds." *Chemical and Engineering News,* May 3, 1993.

Embree, Ainslie. *Utopias in Conflict: Religion and Nationalism in Modern India.* Berkeley: University of California Press, 1990.

Emerson, Steven. *American Jihad: The Terrorists Living among Us.* New York: Simon and Schuster, 2002.

———. "The Threat of Militant Islamic Fundamentalism." In *The Future of Terrorism: Violence in the New Millennium.* Edited by Harvey W. Kushner. Thousand Oaks, Calif.: Sage, 1998.

Enayat, Hamid. *Modern Islamic Political Thought: The Response of the Shi'i and Sunni Moslems to the Twentieth Century.* London: Macmillan, 1982.

Enders, Walter, and Todd Sandler. "Causality between Transnational Terrorism and Tourism: The Case of Spain." *Terrorism* 14 (1991): 49–58.

———. "Is Transnational Terrorism Becoming More Threatening?" *Journal of Conflict Resolution* 44 (2000): 307–332.

———. "Transnational Terrorism in the Post–Cold War Era." *International Studies Quarterly* 43 (1999): 145–167.

Enders, Walter, Todd Sandler, and Jon Cauley. "U.N. Conventions, Technology and Retaliation in the Fight against Terrorism." *Terrorism and Political Violence* 2 (1990): 83–105.

Engel, James B. *Defense against the Military Use of Genetic Engineering.* Norfolk, Va.: Armed Forces Staff College, 1985.

Eppright, Charles T. "'Counterterrorism' and Conventional Military Force: The Relationship between Political Effect and Utility." *Studies in Conflict and Terrorism* 20 (1997): 333–344.

Erickson, Richard J. "What International Law Approach Should Be Taken toward International Terrorism?" *Terrorism* 11 (1988): 113–137.

Esman, Milton J. "Ethnic Actors in International Politics." *Nationalism and Ethnic Politics* 1 (1995): 111–125.

Esman, Milton J., and Shibley Telhami, eds. *International Organizations and Ethnic Conflict.* Ithaca, N.Y.: Cornell University Press, 1995.

Esposito, John L. *Islam and Politics.* Syracuse, N.Y.: Syracuse University Press, 1998.

———. *The Islamic Threat: Myth or Reality?* New York: Oxford University Press, 1992.

———. *Unholy War: Terror in the Name of Islam.* New York: Oxford University Press, 2002.

Esposito, John L., ed. *The Iranian Revolution: Its Global Impact.* Miami: Florida International University Press, 1990.

———. *Voices of Resurgent Islam.* Oxford: Oxford University Press, 1983.

Esty, Daniel C., et al. *State Failure Task Force Report: Phase 2 Findings.* McLean, Va.: Science Applications International Corporation, 1998.

———. *Working Papers: State Failure Task Force Report.* McLean, Va.: Science Applications International Corporation, 1995.

Euban, Roxanne. *Enemy in the Mirror: Islamic Fundamentalism and the Limits of Modern Rationalism.* Princeton: Princeton University Press, 1999.

Evan, William M., and Mark Nanion. *Minding the Machines: Preventing Technological Disasters.* Upper Saddle River, N.J.: Prentice Hall, 2002.

Evangelista, Matthew. *The Chechen Wars: Will Russia Go the Way of the Soviet Union?* Washington: Brookings, 2003.

Ezeldin, Ahmed Galal. "Terrorism in the 1990s: New Strategies and the Nuclear Threat." *International Journal of Comparative and Applied Criminal Justice* 13 (1989): 7–16.

Fadlallah, Mohammed Hussein. *Islam and the Logic of Force.* Beirut: Al-Dar al-Islamiya, 1984.

Faksh, Mahmud A. *The Future of Islam in the Middle East: Fundamentalism in Egypt, Algeria, and Saudi Arabia.* Westport, Conn.: Praeger, 1997.

Falk, Richard. *Global Shock Waves: The Persistence of Terror, Terrorists and Terror-States.* Northampton, Mass.: Interlink, 2002.

———. "In Search of a New World Model." *Current History* 23 (1993): 145–149.

Falkenrath, Richard A. "Confronting Nuclear, Biological, and Chemical Terrorism." *Survival* 40 (1998): 43–65.

Falkenrath, Richard A., Robert D. Newman, and Bradley A. Thayer. *America's Achilles' Heel: Nuclear, Biological, and Chemical Terrorism and Covert Attack.* Cambridge, Mass.: MIT Press, 1998.

Fandy, Mamoun. *Saudi Arabia and the Politics of Dissent.* New York: Palgrave, 2001.

Fattah, Nabil Abdel. *Veiled Violence: Islamic Fundamentalism in Egyptian Politics in the 1990s.* Cairo: Sechat, 1993.

"FBI Says It Foiled a Plan to Sabotage Nuclear Facilities." *Boston Globe,* June 1, 1989.

Feld, Bernard T. "Nuclear Violence at the Non-Governmental Level." In *Contemporary Terror: Studies in Sub-State Violence.* Edited by David Carlton and Carlo Schaerf. New York: St. Martin's, 1978.

Feld, Werner J. *International Relations.* New York: Alfred, 1979.

Ferguson, R. Brian, ed. *The State, Identity and Violence: Political Disintegration in the Post–Cold War Period.* New York: Routledge, 2003.

Ferguson, Wallace K., and Geoffrey Bruun. *A Survey of European Civilization.* Boston: Houghton Mifflin, 1969.

Finger, Seymour Maxwell. "The United Nations and International Terrorism." In *International Terrorism: Characteristics, Causes, Controls.* Edited by Charles W. Kegley, Jr. New York: St. Martin's, 1990.

Firestone, Reuven. *Jihad: The Origin of Holy War in Islam*. New York: Oxford University Press, 1999.

Fisk, Robert. "My Days with Bin Laden." *Gentleman's Quarterly,* November 2001.

Flockhart, Trine, ed. *From Vision to Reality: Implementing Europe's New Security Order*. Boulder, Colo.: Westview, 1998.

"Florida Man Dies of Anthrax." *Dallas Morning News,* October 6, 2001.

Ford, James L. *Nuclear Smuggling: How Serious a Threat?* Washington: National Defense University, 1996.

Forrest, Frank R. "Nuclear Terrorism and the Escalation of International Conflict." *Naval War College Review* 29 (1976): 12–27.

"Four Suspects Held in French Drive on Terrorists." *Boston Globe,* August 31, 1982.

Fowkes, Ben, ed. *Russia and Chechnia: The Permanent Crisis*. New York: St. Martin's, 1998.

Foxell, Joseph W., Jr. "Current Trends in Agroterrorism (Antilivestock, Anticrop, and Antisoil Bioagricultural Terrorism) and Their Potential Impact on Food Security." *Studies in Conflict and Terrorism* 24 (2001): 107–129.

————. "The Debate on the Potential for Mass-Casualty Terrorism: The Challenge to U.S. Security." *Terrorism and Political Violence* 11 (1999): 94–109.

————. "The Prospect of Nuclear and Biological Terrorism." *Journal of Contingencies and Crisis Management* 5 (1997): 98–108.

Franz, David R., et al. "Clinical Recognition and Management of Patients Exposed to Biological Warfare Agents." *Journal of the American Medical Association* 278 (1997): 399–411.

Frazier, Thomas W., and Drew C. Richardson, eds. *Food and Agricultural Security: Guarding against Natural Threats and Terrorist Attacks Affecting Health, National Food Supplies, and Agricultural Economics*. New York: New York Academy of Sciences, 2000.

Freedberg, Sydney J., Jr., and Marylyn Werber Serafine. "Be Afraid, Be Moderately Afraid." *National Journal,* March 27, 1999.

Fregosi, Paul. *Jihad in the West: Muslim Conquests from the 7th to the 21st Centuries*. Amherst, N.Y.: Prometheus, 1998.

Friedman, Jonathan. "Transnationalization, Socio-political Disorder, and Ethnification." *International Political Science Review* 19 (1998): 233–250.

Friedman, Robert I. *Sheik Abdel Rahman, the World Trade Center Bombing and the CIA*. Westfield, N.J.: Open Media, 1993.

Friedman, Steven. "Nuclear Terrorism: How Concerned Should We Be?" In *World Politics*. Edited by Marc Genest. Boulder, Colo.: Coursewise, 1999.

Friedman, Thomas L. *From Beirut to Jerusalem*. New York: Anchor, 1990.

————. *Longitudes and Attitudes: Exploring the World after September 11*. New York: Farrar Straus and Giroux, 2003.

Frist, Bill. *When Every Moment Counts: What You Need to Know about Bioterrorism*. Lanham, Md.: Rowman and Littlefield, 2002.

Fuller, Graham E. *Algeria: The Next Fundamentalist State?* Santa Monica, Calif.: Rand, 1996.

————. *Islamic Fundamentalism in Afghanistan: Its Character and Prospects*. Santa Monica, Calif.: Rand, 1991.

————. *Islamic Fundamentalism in the Northern Tier Countries: An Integrative View*. Santa Monica, Calif.: Rand, 1991.

Gagnon, V. P. "Ethnic Nationalism and International Conflict." In *Nationalism and*

Ethnic Conflict. Edited by Michael E. Brown, Owen R. Cote, Jr., Sean M. Lynn-Jones, and Steven E. Miller. Cambridge, Mass.: MIT Press, 1997.

Galeotti, Mark. *The Age of Anxiety: Security and Politics in Soviet and Post-Soviet Russia.* London: Longman, 1995.

Gall, Carlotta, and Thomas de Waal. *Chechnya: Calamity in the Caucasus.* New York: New York University Press, 2000.

Gard, Carolyn. *The Attacks on the World Trade Center.* New York: Rosen, 2002.

Gargan, Edward A. "Violence, Like Punjab's Wheat, Finds Fertile Soil." In *Violence and Terrorism.* Edited by Bernard Schecterman and Martin Slann. Guilford, Conn.: Dushkin, 1993.

Gartner, Heinz, Adrian Hyde-Price, and Erich Reiter, eds. *Europe's New Security Challenges.* Boulder, Colo.: Lynne Rienner, 2001.

Gates, Mahlon E. "The Nuclear Emergency Search Team." In *Preventing Nuclear Terrorism: The Report and Papers of the International Task Force on Prevention of Nuclear Terrorism.* Edited by Paul Leventhal and Yonah Alexander. Lexington, Mass.: Lexington, 1987.

Geertz, Clifford. *Islam Observed: Religious Development in Morocco and Indonesia.* Chicago: University of Chicago Press, 1971.

Geissler, Erhard. "Implications of Genetic Engineering for Chemical and Biological Warfare." In *World Armaments and Disarmament: SIPRI Yearbook 1984.* Edited by Stockholm International Peace Research Institute. London: Taylor and Francis, 1984.

Gellman, Barton. "Fears Prompt U.S. to Beef up Nuclear Terror Detection." In *Violence and Terrorism.* Edited by Thomas J. Badey. Guilford, Conn.: McGraw-Hill/Dushkin, 2003.

Genest, Marc. "Is Nuclear Terrorism a Realistic Threat?" In *World Politics.* Edited by Marc Genest. Boulder, Colo.: Coursewise, 1999.

Gerges, Fawaz A. *America and Political Islam: Clash of Cultures or Clash of Interests?* New York: Cambridge University Press, 1999.

Ghadbian, Najib. "Political Islam and Violence." In *Developing World.* Edited by Robert J. Griffiths. Guilford, Conn.: Dushkin/McGraw-Hill, 2001.

Giannakos, S. A., ed. *Ethnic Conflict: Religion, Identity, and Politics.* Athens: Ohio University Center for International Studies, 2001.

Gilbert, Paul. *Terrorism, Security, and Nationality.* New York: Routledge, 1995.

Gill, Surjan Singh. *Case for Republic of Khalistan.* Vancouver: Babar Khalsa, 1982.

Girard, Rene. *Violence and the Sacred.* Baltimore: Johns Hopkins University Press, 1977.

Global Organized Crime Project. *The Nuclear Black Market.* Washington: Center for Strategic and International Studies, 1996.

Gohari, M. J. *Taliban: Ascent to Power.* New York: Oxford University Press, 2001.

Goldberg, Steven. "Civil Liberties and Nuclear Terrorism." In *Preventing Nuclear Terrorism: The Report and Papers of the International Task Force on Prevention of Nuclear Terrorism.* Edited by Paul Leventhal and Yonah Alexander. Lexington, Mass.: Lexington, 1987.

Goldsmith, Marsha F. "Preparing for Medical Consequences of Terrorism." *Journal of the American Medical Association* 275 (1996): 1713–1714.

Goodson, Larry P. *Afghanistan's Endless War: State Failure, Regional Politics, and the Rise of the Taliban.* Seattle: University of Washington Press, 2001.

Gordon, Hayim. *Quicksand: Israel, the Intifada, and the Rise of Political Evil in Democracies*. East Lansing: Michigan State University Press, 1994.

Gorenberg, Gershom. *The End of Days: Fundamentalism and the Struggle for the Temple Mount*. Oxford: Oxford University Press, 2000.

Gottlieb, Gidon. *Nation against State: A New Approach to Ethnic Conflicts and the Decline of Sovereignty*. New York: Council on Foreign Relations, 1992.

Graham, Bradley. "Colombia Decrees Antiterrorism Laws." *Washington Post*, January 28, 1988.

Graves, Barbara, ed. *Chem-Bio: Frequently Asked Questions*. Alexandria, Va.: Tempest, 1998.

Gray, Colin. "Weapons of Mass Destruction." In *Strategy in the Contemporary World: Introduction to Strategic Studies*. Edited by John Baylis, James Wirtz, Eliot Cohen, and Colin Gray. New York: Oxford University Press, 2002.

Green, Jerrold. *Revolution in Iran: The Politics of Countermobilization*. New York: Praeger, 1982.

———. "Terrorism and Politics in the Islamic Republic of Iran." Paper presented to the Terrorism in Context Conference, June 8–10, 1989, at Middletown, Connecticut.

Gregory, F. E. C. "Police Cooperation and Integration in the European Community: Proposals, Problems, and Prospects." *Terrorism* 14 (1991): 145–155.

Griffin, Michael. *Reaping the Whirlwind: The Taliban Movement in Afghanistan*. Milford, Conn.: Pluto, 2001.

Griffith, Lee. *The War on Terrorism and the Terror of God*. Grand Rapids, Mich.: Eerdmans, 2002.

Griffiths, Stephen Iwan. *Nationalism and Ethnic Conflict*. Oxford: Oxford University Press, 1993.

Griset, Pamala, and Sue Mahan, eds. *Terrorism in Perspective*. Thousand Oaks, Calif.: Sage, 2003.

Grosscup, Beau. *The Newest Explosions of Terrorism: Latest Sites of Terrorism in the 1990s and Beyond*. Far Hills, N.J.: Horizon, 1998.

Guehenno, Jean-Marie. *The End of the Nation-State*. Minneapolis: University of Minnesota Press, 1995.

Guelke, Adrian. *The Age of Terrorism*. London: I. B. Tauris, 1995.

Guibernau, Montserrat. *Nations without States: Political Communities in a Global Age*. Malden, Mass.: Blackwell, 1999.

Guillemin, Jeanne. *Anthrax: The Investigation of a Deadly Outbreak*. Berkeley: University of California Press, 1999.

Gunaratna, Rohan. *Inside al Qaeda: Global Network of Terror*. New York: Columbia University Press, 2002.

Gunter, Michael M. "The Armenian Terrorist Campaign against Turkey." *Orbis* 27 (1983): 447–477.

———. *The Kurdish Predicament in Iraq: A Political Analysis*. New York: St. Martin's, 1999.

———. *The Kurds of Iraq: Tragedy and Hope*. New York: St. Martin's, 1992.

Gupta, Dipankar. *The Context of Ethnicity: Sikh Identity in a Comparative Perspective*. New York: Oxford University Press, 1996.

Gupta, Suman. *The Replication of Violence: Thoughts on International Terrorism after September 11, 2001*. Herndon, Va.: Pluto, 2002.

Gurr, Nadine, and Benjamin Cole. *The New Face of Terrorism: Threats from Weapons of Mass Destruction.* New York: Palgrave, 2002.

Gurr, Ted Robert. *Minorities at Risk: A Global View of Ethnopolitical Conflicts.* Washington: United States Institute of Peace Press, 1993.

———. "Peoples against States: Ethnopolitical Conflict and the Changing World System." *International Studies Quarterly* 38 (1994): 347–377.

———. *Peoples versus States: Minorities at Risk in the New Century.* Herndon, Va.: United States Institute of Peace Press, 2000.

———. "Why Minorities Rebel: A Global Analysis of Communal Mobilization and Conflict since 1945." *International Political Science Review* 14 (1993): 161–201.

Gurr, Ted Robert, and Barbara Harff. *Ethnic Conflict and World Politics.* Boulder, Colo.: Westview, 1994.

Gutierrez, Miren. "Terror in the Pyrenees." In *Violence and Terrorism.* Edited by Thomas J. Badey. Guilford, Conn.: McGraw-Hill/Dushkin, 2003.

Haber, L. F. *The Poisonous Cloud: Chemical Warfare in the First World War.* Oxford: Clarendon, 1986.

Hacker, Frederick J. *Crusaders, Criminals, Crazies: Terror and Terrorism in Our Time.* New York: W. W. Norton, 1976.

Hafez, Mohammed M. *Why Muslims Rebel: Repression and Resistance in the Islamic World.* Boulder, Colo.: Lynne Rienner, 2003.

Haghayeghi, Mehrdad. *Islam and Politics in Central Asia.* New York: St. Martin's, 1995.

Hall, Thomas D., Christopher Bartalos, Elizabeth Mannebach, and Thomas Perkowitz. "Varieties of Ethnic Conflict in Global Perspective: A Review Essay." *Social Science Quarterly* 77 (1996): 445–452.

Halliday, Fred. *Islam and the Myth of Confrontation: Religion and Politics in the Middle East.* New York: Palgrave, 2002.

———. *Nation and Religion in the Middle East.* London: Saqi, 2000.

———. *Two Hours That Shook the World: September 11, 2001: Causes and Consequences.* London: Saqi, 2002.

Hamady, Sania. *Temperament and Character of the Arabs.* New York: Taywine, 1960.

Hamdi, Mohammed E. *The Making of an Islamic Political Leader: Conversations with Hasan al-Turabi.* Boulder, Colo.: Westview, 1998.

Hampson, Fen, et al. *Madness in the Multitude: Human Security and World Disorder.* New York: Oxford University Press, 2001.

Hanauer, Laurence S. "The Path to Redemption: Fundamentalist Judaism, Territory, and Jewish Settler Violence in the West Bank." *Studies in Conflict and Terrorism* 18 (1995): 245–270.

Handleman, Stephen. *Comrade Criminal: Russia's New Mafia.* New Haven: Yale University Press, 1995.

Hanif, Muhammad. "Islam: Sunnis and Shiites." In *The Middle East.* Edited by William Spencer. Guilford, Conn.: Dushkin/McGraw-Hill, 2000.

Hanley, Charles J. "New States Trading in Radioactive Materials." *New Orleans Times-Picayune,* June 15, 2002.

Hanna, Phillip, Nicholas Duesbery, George Vande Woude, and Stephen Leppla. "How Anthrax Kills." *Science,* June 12, 1998.

Hansen, Birthe, and Bertel Heurlin. *The New World Order: Contrasting Theories.* New York: Palgrave, 2000.

Hardacre, Helen. *Aum Shinrikyo and the Japanese Media: The Pied Piper Meets the Lamb of God.* New York: Columbia University Press, 1995.

Harish, Puri, Paramjit Singh Judge, and Jagrup Sekhon. *Terrorism in Punjab.* New Delhi: Har-Anand, 1999.

Harmon, Christopher. *Terrorism Today.* London: Frank Cass, 2000.

Harris, Christina Phelps. *Nationalism and Revolution in Egypt: The Role of the Muslim Brotherhood.* The Hague: Mouton, 1964.

Harris, George S. "Whither the Kurds?" In *Global Convulsions: Race, Ethnicity, and Nationalism at the End of the Twentieth Century.* Edited by Winston A. Van Horne. Albany: State University of New York Press, 1997.

Harris, Robert, and Jeremy Paxman. *A Higher Form of Killing: The Secret History of Chemical and Biological Warfare.* New York: Random House, 2002.

Harris, Sheldon H. *Factories of Death: Japanese Biological Warfare 1932–45 and the American Cover-Up.* New York: Routledge, 1994.

Hastedt, Glenn P., ed. *American Foreign Policy.* Guilford, Conn.: Dushkin/McGraw-Hill, 2000.

Hatina, Meir. *Islam and Salvation in Palestine: The Islamic Jihad Movement.* Tel Aviv: Daya Center, 2001.

Haught, James A. *Holy Hatred: Religious Conflicts of the '90s.* Amherst, N.Y.: Prometheus, 1995.

Hay, Alastair, and Gwynne Roberts. "The Use of Poison Gas against the Iraqi Kurds: Analysis of Bomb Fragments, Soil, and Wool Samples." *Journal of the American Medical Association* 263 (1990): 1065–1066.

Hayes, Denis. "Nuclear Terrorism." *Gamaliel* 3 (1977): 5–6.

Heemstra, Thomas S. *Anthrax: A Deadly Shot in the Dark.* Lexington, Ky.: Crystal Communications, 2002.

Hefner, Robert W., and Patricia Horavitch, eds. *Islam in an Era of Nation-States: Politics and Religious Renewal in Muslim Southeast Asia.* Honolulu: University of Hawaii Press, 1997.

Heiberg, Marianne. *The Making of the Basque Nation.* Cambridge: Cambridge University Press, 1989.

Heikal, Mohammed. *Autumn of Fury: The Assassination of Sadat.* London: André Deutsch, 1983.

Heinrich, Janet. *Bioterrorism: Public Health and Medical Preparedness.* Washington: General Accounting Office, 2001.

Heller, Arnie. "Uncovering Bioterrorism." *Science and Technology Review,* May 2000.

Helliwell, John F. *How Much Do National Borders Matter?* Washington: Brookings, 1998.

Henderson, D. A., et al. "Smallpox as a Biological Weapon: Medical and Health Management." *Journal of the American Medical Association* 281 (1999): 2127–2137.

Hendrickson, Ryan C. "American War Powers and Terrorists: The Case of Usama Bin Laden." *Studies in Conflict and Terrorism* 23 (2000): 161–174.

———. "The Clinton Administration's Strikes on Usama Bin Laden: Limits to Power." In *Contemporary Cases in U.S. Foreign Policy: From Terrorism to Trade.* Edited by Ralph G. Carter. Washington: CQ Press, 2001.

Heper, Metin, and Raphael Israeli, eds. *Islam and Politics in the Modern Middle East*. London: Croom Helm, 1984.

Heraclides, Alexis. *The Self-Determination of Minorities in International Politics*. Portland, Ore.: Frank Cass, 1991.

Herman, Valentine, and Rob van der Laan Bouma. "Nationalists without a Nation: South Moluccan Terrorism in the Netherlands." In *Terrorism: A Challenge to the State*. Edited by Juliet Lodge. New York: St. Martin's, 1981.

Hewitt, Christopher. *Understanding Terrorism in America: From the Klan to al Qaeda*. New York: Routledge, 2003.

Hewsen, Robert H. "Who Speaks Today of the Armenians?" In *International Terrorism in the Contemporary World*. Edited by Marius Livingston et al. Westport, Conn.: Greenwood, 1978.

Heymann, Philip B. *Terrorism and America: A Commonsense Strategy for a Democratic Society*. Cambridge, Mass.: MIT Press, 1998.

Hibbs, Mark. "Plutonium, Politics, and Panic." *Bulletin of the Atomic Scientists* 50 (1994): 24–31.

Hill, Stuart, Donald Rothchild, and Colin Cameron. "Tactical Information and the Diffusion of Peaceful Protests." In *The International Spread of Ethnic Conflict*. Edited by David A. Lake and Donald Rothchild. Princeton: Princeton University Press, 1998.

Hills, Alice. "Responding to Catastrophic Terrorism." *Studies in Conflict and Terrorism* 25 (2002): 245–261.

Hiro, Dilip. *Iran under the Ayatollahs*. London: Routledge and Kegan Paul, 1987.

———. *Islamic Fundamentalism*. London: Paladin, 1989.

———. *War without End: The Rise of Islamist Terrorism and the Global Response*. New York: Routledge, 2002.

Hirsch, Daniel. "The Truck Bomb and Insider Threats to Nuclear Facilities." In *Preventing Nuclear Terrorism: The Report and Papers of the International Task Force on Prevention of Nuclear Terrorism*. Edited by Paul Leventhal and Yonah Alexander. Lexington, Mass.: Lexington, 1987.

Hobbes, Thomas. *Leviathan: Or the Matter, Form, and Power of a Commonwealth Ecclesiastical and Civil*. New York: Collier, 1977.

Hobbs, Heidi H., ed. *Pondering Postinternationalism: A Paradigm for the Twenty-First Century?* Albany: State University of New York Press, 2000.

Hoffman, Bruce. "Change and Continuity in Terrorism." *Studies in Conflict and Terrorism* 24 (2001): 417–428.

———. "The Debate over Future Terrorist Use of Chemical, Biological, Radiological and Nuclear Weapons." In *Hype or Reality? The "New Terrorism" and Mass Casualty Attacks*. Edited by Brad Roberts. Alexandria, Va.: Chemical and Biological Arms Control Institute, 2000.

———. *"Holy Terror": The Implications of Terrorism Motivated by a Religious Imperative*. Santa Monica, Calif.: Rand, 1993.

———. *Inside Terrorism*. New York: Columbia University Press, 1998.

———. *The Potential Threat to Commercial Nuclear Facilities*. Santa Monica, Calif.: Rand, 1985.

———. *Recent Trends and Future Prospects of Iranian-Sponsored International Terrorism*. Santa Monica, Calif.: Rand, 1988.

———. "Reply to Pluchinsky and Rapoport Comments." *Terrorism and Political Violence* 9 (1997): 18–19.

————. *Responding to Terrorism across the Technological Spectrum.* Carlisle Barracks, Pa.: U.S. Army War College, 1994.

————. "Rethinking Terrorism and Counterterrorism since 9/11." *Studies in Conflict and Terrorism* 25 (2002): 303–316.

————. *Terrorism in the United States and the Potential Threat to Nuclear Facilities.* Santa Monica, Calif.: Rand, 1986.

————. "Terrorism Trends and Prospects." In *Countering the New Terrorism.* Edited by Ian O. Lesser et al. Santa Monica, Calif.: Rand, 1999.

————. *Terrorism and Weapons of Mass Destruction: An Analysis of Trends and Motivations.* Washington: Rand, 1999.

————. "Terrorism and WMD: Some Preliminary Hypotheses." *Nonproliferation Review* 4 (1997): 45–53.

————. "Why Terrorists Don't Claim Credit." *Terrorism and Political Violence* 9 (1997): 1–6.

Hoffman, Bruce, and Peter deLeon. *A Reassessment of Potential Adversaries to U.S. Nuclear Programs.* Santa Monica, Calif.: Rand, 1986.

Hoffman, David. "A Shrunken and Rusty 'Nuclear Stick.'" In *Global Politics in a Changing World.* Edited by Richard W. Mansbach and Edward Rhodes. Boston: Houghton Mifflin, 2000.

Hoffman, Stanley. *World Disorders: Troubled Peace in the Post–Cold War Era.* Lanham, Md.: Rowman and Littlefield, 1998.

Holloway, Harry C., et al. "The Threat of Biological Weapons: Prophylaxis and Mitigation of Psychological and Social Consequences." *Journal of the American Medical Association* 278 (1997): 425–427.

Horowitz, Donald L. *Ethnic Groups in Conflict.* Berkeley: University of California Press, 2000.

Howard, Russell D., and Reid L. Sawyer, eds. *Terrorism and Counterterrorism: Understanding the New Security Environment.* Guilford, Conn.: McGraw-Hill/Dushkin, 2003.

Hroub, Khaled. *Hamas: Political Thought and Practice.* Washington: Institute for Palestine Studies, 2000.

Huband, Mark. *Warriors of the Prophet: The Struggle for Islam.* Boulder, Colo.: Westview, 1998.

Hudson, Rex A. *Who Becomes a Terrorist and Why: The 1999 Government Report on Profiling Terrorists.* Guilford, Conn.: Lyons, 2002.

Hughey, Michael W. *New Tribalisms: The Resurgence of Race and Ethnicity.* New York: New York University Press, 1998.

Human Rights Watch. *Slaughter among Neighbors: The Political Origins of Ethnic, Racial, and Religious Violence.* New Haven: Yale University Press, 1995.

Humphries, R. Stephen. "The Contemporary Resurgence in the Context of Modern Islam." In *Islamic Resurgence in the Arab World.* Edited by Ali E. Hillal Dessouki. New York: Praeger, 1982.

Hunter, Shireen T. *The Algerian Crisis: Origins, Evolution and Lessons for the Maghreeb and Europe.* Brussels: Centre for European Policy Studies, 1996.

————. *Iran after Khomeini.* Westport, Conn.: Praeger, 1992.

————. *Iran and the World.* Bloomington: Indiana University Press, 1990.

Hunter, Shireen T., ed. *The Politics of Islamic Revivalism: Diversity and Unity.* Bloomington: Indiana University Press, 1988.

Huntington, Samuel P. "The Clash of Civilizations." *Foreign Affairs* 72 (1993): 56–73.

———. *The Clash of Civilizations and the Remaking of World Order.* New York: Simon and Schuster, 1996.

Hurley, Jennifer A., ed. *Weapons of Mass Destruction.* San Diego: Greenhaven, 1999.

Hurwitz, Elliot. "Terrorists and Chemical/Biological Weapons." *Naval War College Review* 35 (1982): 36–40.

Hyland, Francis P. *Armenian Terrorism: The Past, the Present, the Prospects.* Boulder, Colo.: Westview, 1991.

Ibrahim, Saad Eddin. "Islamic Militancy as a Social Movement: The Case of Two Groups in Egypt." In *Islamic Resurgence in the Arab World.* Edited by Ali E. Hillal Dessouki. New York: Praeger, 1982.

Ibrahim, Ferhard, and Gulistan Gurbey, eds. *The Kurdish Conflict in Turkey: Obstacles and Chances for Peace and Democracy.* New York: Palgrave, 2001.

Ignatieff, Michael. *Blood and Belonging: Journeys into the New Nationalism.* New York: Farrar, Straus and Giroux, 1993.

———. *The Warrior's Honor: Ethnic War and the Modern Conscience.* New York: Owl, 1998.

Immel, Myra H. "Introduction." In *Ethnic Violence.* Edited by Myra H. Immel. San Diego: Greenhaven, 2000.

Immel, Myra H., ed. *Ethnic Violence.* San Diego: Greenhaven, 2000.

Inglesby, Thomas V., et al. "Anthrax as a Biological Weapon: Medical and Public Health Management." *Journal of the American Medical Association* 281 (1999): 1735–1745.

Institute of Medicine. *Chemical and Biological Terrorism: Research and Development to Improve Civilian Medical Response.* Washington: National Academy Press, 1999.

International Atomic Energy Agency. *Measures against Illicit Trafficking in Nuclear Material and Other Radioactive Sources.* Vienna: International Atomic Energy Agency, 1996.

———. *Second Quarter 1997: Summary Listing of Illicit Trafficking Incidents.* Vienna: International Atomic Energy Agency, 1997.

International Business Publications USA, ed. *Osama Bin Laden: Jihad against the U.S. Intelligence Report.* Cincinnati: International Business Publications, 2001.

"IRA Bomb Suspects Captured in France." *Boston Globe,* July 18, 1989.

Irvin, Cynthia. *Militant Nationalism: Between Movement and Party in Ireland and the Basque Country.* Minneapolis: University of Minnesota Press, 1999.

Israeli, Raphael. "Islamikaze and Their Significance." *Terrorism and Political Violence* 9 (1997): 96–121.

———. *Muslim Fundamentalism in Israel.* London: Brassey's, 1993.

Izady, Mehrdad R. *The Kurds: A Concise Handbook.* Washington: Crane Russak, 1992.

Jaber, Hala. *Hezbollah: Born with a Vengeance.* New York: Columbia University Press, 1997.

Jablonsky, David. *Paradigm Lost? Transitions and the Search for a New World Order.* Westport, Conn.: Praeger, 1995.

Jackson, Brian A. "Technology Acquisition by Terrorist Groups: Threat Assessment Informed by Lessons from Private Sector Technology Adoption." *Studies in Conflict and Terrorism* 24 (2001): 183–213.

Jackson, David, and Alfredo Corchado. "Anthrax Likely in 2 DC Deaths." *Dallas Morning News*, October 23, 2001.

Jackson, Robert H. *Quasi-State Relations and the Third World.* Cambridge: Cambridge University Press, 1990.

Jacob, James Edwin. "The Basques and Occitans of France: A Comparative Study in Ethnic Militancy." Ph.D. dissertation, Cornell University, 1979.

Jacobs, Stanley S. "The Nuclear Threat as a Terrorist Option." *Terrorism and Political Violence* 10 (1998): 149–163.

Jacquard, Roland. *In the Name of Osama bin Laden.* Durham, N.C.: Duke University Press, 2002.

Jaffrelot, Christophe. *The Hindu Nationalist Movement in India, 1925–1993.* New York: Columbia University Press, 1996.

Jaffrelot, Christophe, ed. *Pakistan: Nationalism without a Nation.* New York: Palgrave, 2001.

Jain, Vinod, and Bharati Dhruva. "Chemical and Biological Terrorism Is a Serious Threat." In *Weapons of Mass Destruction.* Edited by Jennifer A. Hurley. San Diego: Greenhaven, 1999.

Jameelah, Maryam. *Islam versus the West.* Lahore: Muhammad Yusuf Khan, 1984.

Janke, Peter F. "Spanish Separatism: ETA's Threat to Basque Democracy." In *Contemporary Terrorism.* Edited by William Gutteridge. New York: Facts on File, 1986.

Jansen, Johannes J. G. *The Dual Nature of Islamic Fundamentalism.* Ithaca, N.Y.: Cornell University Press, 1997.

Jansen, Johannes J. G., ed. *The Neglected Duty: The Creed of Sadat's Assassins and Islamic Resurgence in the Middle East.* New York: Macmillan, 1986.

Japan Times. *Special Report: Terror in the Heart of Japan.* Tokyo: Japan Times, 1995.

"Japanese Cult Member Admits 1994 Gas Attack." *Dallas Morning News,* January 24, 1996.

Jeffery, Robin. *What's Happening to India? Punjab, Ethnic Conflict, Mrs. Gandhi's Death and the Test for Federalism.* Basingstoke, UK: Macmillan, 1988.

Jenkins, Brian M. *High Technology Terrorism and Surrogate War: The Impact of New Technology on Low-Level Violence.* Santa Monica, Calif.: Rand, 1975.

———. "International Cooperation in Locating and Recovering Stolen Nuclear Materials." *Terrorism* 8 (1983): 561–575.

———. "Keynote Address." Paper presented to Terrorism and Beyond: The 21st Century Conference, April 17–19, 2000, at Oklahoma City, Oklahoma.

———. *The Likelihood of Nuclear Terrorism.* Santa Monica, Calif.: Rand, 1985.

———. *Should Our Arsenal against Terrorism Include Assassination?* Santa Monica, Calif.: Rand, 1987.

———. "Terrorism and Beyond: A 21st Century Perspective." *Studies in Conflict and Terrorism* 24 (2001): 321–327.

———. *Terrorism: Current and Long Term Trends.* Santa Monica, Calif.: Rand, 2001.

———. "The Threat of Nuclear Terrorism Is Minimal." In *Urban Terrorism.* Edited by A. E. Sadler and Paul A. Winters. San Diego: Greenhaven, 1996.

———. "Understanding the Link between Motives and Methods." In *Terrorism with Chemical and Biological Weapons: Calibrating Risks and Responses.* Edited by Brad Roberts. Alexandria, Va.: Chemical and Biological Arms Control Institute, 1997.

———. *Will Terrorists Go Nuclear?* Santa Monica, Calif.: Rand, 1975.

———. "Will Terrorists Go Nuclear? A Reappraisal." In *The Future of Terrorism: Violence in the New Millennium.* Edited by Harvey W. Kushner. Thousand Oaks, Calif.: Sage, 1998.

Jha, Rajani Ranjan. "The Origins and Dimensions of Terrorism: The Punjab Case." In *Terrorism in India.* Edited by S. C. Tiwari. New Delhi: South Asian, 1990.

Jiwa, Salim. *The Death of Air India Flight 182.* London: W. H. Allen, 1986.

Johnson, Chalmers. *Blowback: The Costs and Consequences of American Empire.* New York: Henry Holt, 2000.

Johnson, James Turner. *The Holy War Idea in Western and Islamic Thought.* State College: Pennsylvania State University Press, 1997.

Johnston, David, Don van Natta, Jr., and Judith Miller. "Surviving al-Qaeda Seen as Loosely Knit But Potent." *Dallas Morning News,* June 16, 2002.

Jonas, George. *Vengeance: The True Story of an Israeli Counter-Terrorist Team.* New York: Simon and Schuster, 1984.

Joshi, Manoj. "On the Razor's Edge: The Liberation Tigers of Tamil Eelam." *Studies in Conflict and Terrorism* 19 (1996): 19–42.

Juergensmeyer, Mark. "The Logic of Religious Violence: The Case of the Punjab." *Contributions to Indian Sociology* 22 (1988): 65–88.

———. *The New Cold War? Religious Nationalism Confronts the Secular State.* Berkeley: University of California Press, 1993.

———. "The New Religious State." *Comparative Politics* 27 (1995): 379–391.

———"Religious Radicalism Causes Ethnic Conflict." In *Nationalism and Ethnic Conflict.* Edited by Charles P. Cozic. San Diego: Greenhaven, 1994.

———. "Terror Mandated by God." *Terrorism and Political Violence* 9 (1997): 16–23.

———. *Terror in the Mind of God: The Global Rise of Religious Violence.* Berkeley: University of California Press, 2000.

———. "The World-Wide Rise of Religious Nationalism." *Columbia Journal of International Affairs* 50 (1996): 1–20.

Juergensmeyer, Mark, ed. *Violence and the Sacred in the Modern World.* London: Frank Cass, 1992.

Juergensmeyer, Mark, and N. Gerald Barrier, eds. *Sikh Studies: Comparative Perspectives on Changing Tradition.* Berkeley, Calif.: Graduate Theological Union, 1979.

Kakar, Sudhir. *The Colors of Violence: Cultural Identities, Religion, and Conflict.* Chicago: University of Chicago Press, 1996.

Kakutani, Michiko. "The Information Age Processes a Tragedy." *New York Times,* August 28, 2002.

Kamp, Karl Heinz. "The Risk of Nuclear Terrorism Is Overstated." In *Weapons of Mass Destruction.* Edited by Jennifer A. Hurley. San Diego: Greenhaven, 1999.

Kamp, Karl Heinz, Joseph Pilat, Jessica Stern, and Richard A. Falkenrath. "WMD Terrorism: An Exchange." *Survival* 40 (1998): 168–183.

Kaplan, David E. "Aum Shinrikyo (1995)." In *Toxic Terror: Assessing Terrorist Use of Chemical and Biological Weapons.* Edited by Jonathan B. Tucker. Cambridge, Mass.: MIT Press, 2000.

Kaplan, David E., and Andrew Marshall. *The Cult at the End of the World: The Terrifying Story of the Aum Doomsday Cult, from the Subways of Tokyo to the Nuclear Arsenals of Russia.* New York: Crown, 1996.

Kaplan, Jeffrey, and Leonard B. Weinberg. *The Emergence of a Euro-American Radical Right.* New Brunswick, N.J.: Rutgers University Press, 1999.

Kaplan, Lawrence. *Fundamentalisms in Comparative Perspective.* Amherst: University of Massachusetts Press, 1992.

Kaplan, Robert D. *Balkan Ghosts: A Journey through History.* New York: St. Martin's, 1993.

———. *The Coming Anarchy: Shattering the Dreams of the Post–Cold War.* New York: Random House, 2001.

———. *The Ends of the Earth: A Journey to the Frontiers of Anarchy.* New York: Vintage, 1997.

———. *Soldiers of God: With Islamic Warriors in Afghanistan and Pakistan.* New York: Random House, 2001.

Kapur, Rajiv A. *Sikh Separatism: The Politics of Faith.* London: Allen and Unwin, 1986.

Karam, Azza, ed. *Transnational Political Islam: Globalization, Ideology and Power.* Herndon, Va.: Pluto, 2003.

Karan, Vijay. *War by Stealth: Terrorism in India.* New York: Viking, 1997.

Karawn, Ibrahim A. *The Islamist Impasse.* Oxford: Oxford University Press, 1997.

Karim, Karim H. *Islamic Peril, Media and Global Violence.* Cheektowaga, N.Y.: Black Rose, 2001.

Karim, Karim H., ed. *Diaspora and Communication: Mapping the Globe.* New York: Routledge, 2002.

Karmon, Ely. "Islamist Terrorist Activities in Turkey in the 1990s." *Terrorism and Political Violence* 10 (1998): 101–121.

Karpin, Michael, and Ina Friedman. *Murder in the Name of God: The Plot to Kill Yitzhak Rabin.* New York: Metropolitan, 1998.

Kassimeris, George. *Europe's Last Red Terrorists: The Revolutionary Organization 17 November.* New York: New York University Press, 2001.

Katz, Lee Michael. "Terrorism's Money Web: Financial Records Lifting Veil on bin Laden Network." In *Violence and Terrorism.* Edited by Bernard Schecterman and Martin Slann. Guilford, Conn.: Dushkin/McGraw-Hill, 1999.

Katz, Samuel M. *The Hunt for the Engineer: How Israeli Agents Tracked the Hamas Master Bomber.* New York: Fromm International, 1999.

———. *Relentless Pursuit: The DSS and the Manhunt for the al-Qaeda Terrorists.* New York: Forge, 2002.

Kaufman, Arnold D., Martin I. Meltzer, and George P. Schmid. "The Economic Impact of a Bioterrorist Attack: Are Prevention and Postattack Intervention Justifiable?" *Emerging Infectious Diseases* 3 (1997): 1–12.

Kaufman, Michael T. "The Bitter Struggle between Serbs and Albanians." In *Ethnic Violence.* Edited by Myra H. Immel. San Diego: Greenhaven, 2000.

Kaufman, Stuart J. "The Fragmentation and Consolidation of International Systems." *International Organization* 51 (1997): 755–776.

———. *Modern Hatreds.* Ithaca: Cornell University Press, 2001.

Keating, Michael, ed. *Minority Nationalism and the Changing International Order.* New York: Oxford University Press, 2001.

Keddie, Nikki R. *Roots of Revolution: An Interpretive History of Modern Iran.* New Haven: Yale University Press, 1981.

Keddie, Nikki R., ed. *Religion and Politics in Iran: Shi'ism from Quietism to Revolution.* New Haven: Yale University Press, 1983.

Keddie, Nikki R., and Eric Hooglund, eds. *The Iranian Revolution and the Islamic Republic.* Syracuse, N.Y.: Syracuse University Press, 1986.

Kedourie, Elie. "Political Terrorism in the Muslim World." In *Terrorism: How the West Can Win.* Edited by Benjamin Netanyahu. New York: Farrar, Straus, Giroux, 1986.

Keeney, Spurgeon M., Jr. "Tokyo Terror and Chemical Arms Control." *Arms Control Today,* April 1995.

Kegley, Charles W. *A Multipolar Peace.* New York: St. Martin's, 1994.

Keinon, Herb. "Hamas's Sheikh Ahmed Yassin: Is He a Genuine Threat?" In *Violence and Terrorism.* Edited by Bernard Schecterman and Martin Slann. Guilford, Conn.: Dushkin/McGraw-Hill, 1999.

Keller, Edmond J. "Transnational Ethnic Conflict in Africa." In *The International Spread of Ethnic Conflict.* Edited by David A. Lake and Donald Rothchild. Princeton: Princeton University Press, 1998.

Kelly, Kevin. *Out of Control: The Rise of Neo-Biological Civilization.* New York: Addison-Wesley, 1994.

Kelly, Michael J., and Thomas H. Mitchell. "Transnational Terrorism and the Western Press Elite." *Political Communication and Persuasion* 1 (1981): 269–296.

Kelly, Robert J. "Armed Prophets and Extremists: Islamic Fundamentalism." In *The Future of Terrorism: Violence in the New Millennium.* Edited by Harvey W. Kushner. Thousand Oaks, Calif.: Sage, 1998.

Kelsay, John. *Islam and War: A Study in Comparative Ethics.* Louisville, Ky.: Westminster/John Knox, 1993.

Keohane, Robert, and Joseph Nye. *Transnational Relations and World Politics.* Cambridge, Mass.: Harvard University Press, 1972.

Kepel, Gilles. *Allah in the West.* Stanford, Calif.: Stanford University Press, 1994.

———. *Jihad: The Trail of Political Islam.* Cambridge, Mass.: Harvard University Press, 2002.

———. *Muslim Extremism in Egypt: The Prophet and the Pharaoh.* Berkeley: University of California Press, 1985.

———. *The Revenge of God: The Resurgence of Islam, Christianity, and Judaism in the Modern World.* University Park: Pennsylvania State University Press, 1994.

Kerson, Adrian. *Terror in the Towers.* New York: Random House, 1993.

Khadduri, Majid. "Islamic Fundamentalism." *Terrorism* 11 (1988): 357–359.

Khashan, Hilal. "The Labyrinth of Kurdish Self-Determination." *International Journal of Kurdish Studies* 8 (1995): 5–31.

Khatami, Siamak. "Between Class and Nation: Ideology and Radical Basque Ethnonationalism." *Studies in Conflict and Terrorism* 20 (1997): 395–417.

Khomeini, Imam. *Islam and Revolution: Writings and Declarations.* London: Routledge and Kegan Paul, 1985.

Kibble, David G. "The Threat of Militant Islam: A Fundamental Reappraisal." *Studies in Conflict and Terrorism* 19 (1996): 353–364.

Kindilien, Robert E. "Nuclear Plants Confront Modern Terrorism." *Security Management* 29 (1985): 119–120.

King, Charles. "The Myth of Ethnic Warfare: Understanding Conflict in the Post–Cold War World." *Foreign Affairs* 80 (2001): 165–170.

Kirisci, Kemal, and Gareth M. Winrow. *The Kurdish Question and Turkey: An Example of a Trans-state Ethnic Conflict.* London: Frank Cass, 1997.

Kirkwood, Craig W., and Stephen M. Pollack. *Methodology for Characterizing Potential Adversaries of Nuclear Safeguard Systems.* San Francisco: Lawrence Livermore Laboratories, 1978.

Kitabatake, Kiyoyasu. "Aum Shinrikyo: Society Begets an Aberration." *Japan Quarterly* 42 (1995): 376–383.

Kitfield, James. "The Age of Superterrorism." *Government Executive,* July 1995.

Kleiner, Kurt. "U.S. Bioterror Alert Prompts Tighter Rules." *New Scientist,* June 22, 1996.

Knutsen, Torbjorn L. *The Rise and Fall of World Orders.* New York: Manchester University Press, 1999.

Knutson, Jeanne N. "Social and Psychodynamic Pressures toward a Negative Identity: The Case of an American Revolutionary Terrorist." In *Behavioral and Quantitative Perspectives on Terrorism.* Edited by Yonah Alexander and John M. Gleason. New York: Pergamon, 1981.

Kohli, Atul. "Can Democracies Accommodate Ethnic Nationalism? The Rise and Decline of Self-Determination in India." In *The Self-Determination of Peoples: Community, Nation, and State in an Interdependent World.* Edited by Wolfgang Danspeckgruber. Boulder, Colo.: Lynne Rienner, 2000.

Korchak, Alexander. *Totalistic Organizations: From Mafia to Global Terror.* New York: Columbia University Press, 2002.

Kramer, Martin. *Arab Awakening and Islamic Revival: The Politics of Ideas in the Middle East.* New Brunswick, N.J.: Transaction, 1996.

———. *The Islamism Debate.* Tel Aviv: Dayan Center, 1997.

———. "The Moral Logic of Hizballah." In *Origins of Terrorism: Psychologies, Ideologies, Theologies, States of Mind.* Edited by Walter Reich. New York: Cambridge University Press, 1990.

Krasner, Stephen D., ed. *Problematic Sovereignty: Contested Rules and Political Possibilities.* New York: Columbia University Press, 2001.

Kristof, Nicholas. "Japanese Cult Said to Have Planned Nerve-Gas Attacks in U.S." *New York Times,* March 23, 1997.

Kuhn, Thomas S. *The Structure of Scientific Revolutions.* Chicago: University of Chicago Press, 1970.

Kuhr, Steven, and Jerome M. Hauer. "The Threat of Biological Terrorism in the New Millennium." In *Essential Readings on Political Terrorism: Analyses of Problems and Prospects for the 21st Century.* Edited by Harvey W. Kushner. New York: Gordian Knot, 2002.

Kupperman, Robert H. "Emerging Techno-Terrorism." In *Common Ground on Terrorism: Soviet-American Cooperation against the Politics of Terror.* Edited by John Marks and Igor Beliaev. New York: W. W. Norton, 1991.

Kupperman, Robert H., and Jeff Kamen. *Final Warning: Averting Disaster in the New Age of Terrorism.* New York: Doubleday, 1989.

Kuran, Timur. "Ethnic Dissimilation and Its International Diffusion." In *The International Spread of Ethnic Conflict.* Edited by David A. Lake and Donald Rothchild. Princeton: Princeton University Press, 1998.

Kurz, Anat, and Ariel Merari. *ASALA: Irrational Terror or Political Tool.* Jerusalem: Jerusalem Post Press, 1985.

Kurz, Anat, and Tal Nahman. *Hamas: Radical Islam in a National Struggle.* Tel Aviv: Jaffee Center for Strategic Studies, 1997.

Kushner, Harvey W. "The New Terrorism." In *The Future of Terrorism: Violence in the New Millennium.* Edited by Harvey W. Kushner. Thousand Oaks, Calif.: Sage, 1998.

———. "Suicide Bombers: Business as Usual." *Studies in Conflict and Terrorism* 19 (1996): 329–337.

———. *Terrorism in America: A Structured Approach to Understanding the Terrorist Threat.* Springfield, Ill.: Charles C. Thomas, 1998.

Kushner, Harvey W., ed. *Essential Readings on Political Terrorism: Analyses of Problems and Prospects for the 21st Century.* New York: Gordian Knot, 2002.

Labeviere, Richard. *Dollars for Terror: The U.S. and Islam.* New York: Algore, 2000.

Laffin, John. *Holy War: Islam Fights.* London: Grafton, 1988.

Lafraniere, Sharon. "Bomb Strikes Parade in Russia, Killing 36." *Dallas Morning News,* May 10, 2002.

Laguerre, Michael S. *Diasporic Citizenship: Haitian Americans in Transnational America.* New York: St. Martin's, 1998.

Lake, Anthony. *6 Nightmares: Real Threats in a Dangerous World and How America Can Meet Them.* New York: Little, Brown, 2000.

Lake, David A., and Donald Rothchild. "Containing Fear: The Origins and Management of Ethnic Conflict." In *Nationalism and Ethnic Conflict.* Edited by Michael E. Brown, Owen R. Cote, Jr., Sean Lynn-Jones, and Steven E. Miller. Cambridge, Mass.: MIT Press, 1997.

———. "Spreading Fear: The Genesis of Transnational Ethnic Conflict." In *The International Spread of Ethnic Conflict: Fear, Diffusion, and Escalation.* Edited by David A. Lake and Donald Rothchild. Princeton: Princeton University Press, 1998.

Lake, David A., and Donald Rothchild, eds. *The International Spread of Ethnic Conflict: Fear, Diffusion, and Escalation.* Princeton: Princeton University Press, 1998.

Landau, Jacob M. *The Politics of Pan-Islam: Ideology and Organization.* Oxford: Clarendon, 1990.

Langman, Lauren, and Douglas Morris. "Islamic Terrorism: From Retrenchment to Resentment and Beyond." In *Essential Readings on Political Terrorism: Analyses of Problems and Prospects for the 21st Century.* Edited by Harvey W. Kushner. New York: Gordian Knot, 2002.

Lapidus, Gail. "Contested Sovereignty: The Tragedy of Chechnya." *International Security* 23 (1998): 5–49.

Laqueur, Walter. *A History of Terrorism.* New Brunswick, N.J.: Transaction, 2002.

———. *The New Terrorism: Fanaticism and the Arms of Mass Destruction.* New York: Oxford University Press, 1999.

———. "Terror's New Face: The Radicalization and Escalation of Modern Terrorism." In *The Global Agenda: Issues and Perspectives.* Edited by Charles W. Kegley, Jr., and Eugene R. Wittkopf. Boston: McGraw-Hill, 2001.

"Latest Anthrax Baffles Officials." *Dallas Morning News,* November 22, 2001.

Lawrence, Bruce B. *Defenders of God: The Fundamentalist Revolt against the Modern Age.* San Francisco: Harper and Row, 1989.

Layne, Scott P., Tony J. Beugelsdijk, and C. Kumar N. Patel, eds. *Firepower in the Lab: Automation in the Fight against Infectious Diseases and Bioterrorism.* Washington: National Academy of Sciences, 2000.

Leaf, Murray J. "The Punjab Crisis." *Asian Survey* 25 (1985): 475–498.

Lederberg, Joshua. "Infectious Disease and Biological Weapons: Prophylaxis and Mitigation." *Journal of the American Medical Association* 278 (1997): 435–436.

Lee, Rensselaer W., III. *Smuggling Armageddon: The Nuclear Black Market in the Former Soviet Union and Europe.* New York: St. Martin's, 1998.

———. "Smuggling Update." *Bulletin of the Atomic Scientists* 53 (1997): 52–56.

———. "Transnational Organized Crime: An Overview." In *Transnational Crime in the Americas.* Edited by Tom Farer. New York: Routledge, 1999.

Lee, Rensselaer W., III, and James L. Ford. "Nuclear Smuggling." In *Beyond Sovereignty: Issues for a Global Agenda.* Edited by Maryann K. Cusimano. Boston: Bedford/St. Martin's, 2000.

Legrain, Jean-François. "The Islamic Movement and the Intifada." In *Intifada: Palestine at the Crossroads.* Edited by Jamal R. Nassar and Roger Heacock. New York: Praeger, 1990.

Lehman, Susan G. "Islam and Ethnicity in the Republics of Russia." *Post-Soviet Affairs* 13 (1997): 78–103.

Leitenberg, Milton. "Aum Shinrikyo's Efforts to Produce Biological Weapons: A Case Study in the Serial Propagation of Misinformation." In *The Future of Terrorism.* Edited by Maxwell Taylor and John Horgan. London: Frank Cass, 2000.

Lepor, Keith Philip, ed. *After the Cold War: Essays on the Emerging World Order.* Austin: University of Texas Press, 1997.

Lesser, Ian O., et al. *Countering the New Terrorism.* Santa Monica, Calif.: Rand, 1999.

Letamendia, Francisco. *Game of Mirrors: Centre-Periphery National Conflicts.* Burlington, Vt.: Ashgate, 2000.

Leventhal, Paul L., and Yonah Alexander, eds. *Nuclear Terrorism: Defining the Threat.* Washington: Pergamon-Brassey's, 1986.

———. *Preventing Nuclear Terrorism: Report and Papers of the International Task Force on Prevention of Nuclear Terrorism.* Lexington, Mass.: Lexington, 1987.

Leventhal, Paul L., and Brahma Chellaney. "Nuclear Terrorism: Threat, Perception, and Response in South Asia." *Terrorism* 11 (1988): 447–470.

Leventhal, Paul L., and Milton M. Hoenig. "The Hidden Danger: Risks of Nuclear Terrorism." *Terrorism* 10 (1987): 1–22.

Levinson, Macha. "Custom-Made Biological Weapons." *International Defense Review* 19 (1986): 1611–1615.

Levitt, Peggy. *The Transnational Villagers.* Berkeley: University of California Press, 2001.

Lewis, Bernard. "Islamic Fundamentalism?" In *Terrorism: How the West Can Win.* Edited by Benjamin Netanyahu. New York: Farrar, Straus, Giroux, 1986.

———. "License to Kill: Usama bin Ladin's Declaration of Jihad." In *World Politics.* Edited by Helen Purkitt. Guilford, Conn.: Dushkin/McGraw-Hill, 2000.

———. *The Political Language of Islam.* Chicago: University of Chicago Press, 1988.

———. *What Went Wrong?* New York: Oxford University Press, 2002.

Lewis, Kathy. "Nations Back Anti-Terror Moves." *Dallas Morning News,* June 29, 1996.

———. "U.S., Israel Sign Anti-Terrorism Accord." *Dallas Morning News,* May 1, 1996.

Lewis, William H., and Stuart E. Johnson, eds. *Weapons of Mass Destruction: New Perspectives on Counterproliferation.* Washington: National Defense University Press, 1995.

Lia, Brynjar. *The Society of the Muslim Brothers in Egypt: The Rise of an Islamic Mass Movement, 1928–1982.* London: Ithaca, 1998.

Liefer, John. "The Risk of Nuclear Terrorism Is High." In *Weapons of Mass Destruction.* Edited by Jennifer A. Hurley. San Diego: Greenhaven, 1999.

Lieven, Anatol. *Chechnya: Tombstone of Russian Power.* New Haven: Yale University Press, 1998.

———. "What Is the Future of Chechnya?" In *Russia after the Fall.* Edited by Andrew C. Kuchins. Washington: Carnegie Endowment for International Peace, 2002.

Lifton, Robert Jay. *Destroying the World to Save It: Aum Shinrikyo, Apocalyptic Violence, and the New Global Terrorism.* New York: Metropolitan, 1999.

Lipschutz, Ronnie D. *After Authority: War, Peace, and Global Politics in the 21st Century.* Albany: State University of New York Press, 2000.

Livingstone, Neil C. "The Impact of Technological Innovation." In *Hydra of Carnage: The International Linkages of Terrorism and Other Low-Intensity Operations—The Witnesses Speak.* Edited by Uri Ra'anan et al. Lexington, Mass.: Lexington: 1986.

———. *The War against Terrorism.* Lexington, Mass.: Lexington, 1982.

Livingstone, Neil C., and Joseph D. Douglass, Jr. *CBW: The Poor Man's Atomic Bomb.* Cambridge, Mass.: Institute for Foreign Policy Analysis, 1984.

Lliora, Francisco, Joseph M. Mata, and Cynthia L. Irvin. "ETA: From Secret Army to Social Movement." *Terrorism and Political Violence* 5 (1993): 106–134.

Loeb, Vernon. "The Man Who Pulls the Terrorists' Strings." In *Violence and Terrorism.* Edited by Bernard Schecterman and Martin Slann. Guilford, Conn.: Dushkin/McGraw-Hill, 1999.

Loehmer, Andrew. "The Nuclear Dimension." In *Technology and Terrorism.* Edited by Paul Wilkinson. Portland, Ore.: Frank Cass, 1993.

Long, David E. "Countering Terrorism beyond Sovereignty." In *Beyond Sovereignty: Issues for a Global Agenda.* Edited by Maryann K. Cusimano. Boston: Bedford/St. Martin's, 2000.

———. "The Land and Peoples of the Middle East." In *The Government and Politics of the Middle East and North Africa.* Edited by David E. Long and Bernard Reich. Boulder, Colo.: Westview, 1986.

Lowe, Karl. "Analyzing Technical Constraints on Bio-Terrorism: Are They Still Important?" In *Terrorism with Chemical and Biological Weapons: Calibrating Risks and Responses.* Edited by Brad Roberts. Alexandria, Va.: Chemical and Biological Arms Control Institute, 1997.

Lugar, Richard. "Safeguarding Russian Nuclear Stockpiles Will Prevent a Nuclear Attack." In *Weapons of Mass Destruction.* Edited by Jennifer A. Hurley. San Diego: Greenhaven, 1999.

Lugo, Luis E., ed. *Sovereignty at the Crossroads?* Lanham, Md.: Rowman and Littlefield, 1996.

Lupsha, Peter. "Gray Area Phenomenon: New Threats and Policy Dilemmas." Paper presented to the Conference on High Intensity Crime/Low Intensity Conflict, September 27–30, 1992, at Chicago, Illinois.

Lustick, Ian. *For the Land and the Lord: Jewish Fundamentalism in Israel.* New York: Council on Foreign Relations, 1988.

MacBride, Sean. "Nuclear Terrorism." In *Terrorism and National Liberation: Proceedings of the International Conference on the Question of Terrorism.* Edited by Hans Kochler. Frankfort: Verlag Peter Lang, 1988.

McCuen, Gary E., ed. *Biological Terrorism and Weapons of Mass Destruction.* Hudson, Wisc.: Gem, 1999.

MacDonald, Scott B. "The New 'Bad Guys': Exploring the Parameters of the Violent New World Order." In *Gray Area Phenomena: Confronting the New World Disorder.* Edited by Max G. Manwaring. Boulder, Colo.: Westview, 1993.

McDowall, David. *A Modern History of the Kurds.* Ithaca, N.Y.: Cornell University Press, 1996.

McGeorge, Harvey J., II. "Chemical and Biological Terrorism: Analyzing the Problem." *Applied Science and Analysis Newsletter,* June 16, 1994.

———. "The Deadly Mixture: Bugs, Gas, and Terrorists." *Nuclear, Biological, and Chemical Defense and Technology* 1 (1986): 56–61.

McGowan, William. *Only Man Is Vile: The Tragedy of Sri Lanka.* New York: Farrar, Straus and Giroux, 1993.

McGuire, Patrick A. "The Roots of Ethnic Violence." In *Ethnic Violence.* Edited by Myra H. Immel. San Diego: Greenhaven, 2000.

Macintyre, Anthony G., et al. "Weapons of Mass Destruction: Events with Contaminated Casualties." *Journal of the American Medical Association* 263 (2000): 242–249.

McKean, Lise. *Divine Enterprise: Gurus and the Hindu Nationalist Movement.* Chicago: University of Chicago Press, 1995.

McKinley, Michael. "The International Dimensions of Terrorism in Ireland." In *Terrorism in Ireland.* Edited by Yonah Alexander and Alan O'Day. New York: St. Martin's, 1984.

McMahon, K. Scott. "Unconventional Nuclear, Biological, and Chemical Weapons Delivery Methods: Whither the 'Smuggled Bomb.'" *Comparative Strategy* 15 (1996): 123–134.

McMullen, Ronald K. "Ethnic Conflict in Russia: Implications for the United States." *Studies in Conflict and Terrorism* 16 (1993): 201–218.

McPhilemy, Sean. *The Committee: Political Assassination in Northern Ireland.* Boulder, Colo.: Roberts Rinehart, 1999.

Maddy-Weitzman, Bruce, and Efraim Inbar, eds. *Religious Radicalism in the Greater Middle East.* London: Frank Cass, 1997.

Madeley, John, ed. *Religion and Politics.* Burlington, Vt.: Ashgate, 2002.

Madhok, Balraj. *Punjab Problem: The Muslim Connection.* New Delhi: Hindu World, 1985.

Magnus, Ralph H., and Eden Naby. *Afghanistan: Mullah, Marx and Mujahid.* New Delhi: HarperCollins, 1998.

Mahdi, Muhsin. *Alfarabi and the Foundation of Islamic Political Philosophy.* Chicago: University of Chicago Press, 2001.

Mahmood, Cynthia Keppley. *Fighting for Faith and Nation: Dialogues with Sikh Militants.* University Park: Pennsylvania State University Press, 1997.

"Malaysia Accuses Man of Terrorist Ties." *Dallas Morning News,* September 28, 2002.

Maley, William, ed. *Fundamentalism Reborn? Afghanistan and the Taliban.* New York: New York University Press, 1998.

Malik, Omar. *Enough of the Definition of Terrorism.* London: Royal Institute of International Affairs, 2000.

Malley, Robert. *The Call from Algeria: Third Worldism, Revolution, and the Turn to Islam.* Berkeley: University of California Press, 1996.

Malvesti, Michele L. "Explaining the United States' Decision to Strike Back at Terrorists." *Terrorism and Political Violence* 13 (2001): 85–106.

Mandaville, Peter G. *Transnational Muslim Politics: Reimagining the Umma*. New York: Routledge, 2001.

Mandel, Robert. *Deadly Transfers and the Global Playground: Transnational Security Threats in a Disorderly World*. Westport, Conn.: Greenwood, 1999.

Mandelbaum, Michael, ed. *The New European Diasporas: National Minorities and Conflicts in Eastern Europe*. Washington: Brookings, 2000.

Manisalco, Paul M., and Hank T. Christen. *Understanding Terrorism and Managing the Consequences*. Upper Saddle River, N.J.: Pearson, 2002.

Mansbach, Richard W., and Edward Rhodes, eds. *Global Politics in a Changing World*. Boston: Houghton Mifflin, 2000.

Manwaring, Max G., ed. *Gray Area Phenomena: Confronting the New World Disorder*. Boulder, Colo.: Westview, 1993.

———. *Uncomfortable Wars: Toward a New Paradigm of Low-Intensity Conflict*. Boulder, Colo.: Westview, 1991.

Manwaring, Max G., and William J. Olson, eds. *Managing Contemporary Conflict: Pillars of Success*. Boulder, Colo.: Westview, 1996.

Marhwah, Ved. *Uncivil Wars: Pathology of Terrorism in India*. New Delhi: Indus, 1995.

Marlo, Francis H. "WMD Terrorism and U.S. Intelligence Collection." *Terrorism and Political Violence* 11 (1999): 53–71.

Marrs, Robert W. *Nuclear Terrorism: Rethinking the Unthinkable*. Monterey, Calif.: Naval Postgraduate School, 1994.

Marsden, Peter. *The Taliban: War, Religion and the New Order in Afghanistan*. New York: St. Martin's, 1998.

Martin, Gus. *Understanding Terrorism: Challenges, Perspectives, and Issues*. Thousand Oaks, Calif.: Sage, 2003.

Martin, John M., and Anne T. Romano. *Multinational Crime: Terrorism, Espionage, Drug and Arms Trafficking*. Newbury Park, Calif.: Sage, 1992.

Martin, Richard C. "Religious Violence in Islam: Towards an Understanding of the Discourse on 'Jihad' in Modern Egypt." In *Contemporary Research on Terrorism*. Edited by Paul Wilkinson and A. M. Stewart. Aberdeen, UK: Aberdeen University Press, 1987.

Martinez, Luis. *The Algerian Civil War: 1990–1998*. New York: Columbia University Press, 2000.

Marty, Martin E. *The Glory and the Power: The Fundamentalist Challenge to the Modern World*. Boston: Beacon, 1992.

Marty, Martin E., and R. Scott Appleby, eds. *Accounting for Fundamentalisms: The Dynamic Character of Movements*. Chicago: University of Chicago Press, 1994.

———. *Fundamentalisms Comprehended*. Chicago: University of Chicago Press, 1995.

———. *Fundamentalisms Observed*. Chicago: University of Chicago Press, 1991.

———. *Fundamentalisms and Society: Reclaiming the Sciences, the Family, and Education*. Chicago: University of Chicago Press, 1991.

———. *Fundamentalisms and the State: Remaking Polities, Militance, and Economics*. Chicago: University of Chicago Press, 1993.

Matinuddin, Kamal. *The Taliban Phenomenon: Afghanistan 1994–1997*. New York: Oxford University Press, 1999.

Matthew, Richard A. *Dichotomy of Power: Nation versus State in World Politics.* Lanham, Md.: Rowman and Littlefield, 2002.

Matveeva, Anna. *The North Caucasus: Russia's Fragile Borderland.* Washington: Brookings, 1999.

Mayer, Jean-François. "Cults, Violence and Religious Terrorism at the Dawn of the 21st Century: An International Perspective." Paper presented to Terrorism and Beyond: The 21st Century Conference, April 17–19, 2000, at Oklahoma City, Oklahoma.

Medd, Roger, and Frank Goldstein. "International Terrorism on the Eve of a New Millennium." *Studies in Conflict and Terrorism* 20 (1997): 281–316.

Meddeb, Adelwahab. *The Malady of Islam.* New York: Basic Books, 2003.

Medoff, Rafael. "Gush Emunim and the Question of Jewish Counterterror." *Middle East Review* 18 (1986): 17–23.

Mehlman, Maxwell J., and Jeffrey R. Botkin. *Access to the Genome: The Challenge to Equality.* Washington: Georgetown University Press, 1998.

Melander, Erik. *Anarchy Within: The Security Dilemma between Ethnic Groups in Emerging Anarchy.* Uppsala, Sweden: Uppsala University, 1999.

Menashri, David, ed. *The Iranian Revolution and the Muslim World.* Boulder, Colo.: Westview, 1990.

Mendoza, Susanah Lily L. *Between the Home and the Diaspora: The Politics of Theorizing Filipino and Filipino American Identities.* New York: Routledge, 2001.

Mengel, R. William. "The Impact of Nuclear Terrorism on the Military's Role in Society." In *International Terrorism in the Contemporary World.* Edited by Marius H. Livingston. Westport, Conn.: Greenwood, 1978.

———. "Terrorism and New Technologies of Destruction: An Overview of the Potential Risk." In *Disorders and Terrorism: Report of the Task Force on Disorders and Terrorism.* Edited by the National Advisory Committee on Criminal Justice Standards and Goals. Washington: U.S. Government Printing Office, 1976.

Merari, Ariel. "The Readiness to Kill and Die: Suicidal Terrorism in the Middle East." In *Origins of Terrorism: Psychologies, Ideologies, Theologies, States of Mind.* Edited by Walter Reich. New York: Cambridge University Press, 1990.

Merari, Ariel, Tamar Prat, and David Tal. "The Palestinian Intifada: An Analysis of a Popular Uprising after Seven Months." *Terrorism and Political Violence* 1 (1989): 177–201.

Mercier, Charles L. "Terrorists, WMD, and the U.S. Army Reserve." *Parameters* 27 (1997): 98–118.

Mernisi, Fatima. *Islam and Democracy: Fear of the Modern World.* New York: Addison-Wesley, 1992.

Meselman, Matthew. "Bioterror: What Can Be Done?" In *Striking Terror: America's New War.* Edited by Robert B. Silvers and Barbara Epstein. New York: New York Review of Books, 2002.

Metraux, Daniel A. *Aum Shinrikyo and Japanese Youth.* Lanham, Md.: University Press of America, 1999.

———. *Aum Shinrikyo's Impact on Japanese Society.* Lewis, N.Y.: Mellen, 2000.

Midlarsky, Manus I., ed. *The Internationalization of Communal Strife.* London: Routledge, 1992.

Migdal, Joel S. *Strong Societies and Weak States.* Princeton: Princeton University Press, 1988.

Milani, Mohsen. *The Making of Iran's Islamic Revolution: From Monarchy to Islamic Republic.* London: Westview, 1988.

Milbank, David L. *International and Transnational Terrorism: Diagnosis and Prognosis.* Washington: Central Intelligence Agency, 1976.

"Militants' Money Man Warns U.S." *Dallas Morning News,* May 11, 1997.

Miller, John. "American Policies in the Middle East Justify Islamic Terrorism: Osama bin Laden, Interviewed by John Miller." In *Terrorism.* Edited by Laura K. Egendorf. San Diego: Greenhaven, 2000.

Miller, John, and Michael Stone. *The Cell: Inside the 9/11 Plot, and Why the FBI and CIA Failed to Stop It.* New York: Hyperion, 2002.

Miller, Judith. "The Challenge of Radical Islam." *Foreign Affairs* 77 (1993): 43–57.

———. "Even a Jihad Has Its Rules." In *Violence and Terrorism.* Edited by Bernard Schecterman and Martin Slann. Guilford, Conn.: Dushkin/McGraw-Hill, 1999.

———. *God Has Ninety-nine Names: Reporting from a Militant Middle East.* New York: Simon and Schuster, 1996.

Miller, Judith, Stephen Engelberg, and William J. Broad. *Germs: Biological Weapons and America's Secret War.* New York: Simon and Schuster, 2001.

Miscevic, Nenad, ed. *Nationalism and Ethnic Conflict: Philosophical Perspectives.* Chicago: Open Court, 2000.

Mishal, Shaul, and Avraham Sela. *Hamas: A Behavioral Profile.* Tel Aviv: Tami Steinmetz Center for Peace Research, 1997.

———. *The Palestinian Hamas: Vision, Violence, and Coexistence.* New York: Columbia University Press, 2000.

Mitchell, Richard P. *The Society of the Muslim Brothers.* Oxford: Clarendon, 1969.

Mittelstadt, Michelle. "Anthrax Victim's Last Days Retraced." *Dallas Morning News,* November 1, 2001.

Mohaddessin, Mohammad. *Islamic Fundamentalism: The New Global Threat.* Washington: Seven Locks, 1993.

Mole, Robert L., and Dale M. Mole. *For God and Country: Operation Whitecoat, 1954–1973.* Brushton, N.Y.: Teach Services, 1998.

Monroe, Kristen Renwick, and Lina Haddad Kreidie. "The Perspective of Islamic Fundamentalists and the Limits of Rational Choice Theory." *Political Psychology* 18 (1997): 19–43.

Moodie, Michael L. "The Chemical Weapons Threat." In *The New Terror: Facing the Threat of Biological and Chemical Weapons.* Edited by Sidney D. Drell, Abraham D. Sofaer, and George D. Wilson. Stanford, Calif.: Hoover Institution Press, 1999.

Moore, Martha T., and Dennis Cauchon. "Inches Decide Life, Death on 78." *USA Today,* September 4, 2002.

Moore, Molly. "India's Infamous Anti-Terrorism Law under Attack." *New Orleans Times-Picayune,* December 11, 1994.

Mortimer, Edward. *Faith and Power.* New York: Vintage, 1982.

Mottahedeh, Roy. *The Mantle of the Prophet: Religion and Politics in Iran.* New York: Pantheon, 1985.

Moussalli, Ahmad S. *Moderate and Radical Islamic Fundamentalism: The Quest for Modernity, Legitimacy, and the Islamic State.* Gainesville: University Press of Florida, 1999.

———. *Radical Islamic Fundamentalism: The Ideological and Political Discourse of Sayyid Qutb.* Syracuse, N.Y.: Syracuse University Press, 1993.

Moynihan, Daniel Patrick. *Pandaemonium: Ethnicity in International Politics.* Oxford: Oxford University Press, 1993.

Muir, Angus M. "Terrorism and Weapons of Mass Destruction: The Case of Aum Shinrikyo." *Studies in Conflict and Terrorism* 22 (1999): 79–91.

Mulgrew, Ian. *Unholy Terror: The Sikhs and International Terrorism.* Toronto: Key Porter, 1988.

Mullen, Robert K. *The International Clandestine Nuclear Threat.* Gaithersburg, Md.: International Association of Chiefs of Police, 1975.

———. "Low-Intensity Terrorism against Technological Infrastructures." In *Beyond the Iran-Contra Crisis: The Shape of U.S. Anti-Terrorism Policy in the Post-Reagan Era.* Edited by Neil C. Livingstone and Terrell E. Arnold. Lexington, Mass.: Lexington, 1988.

———. "Mass Destruction and Terrorism." *Journal of International Affairs* 32 (1978): 63–89.

Mullins, Wayman C. "An Overview and Analysis of Nuclear, Biological, and Chemical Terrorism: The Weapons, Strategies, and Solutions to a Growing Problem." *American Journal of Criminal Justice* 16 (1992): 95–119.

Munson, Henry, Jr. *Islam and Revolution in the Middle East.* New Haven: Yale University Press, 1988.

Murakami, Haruki. *Underground: The Tokyo Gas Attack and the Japanese Psyche.* New York: Vintage, 2000.

Murden, Simon W. *Islam, the Middle East, and the New Global Hegemony.* Boulder, Colo.: Lynne Rienner, 2002.

Murphy, John Francis. *Sword of Islam: Muslim Extremism from the Arab Conquests to the Attack on America.* Amherst, N.Y.: Prometheus, 2002.

Mustikhan, Ahmar. "Different Faces of Islamic Fundamentalism." In *The Middle East.* Edited by William Spencer. Guilford, Conn.: Dushkin/McGraw-Hill, 2000.

Mylroie, Laurie. *The War against America: Saddam Hussein and the World Trade Center Attacks.* New York: HarperCollins, 2001.

Nagat, Judith. *The Reflowering of Malaysia: Modern Religious Radicals and Their Roots.* Vancouver: University of British Columbia Press, 1984.

Naipaul, V. S. *Beyond Belief.* New York: Vintage, 1998.

Nash, Manning. *The Cauldron of Ethnicity in the Modern World.* Chicago: University of Chicago Press, 1989.

Nasr, Kameel B. *Arab and Israeli Terrorism: The Causes and Effects of Political Violence, 1936–1993.* Jefferson, N.C.: McFarland, 1997.

Nasr, Seyyed Vali Reza. *Islamic Leviathan: Islam and the Making of State Power.* New York: Oxford University Press, 2001.

———. *Mawdudi and the Making of Islamic Revivalism.* Oxford: Oxford University Press, 1996.

———. *The Vanguard of the Islamic Revolution: The Jama'at-i Islami of Pakistan.* Berkeley: University of California Press, 1994.

National Consortium for Genomic Resources Management and Services. *The 1997 GenCom Conference on Improving U.S. Capabilities for Defense from Bioterrorism.* Montros, Va.: National Consortium for Genomic Resources Management and Services, 1997.

National Research Council. *Proliferation Concerns: Assessing U.S. Efforts to Help Control Nuclear and Other Dangerous Materials and Technologies in the Former Soviet Union.* Washington: National Academy Press, 1997.

Nayar, Kuldip, and Khushwant Singh. *Tragedy of Punjab: Operation Bluestar and After.* New Delhi: Vision, 1984.

Nettler, Ronald P. *Past Trials and Present Tribulations: A Muslim Fundamentalist's View of the Jews.* New York: Pergamon, 1987.

Newman, David, ed. *The Impact of Gush Emunim.* London: Croom Helm, 1985.

Newman, Saul. "Does Modernization Breed Ethnic Conflict?" *World Politics* 43 (1991): 451–478.

Nima, Ramy. *The Wrath of Allah.* London: Pluto, 1983.

Nojumi, Neamatollah. *The Rise of the Taliban in Afghanistan: Mass Mobilization, Civil War, and the Future of the Region.* New York: Palgrave, 2002.

Norman, Daniel. *Islam and the West: The Making of an Image.* Edinburgh: Edinburgh University Press, 1960.

Norton, Augustus R. *Amal and the Shi'a: Struggle for the Soul of Lebanon.* Austin: University of Texas Press, 1987.

———. *Harakat Amal and the Political Mobilization of the Shi'a of Lebanon.* Chicago: University of Chicago Press, 1985.

———. "Nuclear Terrorism and the Middle East." *Military Review* 56 (1976): 3–11.

———. *Understanding the Nuclear Terrorism Problem.* Gaithersburg, Md.: International Association of Chiefs of Police, 1979.

Norton, Augustus R., and Martin H. Greenberg, eds. *Studies in Nuclear Terrorism.* Boston: G. K. Hall, 1979.

Norval, Morgan. *Triumph of Disorder: Islamic Fundamentalism, the New Face of War.* Bend, Ore.: Sligo, 1998.

Novick, Richard, and Seth Shulman. "New Forms of Biological Warfare?" In *Preventing a Biological Arms Race.* Edited by Susan Wright. Cambridge, Mass.: MIT Press, 1990.

Noyon, Jennifer. *Islam, Politics, and Pluralism.* Washington: Brookings, 2001.

Nunn, Sam. "Weapons of Mass Destruction Pose a Terrorist Threat." In *Terrorism.* Edited by Laura K. Egendorf. San Diego: Greenhaven, 2000.

Nusse, Andrea. *Muslim Palestine: The Ideology of Hamas.* London: Harwood, 1999.

O'Ballance, Edgar. *Islamic Fundamentalist Terrorism, 1979–1995: The Iranian Connection.* New York: New York University Press, 1997.

———. *The Kurdish Struggle: 1920–94.* London: Macmillan, 1996.

———. *Sudan, Civil War and Terrorism: 1956–99.* New York: St. Martin's, 2000.

Oberoi, Harjot Singh. "Sikh Fundamentalism: Translating History into Theory." In *Fundamentalisms and the State.* Edited by Martin E. Marty and R. Scott Appleby. Chicago: University of Chicago Press, 1993.

Oberst, Robert C. "Sri Lanka's Tamil Tigers." *Conflict* 8 (1988): 185–202.

O'Dwyer, Thomas. "Hizbullah's Ruthless Realist." In *Violence and Terrorism.* Edited by Bernard Schecterman and Martin Slann. Guilford, Conn.: Dushkin/McGraw-Hill, 1999.

Ogan, Christine. *Communication and Identity in the Diaspora: Turkish Migrants in Amsterdam and Their Use of Media.* Lanham, Md.: Rowman and Littlefield, 2001.

Ohmae, Kenichi. *The Borderless World.* New York: HarperCollins, 1990.

Ojeda, Auriana, ed. *Islamic Fundamentalism.* San Diego: Greenhaven, 2003.

Okamura, Jonathan Y. *The End of the Nation State.* New York: Free Press, 1995.

———. *Imagining the Filipino American Diaspora: Transnational Relations, Identities, and Communities.* New York: Garland, 1998.

Okumura, Tetsu, et al. "Report on 640 Victims of the Tokyo Subway Sarin Attack." *Annals of Emergency Medicine* 28 (1996): 129–135.

Olesen, Asta. *Islam and Politics in Afghanistan.* Richmond, UK: Curzon, 1995.

Oliker, Olga. *Russia's Chechen Wars, 1994–2000.* Santa Monica, Calif.: Rand, 2001.

Oliker, Olga, and Tanya Charlick-Paley. *The Extended Implications of Russian Infrastructure Deterioration: Why Moscow's Problems Should Worry the USAF.* Santa Monica, Calif.: Rand, 2002.

Olson, Robert W., ed. *The Kurdish Nationalist Movement in the 1990s: Its Impact on Turkey and the Middle East.* Lexington: University Press of Kentucky, 1997.

Onwudiwe, Ihekwoaba D. *The Globalization of Terrorism.* Brookfield, Vt.: Ashgate, 2001.

Oots, Kent Layne. *A Political Organization Approach to Transnational Terrorism.* New York: Greenwood, 1986.

Orlov, Vladimir A. "Export Controls and Nuclear Smuggling in Russia." In *Dangerous Weapons, Desperate States: Russia, Belarus, Kazakhstan, and Ukraine.* Edited by Gary K. Bertsch and William C. Potter. New York: Routledge, 1999.

Ostergaard-Nielsen, Eva, ed. *Trans-State Loyalties and Policies: Turks and Kurds in Germany.* New York: Routledge, 2002.

Osterholm, Michael T., and John Schwartz. *Living Terrors: What America Needs to Know to Survive the Coming Bioterrorist Catastrophe.* New York: Delacorte, 2000.

Otis, Pauletta. "The Nature of Religious Terrorism." *Defense Intelligence Journal* 11 (2002): 27–36.

Paltin, D. M. "Chemical and Biological Violence: Predictive Patterns in State and Terrorist Behavior." In *Collective Violence: Effective Strategies for Assessing and Intervening in Fatal Group and Institutional Aggression.* Edited by Harold V. Hall and Leighton C. Whitaker. Boca Raton, Fla.: CRC Press, 1998.

"Panel Hears Testimony on Secret-Evidence Law." *Dallas Morning News,* May 24, 2000.

Pangi, Robyn. "Consequence Management in the 1995 Sarin Attacks on the Japanese Subway System." *Studies in Conflict and Terrorism* 25 (2002): 421–448.

Paone, Rocco M. *Evolving New World Order/Disorder.* Lanham, Md.: University Press of America, 2001.

Parachini, John V. *Combating Terrorism: Assessing the Threat of Biological Terrorism.* Santa Monica, Calif.: Rand, 2001.

———. "Mass Casualty Terrorism: Comparing Means, Motives, and Outcomes." Paper presented to Terrorism and Beyond: The 21st Century Conference, April 17–19, 2000, at Oklahoma City, Oklahoma.

———. "World Trade Center Bombers." In *Toxic Terror: Assessing Terrorist Use of Chemical and Biological Weapons.* Edited by Jonathan B. Tucker. Cambridge, Mass.: MIT Press, 2000.

Parfrey, Adam, ed. *Extreme Islam: Anti-American Propaganda of Muslim Fundamentalism.* Los Angeles: Feral House, 2001.

Parish, Scott. *Are Suitcase Nukes on the Loose? The Story behind the Controversy.* Monterey, Calif.: Monterey Institute of International Studies, 1997.

Parsons, Talcott. "Some Theoretical Considerations on the Nature and Trends of Change of Ethnicity." In *Ethnicity: Theory and Experience.* Edited by Nathan Glazer and Daniel P. Moynihan. Cambridge, Mass.: Harvard University Press, 1975.

Partner, Peter. *God of Battles: Holy Wars of Christianity and Islam.* Princeton: Princeton University Press, 1998.

Patai, Raphael. *The Arab Mind.* New York: Scribner's, 1983.

Pate, Jason, and Gavin Cameron. *Covert Biological Weapons Attacks against Agricultural Targets: Assessing the Impact against U.S. Agriculture.* Cambridge, Mass.: John F. Kennedy School of Government, 2001.

Paz, Reuven. *Tangled Web: International Networking of the Islamist Struggle.* Washington: Brookings, 2002.

Pearlstein, Richard M. "Common Sense about Nuclear Power: Interjurisdictional Agreements and the Institutionalization of Evacuation Procedure." Unpublished manuscript.

———. "The Counterterrorist Effort: Coups and Controversies." Paper presented to the Annual Meeting of the Society for the Study of Social Problems, August 20–22, 1998, at San Francisco, California.

———. "Of Fear, Uncertainty, and Boldness: The Life and Thought of Thomas Hobbes." *Journal of Psychohistory* 13 (1986): 309–324.

———. "The Future of Political Terrorism: New Targets, Tactics, Opportunities, and Vulnerabilities." Paper presented to the Annual Meeting of the Southwestern Social Science Association, March 22–25, 1995, at Dallas, Texas.

———. "Holy Rage: The Epitome of Contemporary Political Terrorism." Paper presented to the Annual Meeting of the Southwestern Social Science Association, March 20–23, 1996, at Houston, Texas.

———. "Lives of Disquieting Desperation: An Inquiry into the Mind of the Political Terrorist." Ph.D. dissertation, University of North Carolina at Chapel Hill, 1986.

———. *The Mind of the Political Terrorist.* Wilmington, Del.: Scholarly Resources, 1991.

———. "Tuned-in Narcissus: The Gleam in the Camera's Eye." In *In the Camera's Eye: News Coverage of Terrorist Events.* Edited by Yonah Alexander and Robert G. Picard. Washington: Brassey's, 1991.

Peleg, Samuel. "They Shoot Prime Ministers Too, Don't They? Religious Violence in Israel: Premises, Dynamics, and Prospects." *Studies in Conflict and Terrorism* 20 (1997): 227–247.

———. *Zealotry and Vengeance: Quest of a Religious Identity Group.* Lanham, Md.: Rowman and Littlefield, 2002.

Perry, Gabrielle, ed. *Terrorism Reader.* Huntington, N.Y.: Nova Science, 2001.

Peters, Rudolph. *Islam and Colonialism: The Doctrine of Jihad in Modern History.* The Hague: Mouton, 1979.

———. *Jihad in Classical and Modern Islam.* Princeton: Princeton University Press, 1996.

Peterson, Scott. "How Reporters Cheat Assassins in Algeria's War with Islamists." In *Violence and Terrorism.* Edited by Bernard Schecterman and Martin Slann. Guilford, Conn.: Dushkin/McGraw-Hill, 1999.

Pettigrew, Joyce. *The Sikhs of Punjab: Unheard Voices of the State and Guerrilla Violence.* Atlantic Highlands, N.J.: Zed, 1995.

Phillips, James. "Islamic Terrorists Pose a Threat." In *Urban Terrorism.* Edited by A. E. Sadler and Paul A. Winters. San Diego: Greenhaven, 1996.

Photos, Abbas, and Magnum Photos. *Allah O Akbar: A Journey through Militant Islam.* London: Phaidon, 1994.

Pierre, Andrew J., and William B. Quandt. *The Algerian Crisis: Policy Options for the West*. Washington: Brookings, 1996.

———. *Between Bullets and Ballots*. Washington: Brookings, 1998.

Pillar, Paul. *Terrorism and U.S. Foreign Policy*. Washington: Brookings, 2001.

Piller, Charles, and Keith R. Yamamoto. *Gene Wars: Military Control over the New Genetic Technologies*. New York: Beech Tree, 1988.

Pinto, Maria do Ceu. *Political Islam and the United States: A Study of U.S. Policy towards Islamist Movements in the Middle East*. London: Ithaca, 1999.

Pipes, Daniel. *Militant Islam Reaches America*. New York: W. W. Norton, 2002.

———. *In the Path of God: Islam and Political Power*. New York: Basic Books, 1983.

———. "There Are No Moderates: Dealing with Fundamentalist Islam." *National Interest* 41 (1995): 48–57.

Piscatori, James P., ed. *Islam in the Political Process*. Cambridge: Cambridge University Press, 1993.

———. *Islamic Fundamentalisms and the Gulf Crisis*. Chicago: American Academy of Arts and Sciences, 1991.

Pluchinsky, Dennis A. "Middle East Terrorist Activity in Western Europe during the 1980s: A Decade of Violence." In *European Terrorism: Today and Tomorrow*. Edited by Yonah Alexander and Dennis A. Pluchinsky. Washington: Brassey's, 1992.

———. "The Terrorism Puzzle: Missing Pieces and No Boxcover." *Terrorism and Political Violence* 9 (1997): 7–10.

Podeh, Elie. "Egypt's Struggle against the Militant Islamic Groups." *Terrorism and Political Violence* 8 (1996): 43–61.

Polesetsky, Matthew, ed. *The New World Order*. San Diego: Greenhaven, 1991.

Polonskaya, Ludmilla, and Alexei Malashenko. *Islam in Central Asia*. Reading, UK: Ithaca, 1994.

Posen, Barry. "The Security Dilemma and Ethnic Conflict." *Survival* 35 (1993): 27–47.

Post, Jerrold M. "Fundamentalism and the Justification of Terrorist Violence." *Terrorism* 11 (1988): 369–371.

———. "Prospects for Nuclear Terrorism: Psychological Motivations and Constraints." In *Preventing Nuclear Terrorism: The Report and Papers of the International Task Force on Prevention of Nuclear Terrorism*. Edited by Paul L. Leventhal and Yonah Alexander. Lexington, Mass.: Lexington, 1987.

———. "Rewarding Fire with Fire? Effects of Retaliation on Terrorist Group Dynamics." In *Contemporary Trends in World Terrorism*. Edited by Anat Kurz. New York: Praeger, 1987.

———. "Superterrorism." *Terrorism* 13 (1990): 165–176.

Post, Jerrold M., ed. *Military Studies in the Jihad against the Tyrants: The al-Qaeda Training Manual*. Portland, Ore.: Frank Cass, 2002.

Post, Jerrold M., and Ehud Sprinzak. "Searching for Answers: Why Haven't Terrorists Used Weapons of Mass Destruction?" *Armed Forces Journal International*, April 1998.

Potomac Institute for Policy Studies. *Conference on Countering Biological Terrorism: Proceedings Report*. Arlington, Va.: Potomac Institute for Policy Studies, 1997.

———. *Countering Biological Terrorism in the United States: An Understanding of Issues and Status.* Dobbs Ferry, N.Y.: Oceana, 1999.

———. *Seminar on Emerging Threats of Biological Terrorism: Proceedings Report.* Arlington, Va.: Potomac Institute for Policy Studies, 1998.

Potter, William C. *Less Well-Known Cases of Nuclear Terrorism and Nuclear Diversions in the Former Soviet Union.* Monterey, Calif.: Monterey Institute of International Studies, 1997.

"Premier Says Terrorist Group Dismantled." *Dallas Morning News,* September 9, 2002.

Preston, Richard. "The Bioweaponeers: In the Last Few Years, Russian Scientists Have Invented the World's Deadliest Plagues—Have We Learned about This Too Late to Stop It?" *New Yorker,* March 9, 1998.

———. *The Cobra Event.* New York: Random House, 1997.

———. *The Demon in the Freezer.* New York: Random House, 2002.

———. "A Strong Public Health System Can Manage the Consequences of a Biological Attack." In *Weapons of Mass Destruction.* Edited by Jennifer A. Hurley. San Diego: Greenhaven, 1999.

Probst, Peter S. "Islamic Extremism and U.S. Security Interests." *Terrorism* 11 (1988): 371–374.

"Pro-Chechen Gunmen Hijack Plane with 109 on Board, Land in Munich." *Dallas Morning News,* March 9, 1996.

Prusher, Ilene R. "Also Terrorism: Budget Weddings by Hamas." In *Violence and Terrorism.* Edited by Bernard Schecterman and Martin Slann. Guilford, Conn.: Dushkin/McGraw-Hill, 1999.

Purewal, Shinder. *Sikh Ethnonationalism and the Political Economy of Punjab.* New York: Oxford University Press, 2000.

Puri, Harish, Paramjit Singh Judge, and Jagrup Singh Sekhon. *Terrorism in Punjab: Understanding Grassroots Reality.* New Delhi: Har-anand, 1999.

———. "Terrorism in Punjab: Understanding Reality at the Grass-Roots Level." *Guru Nanak Journal of Sociology* 18 (1997): 5–12.

Purver, Ron. *Chemical and Biological Terrorism: The Threat According to the Open Literature.* Ottawa: Canadian Security Intelligence Service, 1995.

———. *Chemical Terrorism in Japan.* Ottawa: Canadian Security Intelligence Service, 1995.

Quandt, William B. *Between Bullets and Ballots: Algeria's Transition from Authoritarianism.* Washington: Brookings, 1998.

Quillen, Chris. "A Historical Analysis of Mass Casualty Bombers." *Studies in Conflict and Terrorism* 25 (2002): 279–292.

———. "Terrorism with Weapons of Mass Destruction: The Congressional Response." *Terrorism and Political Violence* 13 (2001): 47–65.

Qutb, Sayyid. *Milestones.* Indianapolis: American Trust, 1990.

———. *In the Shade of the Quran.* Falls Church, Va.: Wamy International, 1995.

Ra'anan, Uri, et al., eds. *Hydra of Carnage: The International Linkages of Terrorism.* Lexington, Mass.: Lexington, 1986.

Rabi, Ibrahim M. Abu. *Intellectual Origins of Islamic Resurgence in the Muslim Arab World.* Albany: State University of New York Press, 1996.

"Radioactive Container Found at Park in Moscow Not Dangerous, Officials Say." *Dallas Morning News,* November 25, 1995.

Radulescu, Dominica, ed. *Realms of Exile: Nomadism, Diasporas, and Eastern European Voices*. Lanham, Md.: Rowman and Littlefield, 2002.

Rahnema, Ali, ed. *Pioneers of Islamic Revival*. London: Zed, 1994.

Ram, Haggay. "Exporting Iran's Islamic Revolution: Steering a Path between Pan-Islam and Nationalism." *Terrorism and Political Violence* 8 (1996): 7–24.

Ramazani, R. K. *Revolutionary Iran*. Baltimore: Johns Hopkins University Press, 1986.

Ramazani, R. K., ed. *Iran's Revolution: The Search for Consensus*. Bloomington: Indiana University Press, 1990.

Ranstorp, Magnus. *Hizb'Allah in Lebanon: The Politics of the Western Hostage Crisis*. New York: St. Martin's, 1996.

———. "Interpreting the Broader Context and Meaning of Bin-Laden's Fatwa." *Studies in Conflict and Terrorism* 21 (1998): 321–330.

———. "Radical Islamic Movements and Terrorism: A Trans-National Problem." Paper presented to Terrorism and Beyond: The 21st Century Conference, April 17–19, 2000, at Oklahoma City, Oklahoma.

———. "Religious Fanaticism Motivates Terrorists." In *Terrorism*. Edited by Laura K. Egendorf. San Diego: Greenhaven, 2000.

———. "Terrorism in the Name of Religion." *Journal of International Affairs* 50 (1996): 41–62.

Rapoport, David C. "To Claim or Not to Claim: That Is the Question—Always!" *Terrorism and Political Violence* 9 (1997): 11–17.

———. "Fear and Trembling: Terrorism in Three Religious Traditions." *American Political Science Review* 78 (1984): 655–677.

———. "Religion and Terror: Thugs, Assassins, and Zealots." In *International Terrorism: Characteristics, Causes, Controls*. Edited by Charles W. Kegley, Jr. New York: St. Martin's, 1990.

———. "The Role of External Forces in Supporting Ethno-Religious Conflict." In *Violence and Terrorism*. Edited by Bernard Schecterman and Martin Slann. Guilford, Conn.: Dushkin/McGraw-Hill, 1999.

———. "Sacred Terror: A Contemporary Example from Islam." In *Origins of Terrorism: Psychologies, Ideologies, Theologies, States of Mind*. Edited by Walter Reich. Cambridge: Cambridge University Press, 1990.

———. "Some General Observations on Religion and Violence." In *Violence and the Sacred in the Modern World*. Edited by Mark Juergensmeyer. London: Frank Cass, 1992.

———. "Terrorism and Weapons of the Apocalypse." *Georgetown National Security Studies Quarterly* 5 (1999): 49–67.

———. "Why Does Religious Messianism Produce Terror?" In *Contemporary Research on Terrorism*. Edited by Paul Wilkinson and A. M. Stewart. Aberdeen, UK: Aberdeen University Press, 1987.

Rapoport, David C., and Yonah Alexander, eds. *The Morality of Terrorism: Religious and Secular Justifications*. New York: Pergamon, 1982.

Rashid, Ahmed. *Jihad: The Rise of Militant Islam in Central Asia*. New Haven: Yale University Press, 2002.

———. *The Resurgence of Central Asia: Islam or Nationalism?* London: Zed, 1994.

———. *Taliban: Militant Islam, Oil and Fundamentalism in Central Asia*. New Haven: Yale University Press, 2000.

Rasler, Karen A., and William R. Thompson. *The Great Powers and Global Struggle, 1490–1990*. Lexington: University Press of Kentucky, 1994.

Raufer, Xavier. "New World Disorder, New Terrorisms: New Threats for Europe and the Western World." In *The Future of Terrorism*. Edited by Maxwell Taylor and John Horgan. London: Frank Cass, 2000.

Reader, Ian. "Imagined Persecution: Aum Shinrikyo, Millennialism, and the Justification of Violence." In *Millennialism, Persecution and Violence: Historical Cases*. Edited by Catherine Wessinger. Syracuse, N.Y.: Syracuse University Press, 2000.

———. *A Poisonous Cocktail? Aum Shinrikyo's Path to Violence*. Copenhagen: NIAS, 1996.

———. *Religious Violence in Contemporary Japan: The Case of Aum Shinrikyo*. Honolulu: University of Hawaii Press, 2000.

Redlick, Amy Sands. "Transnational Factors Affecting Quebec Separatist Terrorism." Paper presented to the Annual Convention of the International Studies Association, February 25–29, 1976, at Toronto, Canada.

———. "The Transnational Flow of Information as a Cause of Terrorism." In *Terrorism: Theory and Practice*. Edited by Yonah Alexander, David Carlton, and Paul Wilkinson. Boulder, Colo.: Westview, 1979.

Reed, Stanley. "The Battle for Egypt." *Foreign Affairs* 72 (1993): 94–107.

Reeve, Simon. *The New Jackals: Ramzi Yousef, Osama bin Laden and the Future of Terrorism*. Boston: Northeastern University Press, 1999.

Regis, Ed. *The Biology of Doom: The History of America's Secret Germ Warfare Project*. New York: Henry Holt, 1999.

Reich, Walter, ed. *Origins of Terrorism: Psychologies, Ideologies, Theologies, States of Mind*. New York: Cambridge University Press, 1990.

Reid, T. R. "Cult Leader: The U.S. Did It." *New Orleans Times-Picayune*, March 25, 1995.

Reinares, Fernando, ed. *European Democracies against Terrorism: Governmental Policies and Intergovernmental Cooperation*. Brookfield, Vt.: Ashgate, 2001.

Rejwan, Nissim. *Arabs Face the Modern World: Religious, Cultural and Political Responses to the West*. Gainesville: University Press of Florida, 1998.

Rekhes, Elie. "Resurgent Islam in Israel." Paper presented to the Conference on the Arab Minority in Israel, June 3–4, 1991, at Tel Aviv.

Richar, Yann. *Shiite Islam: Polity, Ideology, and Creed*. Oxford: Blackwell, 1995.

Richardson, James T. "Minority Religions and the Context of Violence: A Conflict/Interactionist Perspective." *Terrorism and Political Violence* 13 (2001): 103–133.

Richardson, Louise. "Global Rebels: Terrorist Organizations as Trans-National Actors." In *Terrorism and Counterterrorism: Understanding the New Security Environment*. Edited by Russell D. Howard and Reid L. Sawyer. Guilford, Conn.: McGraw-Hill/Dushkin, 2003.

Richter, Paul. "U.S. Has Right to Kill Terrorists, Officials Say." *Dallas Morning News*, October 29, 1998.

Ridley, Matt. *Genome: The Autobiography of a Species in 23 Chapters*. New York: HarperCollins, 2000.

Rifkin, Jeremy. *The Biotech Century: Harnessing the Gene and Remaking the World*. New York: Putnam, 1998.

Risen, James, and David Johnston. "CIA Authorized to Kill Top Terrorism Suspects." *Dallas Morning News,* December 15, 2002.

Risse-Kappen, Thomas. *Bringing Transnational Relations Back In: Non-State Actors, Domestic Structures and International Institutions.* Cambridge: Cambridge University Press, 1995.

Robbins, James S. "Bin Laden's War." In *Terrorism and Counterterrorism: Understanding the New Security Environment.* Edited by Russell D. Howard and Reid L. Sawyer. Guilford, Conn.: McGraw-Hill/Dushkin, 2003.

Roberts, Brad, ed. *Biological Weapons: Weapons of the Future?* Washington: Center for Strategic and International Studies, 1993.

———. *Hype or Reality? The "New Terrorism" and Mass Casualty Attacks.* Alexandria, Va.: Chemical and Biological Arms Control Institute, 2000.

———. *Terrorism with Chemical and Biological Weapons: Calibrating Risks and Responses.* Alexandria, Va.: Chemical and Biological Arms Control Institute, 1997.

Roberts, Brad, and Michael Moodie. *Combating NBC Terrorism: An Agenda for Enhancing International Cooperation.* Alexandria, Va.: Chemical and Biological Arms Control Institute, 1998.

Robertson, Ken. "Terrorism: Europe without Borders." *Terrorism* 14 (1991): 105–110.

Robinson, Adam. *Bin Laden: Behind the Mask of a Terrorist.* New York: Arcade, 2002.

Rogers, John D., Jonathan Spencer, and Jayadeva Uyangoda. "Sri Lanka: Political Violence and Ethnic Conflict." *American Psychologist* 58 (1998): 771–777.

Ronfeldt, David, and William Sater. "The Mindsets of High-Technology Terrorists: Future Implication from an Historical Analog." In *Political Terrorism and Energy: The Threat and the Response.* Edited by Yonah Alexander and Charles K. Ebinger. New York: Praeger, 1982.

Root-Bernstein, Robert S. "Infectious Terrorism: It Is Time to Think Seriously about How Biological Agents Could Be Deployed against Innocent Citizens." *Atlantic,* May 1991.

Rose, Stephen. "Biotechnology at War." *New Scientist* 113 (1987): 33–37.

Rosenau, James N. *Turbulence in World Politics: A Theory of Change and Continuity.* Princeton: Princeton University Press, 1990.

Rosenau, William. "Aum Shinrikyo's Biological Weapons Program: Why Did It Fail?" *Studies in Conflict and Terrorism* 24 (2001): 289–301.

Rosenau, William, et al. "Transnational Threats and U.S. National Security." *Low Intensity Conflict and Law Enforcement* 6 (1997): 144–161.

Rothchild, J. H. *Tomorrow's Weapons: Chemical and Biological.* New York: McGraw-Hill, 1964.

Rourke, John T. *International Politics on the World Stage.* Guilford, Conn.: Dushkin/McGraw-Hill, 1999.

Roy, Olivier. *The Failure of Political Islam.* London: I. B. Tauris, 1994.

———. *Islam and Resistance in Afghanistan.* Cambridge: Cambridge University Press, 1986.

Rubin, Barnett. *The Fragmentation of Afghanistan: State Formation and Collapse in the International System.* New Haven: Yale University Press, 1995.

———. *Islamic Fundamentalism in Egyptian Politics.* New York: Palgrave, 2002.

———. *The Search for Peace in Afghanistan: From Buffer State to Failed State.* New Haven: Yale University Press, 1995.

Rubin, Barry, and Judith Colp Rubin, eds. *Anti-American Terrorism and the Middle East: A Documentary Reader.* New York: Oxford University Press, 2002.

Rudolph, Hoeber, Susanne Piscatori, and James Piscatori, eds. *Transnational Religion and the Fading State.* Boulder, Colo.: Westview, 1996.

Ruedy, John, ed. *Islamism and Secularism in North Africa.* New York: St. Martin's, 1994.

Rupesinghe, Kumar, Peter King, and Olga Vorkunova, eds. *Ethnicity and Conflict in a Post-Communist World: The Soviet Union, Eastern Europe, and China.* New York: St. Martin's, 1992.

"Russian Embassy Attacked in Beirut." *Dallas Morning News,* January 4, 2000.

Russo, Enzo, and David Cove. *Genetic Engineering: Dreams and Nightmares.* Oxford: W. H. Freeman, 1995.

Ruthven, Malise. *A Fury for God: The Islamist Attack on America.* London: Granta, 2002.

———. *Islam in the World.* New York: Oxford University Press, 2000.

Ryan, Stephen. *Ethnic Conflict and International Relations.* Aldershot, UK: Dartmouth, 1990.

———. "Political Crises Intensify Ethnic Conflict." In *Nationalism and Ethnic Conflict.* Edited by Charles P. Cozic. San Diego: Greenhaven, 1994.

Rydell, Randy J. "Preventing Nuclear Terrorism: The Report and Papers of the International Task Force on Prevention of Nuclear Terrorism." *Science* 236 (1987): 977–978.

Saad-Ghorayeb, Amal. *Hizbu'llah: Politics and Religion.* Herndon, Va.: Pluto, 2002.

Sabaratnam, Lakshmanan. *Ethnic Attachments in Sri Lanka: Social Change and Cultural Continuity.* New York: Palgrave, 2001.

Sadler, A. E., and Paul A. Winters, eds. *Urban Terrorism.* San Diego: Greenhaven, 1996.

Sadowski, Yahya. *The Myth of Global Chaos.* Washington: Brookings, 1998.

Saha, Santosh C., and Thomas K. Carr, eds. *Religious Fundamentalism in Developing Countries.* Westport, Conn.: Greenwood, 2001.

Said, Abdul Aziz. "Western Arrogance, Islamic Fanaticism, and Terrorism." *Terrorism* 11 (1988): 378–384.

Saideman, Stephen M. "Explaining the International Relations of Secessionist Conflicts: Vulnerability versus Ethnic Ties." *International Organization* 51 (1997): 721–754.

———. *The Ties That Divide: Ethnic Politics, Foreign Policy, and International Conflict.* New York: Columbia University Press, 2001.

Sakomoto, Yoshikazu. *Global Transformation: Challenges to the State System.* Lanham, Md.: United Nations University Press, 1994.

Salame, Ghassan. "Islam and the West." *Foreign Policy* 90 (1993): 22–37.

Salame, Ghassan, ed. *Democracy without Democrats: The Renewal of Politics in the Muslim World.* London: I. B. Tauris, 1994.

Samaranayake, Gamini. "Ethnic Conflict in Sri Lanka and Prospects of Management: An Empirical Inquiry." In *Violence and Terrorism.* Edited by Bernard Schecterman and Martin Slann. Guilford, Conn.: Dushkin, 1993.

Sandia National Laboratories. *Physical Protection of Nuclear Facilities and Materials.* Albuquerque: Sandia National Laboratories, 1989.

Sandler, Todd, John T. Tschirhart, and Jon Cauley. "A Theoretical Analysis of Transnational Terrorism." *American Political Science Review* 77 (1983): 33–54.

Sandole, Dennis J. D. *Capturing the Complexity of Conflict: Dealing with Violent Ethnic Conflicts in the Post–Cold War Era.* New York: Pinter, 2000.

Sapir, Jacques. "State Weakening and Proliferation: The Russian Case." Paper presented to the Fissile Material Workshop, February 3–4, 1998, at Livermore, California.

Sardar, Zauddin, S. Z. Abedin, and M. A. Anees. *Christian-Muslim Relations: Yesterday, Today and Tomorrow.* London: Grey Seal, 1991.

Satloff, Robert B., ed. *Campaign against Terror: The Middle East Dimension.* Washington: Brookings, 2002.

Sayari, Sabri. *Generational Changes in Terrorist Movements: The Turkish Case.* Santa Monica, Calif.: Rand, 1985.

Schaper, Annette. "Nuclear Smuggling in Europe: Real Dangers and Enigmatic Deception." Paper presented to the Forum on Illegal Nuclear Traffic: Risks, Safeguards, and Countermeasures, June 11–13, 1997, at Como, Italy.

Schbley, Ayla Hammond. "Religious Terrorists: What They Aren't Going to Tell Us." *Terrorism* 13 (1990): 237–241.

———. "Resurgent Religious Terrorism: A Study of Some of the Lebanese Shi'a Contemporary Terrorism." *Terrorism* 12 (1989): 213–247.

———. "Torn between God, Family, and Money: The Changing Profile of Lebanon's Religious Terrorists." *Studies in Conflict and Terrorism* 23 (2000): 175–196.

Schecterman, Bernard, and Martin Slann. *The Ethnic Dimension in International Relations.* Westport, Conn.: Praeger, 1993.

Schelling, Thomas. "Thinking about Nuclear Terrorism." *International Security* 6 (1982): 6–67.

Schiff, Ze'ev, and Ehud Ya'ari. *Intifada: The Palestinian Uprising.* New York: Simon and Schuster, 1990.

Schiller, Nina Glick, Cristina Blanc-Szanton, and Linda Baasch, eds. *Towards a Transnational Perspective on Migration: Race, Class, Ethnicity, and Nationalism.* Baltimore: Johns Hopkins University Press, 1998.

Schlefer, Jonathan. "Nuclear Terrorism." *Technology Review,* April 1991.

Schlesinger, Robert. "Markey Decries Lack of Security Checks on Radiation Facility Staff." *Boston Globe,* July 31, 2002.

Schmid, Alex P. "Terrorism and the Use of Weapons of Mass Destruction: From Where the Risk?" In *The Future of Terrorism.* Edited by Maxwell Taylor and John Horgan. London: Frank Cass, 2000.

Schmitt, David. *Violence in Northern Ireland: Ethnic Conflict and Radicalization in an International Setting.* Morristown, N.J.: General Learning, 1974.

Schumacher, Ulrike, ed. *Structure, Order, and Disorder in World Politics: Papers Presented at the Summer Course 1998 on International Security.* New York: Peter Lang, 1999.

Schwartz, Stephen. *The Two Faces of Islam: The House of Sa'ud from Tradition to Terror.* New York: Doubleday, 2002.

Schwartz, T. P. "Terror and Terrorism in the Koran." In *Essential Readings on Political Terrorism: Analyses of Problems and Prospects for the 21st Century.* Edited by Harvey W. Kushner. New York: Gordian Knot, 2002.

Schweitzer, Glenn E. *Superterrorism: Assassins, Mobsters, and Weapons of Mass Destruction.* New York: Plenum, 1998.

Schweller, Randall L. *Deadly Imbalances: Tripolarity and Hitler's Strategy of World Conquest.* New York: Columbia University Press, 1998.

Scott, Janny. "From 'Ground Zero,' a "Debris Surge' of '9/11' Terms." *Dallas Morning News*, February 24, 2002.

"Secretive Court to Rule on Prosecutor's Powers." *Dallas Morning News*, September 2, 2002.

"Security Beefed up after New Moscow Bombing." *Dallas Morning News*, July 13, 1996.

"Sending Police to Jail." *Time*, June 3, 1985.

Sergeyev, Victor M. *The Wild East: Crime and Lawlessness in Post-Communist Russia*. Armonk, N.Y.: M. E. Sharpe, 1997.

Sessions, William S. "Terrorism: The Chemical-Biological Threat." *Police Chief*, March 1991.

Shabad, Goldie A., and Francisco José Llera Ramo. "Basque Terrorism in Spain." Paper presented to the Terrorism in Context Conference, June 8–10, 1989, at Middletown, Connecticut.

Shabi, Aviva, and Roni Shaked. *Hamas: From Belief in Allah to Routes of Terror*. Jerusalem: Keter, 1994.

Shadid, Anthony. *Legacy of the Prophet: Despots, Democrats, and the New Politics of Islam*. Boulder, Colo.: Westview, 2001.

Shafir, Gershon. *Immigrants and Nationalists: Ethnic Conflict and Accommodation in Catalonia, the Basque Country, Latvia, and Estonia*. Albany: State University of New York Press, 1995.

Shah, Sonia. "The Political Exploitation of Ethnicity Causes Ethnic Conflict." In *Nationalism and Ethnic Conflict*. Edited by Charles P. Cozic. San Diego: Greenhaven, 1994.

Shahak, Israel, and Norton Mezvinsky. *Jewish Fundamentalism in Israel*. Herndon, Va.: Pluto, 1999.

Shah-Kazemi, Reza, ed. *Algeria: Revolution Revisited*. New York: St. Martin's, 1998.

Shapiro, Michael J., and Haywood R. Alker, eds. *Challenging Boundaries: Global Flows, Territorial Identities*. Minneapolis: University of Minnesota Press, 1995.

Shapiro, Roger L., Charles Hatheway, John Becher, and David L. Swerdlow. "Botulism Surveillance and Emergency Response." *Journal of the American Medical Association* 278 (1997): 433–435.

Sharma, D. P. *The Punjab Story: Decade of Turmoil*. New Delhi: APH, 1996.

Sheffer, Gabriel, ed. *Modern Diasporas in International Politics*. New York: Palgrave-Macmillan, 1986.

Shields, Charles J. *The 1993 World Trade Center Bombing*. Broomall, Pa.: Chelsea House, 2001.

Shimazono, Susumu. "In the Wake of Aum: The Formation and Transformation of a Universe of Beliefs." *Japanese Journal of Religious Studies* 22 (1995): 381–415.

Shirley, Edward G. "The Etiquette of Killing bin Laden." In *Violence and Terrorism*. Edited by Bernard Schecterman and Martin Slann. Guilford, Conn.: Dushkin/McGraw-Hill, 1999.

Shultz, Richard, and William Olson. *Ethnic and Religious Conflict*. Washington: National Strategy Information Center, 1994.

Sidahmed, Abdel Salam, and Anoushiravan Ehteshami. *Islamic Fundamentalism*. Boulder, Colo.: Westview, 1996.

Sidell, Frederick R. "Chemical Agent Terrorism." *Annals of Emergency Medicine* 28 (1996): 223–224.

Sidell, Frederick R., Ernest T. Takafuji, and David L. Franz, eds. *Medical Aspects of Chemical and Biological Warfare*. Falls Church, Va.: United States Army, Office of the Surgeon General, 1997.

Sil, Rudra, and Eileen M. Doherty, eds. *Beyond Boundaries? Disciplines, Paradigms, and Theoretical Integration in International Studies*. Albany: State University of New York Press, 2000.

Simon, Jeffrey D. "Biological Terrorism: Preparing to Meet the Threat." *Journal of the American Medical Association* 278 (1997): 428–430.

———. *Terrorists and the Potential Use of Biological Weapons: A Discussion of Possibilities*. Santa Monica, Calif.: Rand, 1989.

———. *The Terrorist Trap: America's Experience with Terrorism*. Bloomington: Indiana University Press, 1994.

Simone, T. Abdou Maliqalim. *In Whose Image? Political Islam and Urban Practices in Sudan*. Chicago: University of Chicago Press, 1994.

Simons, Anna. "Making Sense of Ethnic Cleansing." *Studies in Conflict and Terrorism* 22 (1999): 1–20.

Simonsen, Clifford E., and Jeremy R. Spindlove. *Terrorism Today: The Past, the Players, the Future*. Upper Saddle River, N.J.: Prentice Hall, 2000.

"Singapore: Man Met with Moussaoui." *Dallas Morning News*, September 28, 2002.

Singer, Max, and Aaron Wildavsky. *The Real World Order: Zones of Peace/Zones of Turmoil*. Chatham, N.J.: Chatham House, 1996.

Singh, Gurdev. *Punjab Politics*. New Delhi: B. R. Publishing, 1986.

Singh, Gurharpal. *Ethnic Conflict in India: A Case-Study of Punjab*. New York: Palgrave, 2000.

———. "The Punjab Crisis since 1984: A Reassessment." *Ethnic and Racial Studies* 18 (1995): 476–493.

———. "Understanding the 'Punjab Problem.'" *Asian Survey* 27 (1987): 1268–1277.

Singh, Satinder. *Khalistan: An Academic Analysis*. New Delhi: Amar Prakashan, 1982.

———. "Terrorism in Punjab." *Guru Nanak Journal of Sociology* 18 (1997): 5–12.

Sivan, Emmanuel. *Radical Islam: Medieval Theology and Modern Politics*. New Haven: Yale University Press, 1985.

Sivan, Emmanuel, and Menachem Friedman, eds. *Religious Radicalism and Politics in the Middle East*. Albany: State University of New York Press, 1990.

Sloan, Stephen. *Anatomy of Non-Territorial Terrorism*. Gaithersburg, Md.: International Association of Chiefs of Police, 1978.

———. "Terrorism: How Vulnerable Is the United States?" In *Terrorism*. Edited by Stephen C. Pelletiere. Carlisle, Pa.: U.S. Army War College Strategic Studies Institute, 1995.

Sloan, Susan R. *Act of God*. New York: Warner, 2002.

Smith, Brent L. *Terrorism in America: Pipe Bombs and Pipe Dreams*. Albany: State University of New York Press, 1994.

Smith, Joseph Wayne, Graham Lyons, and Evonne Moore. *Global Anarchy in the Third Millennium? Race, Place and Power at the End of the Modern Age*. New York: Palgrave, 2000.

Smith, Paul, et al. *Ethnic Groups in International Relations*. New York: New York University Press, 1991.

Smith, Sebastian. *Allah's Mountains: The Battle for Chechnya*. New York: Palgrave, 2001.

Smithson, Amy E., and Leslie-Anne Levy. *Ataxia: The Chemical and Biological Terrorism Threat and the U.S. Response.* Washington: Henry L. Stimson Center, 2000.

Smock, David R. *Religious Perspectives on War: Christian, Muslim, and Jewish Attitudes toward Force.* Herndon, Va.: United States Institute of Peace Press, 2002.

Snyder, Louis L. *Global Mini-Nationalisms: Autonomy or Independence.* Westport, Conn.: Greenwood, 1982.

Sonn, Tamara. *Between the Qur'an and the Crown: The Challenge of Political Legitimacy in the Arab World.* Boulder, Colo.: Westview, 1990.

Sopko, John F. "The Changing Proliferation Threat." In *The Global Agenda: Issues and Perspectives.* Edited by Charles W. Kegley, Jr., and Eugene R. Wittkopf. Boston: McGraw-Hill, 1998.

Sorensen, Georg. *Changes in Statehood: The Transformation of International Relations.* New York: Palgrave, 2001.

Soroos, Marvin S. *Beyond Sovereignty: The Challenge of Global Policy.* Columbia: University of South Carolina Press, 1986.

"Spain Official, 11 Others Convicted of Kidnapping." *Dallas Morning News,* August 30, 1998.

Spector, Leonard S. "Clandestine Nuclear Trade and the Threat of Nuclear Terrorism." In *Preventing Nuclear Terrorism: The Report and Papers of the International Task Force on Prevention of Nuclear Terrorism.* Edited by Paul L. Leventhal and Yonah Alexander. Lexington, Mass.: Lexington, 1987.

Spencer, Robert. *Islam Unveiled: Disturbing Questions about the World's Fastest-Growing Faith.* San Francisco: Encounter, 2002.

Spielman, Andrew, and Michael D'Antonio. *Mosquito: The Story of Man's Deadliest Foe.* New York: Hyperion, 2001.

Sprinzak, Ehud. *The Ascendance of Israel's Radical Right.* New York: Oxford University Press, 1991.

———. *Brother against Brother: Violence and Extremism in Israeli Politics from Altalena to the Rabin Assassination.* New York: Free Press, 1999.

———. "Extremism and Violence in Israeli Democracy." *Terrorism and Political Violence* 12 (2000): 209–236.

———. *Fundamentalism, Terrorism, and Democracy: The Case of the Gush Emunim Underground.* Washington: Smithsonian Institution, 1986.

———. "The Great Superterrorism Scare." In *American Foreign Policy.* Edited by Glenn P. Hastedt. Guilford, Conn.: Dushkin/McGraw-Hill, 2000.

———. *Gush Emunim: The Politics of Zionist Fundamentalism in Israel.* New York: American Jewish Committee, 1986.

———. "Gush Emunim: The Tip of the Iceberg." *Jerusalem Quarterly* 21 (1981): 28–47.

———. "From Messianic Pioneering to Vigilante Terrorism: The Case of the Gush Emunim Underground." In *Inside Terrorist Organizations.* Edited by David C. Rapoport. New York: Columbia University Press, 1988.

———. "Rational Fanatics." *Foreign Policy,* September 2000.

———. "Weapons of Mass Destruction Do Not Pose a Terrorist Threat." In *Terrorism.* Edited by Laura K. Egendorf. San Diego: Greenhaven, 2000.

Spruyt, Hendrik. *The Sovereign State and Its Competitors: An Analysis of System Change.* Princeton: Princeton University Press, 1995.

Stack, John F., Jr., and Lui Hebron, eds. *The Ethnic Entanglement: Conflict and Intervention in World Politics.* Westport, Conn.: Greenwood, 1999.

Stavenhagen, Rodolfo. *Ethnic Conflicts and the Nation-State*. New York: Palgrave, 1996.

Steinberg, Paul, and Annmarie Oliver. *Rehearsals for a Happy Death: The Testimonies of Hamas Suicide Bombers*. New York: Oxford University Press, 1997.

Stemplowski, Ryszard, et al., eds. *Transnational Terrorism in the World System Perspective*. Warsaw: Polish Institute of International Affairs, 2002.

Stephens, Ralph Eugene. "Cyber-Biotech Terrorism: Going High Tech in the 21st Century." In *The Future of Terrorism: Violence in the New Millennium*. Edited by Harvey W. Kushner. Thousand Oaks, Calif.: Sage, 1998.

Sterling, Claire. *The Terror Network: The Secret War Of International Terrorism*. New York: Berkley, 1982.

Stern, Jessica. "Moscow Meltdown: Can Russia Survive?" *International Security* 18 (1994): 40–65.

———. "Pakistan's Jihad Culture." In *Essential Readings on Political Terrorism: Analyses of Problems and Prospects for the 21st Century*. Edited by Harvey W. Kushner. New York: Gordian Knot, 2002.

———. *The Ultimate Terrorists*. Cambridge, Mass.: Harvard University Press, 1999.

———. "Will Terrorists Turn to Poison?" *Orbis* 37 (1993): 393–410.

Stone, Martin. *The Agony of Algeria*. New York: Columbia University Press, 1997.

Strindberg, N. T. Anders. "Challenging the 'Received View': Dedemonizing Hamas." *Studies in Conflict and Terrorism* 25 (2002): 263–273.

Stuller, Jay. "Nationalism Causes Ethnic Conflict." In *Nationalism and Ethnic Conflict*. Edited by Charles P. Cozic. San Diego: Greenhaven, 1994.

Stump, Roger W. *Boundaries of Faith: Geographical Perspectives on Religious Fundamentalism*. Oxford: Rowman and Littlefield, 2000.

Sudetic, Chuck. "Bosnia: An Ethnic Battleground." In *Ethnic Violence*. Edited by Myra H. Immel. San Diego: Greenhaven, 2000.

Suhrke, Astri, and Lela Garner Noble, eds. *Ethnic Conflict in International Relations*. New York: Praeger, 1977.

Sullivan, Denis J., and Sana Abed-Kotob. *Islam in Contemporary Egypt: Civil Society vs. the State*. Boulder, Colo.: Lynne Rienner, 1999.

Sullivan, John. *ETA and Basque Nationalism: The Fight for Euskadi, 1890–1986*. New York: Routledge, 1988.

Sutherland, Charles W. *Disciples of Destruction: The Religious Origins of War and Terrorism*. Amherst, N.Y.: Prometheus, 1987.

Taheri, Amir. *Holy Terror: Inside the World of Islamic Terrorism*. Bethesda, Md.: Adler and Adler, 1987.

———. *The Spirit of Allah: Khomeini and the Islamic Revolution*. Chevy Chase, Md.: Adler and Adler, 1986.

Talbott, Strobe, and Nayan Chanda, eds. *The Age of Terror: America and the World after September 11*. New York: Basic Books, 2002.

Tambiah, Stanley Jeyaraja. *Buddhism Betrayed? Religion, Politics, and Violence in Sri Lanka*. Chicago: University of Chicago Press, 1992.

———. *Leveling Crowds: Ethnonationalist Conflicts and Collective Violence in South Asia*. Berkeley: University of California Press, 1996.

———. *Sri Lanka: Ethnic Fratricide and the Dismantling of Democracy*. Chicago: University of Chicago Press, 1991.

Tanter, Raymond. *Rogue Regimes: Terrorism and Proliferation*. New York: St. Martin's, 1998.

Taras, Raymond C., and Rajat Ganguly. *Understanding Ethnic Conflict: The International Dimension.* New York: Longman, 1998.

Tatla, Darshan Singh. *The Sikh Diaspora: Search for Statehood.* Seattle: University of Washington Press, 2001.

Taylor, Eric R. *Lethal Mists: An Introduction to the Natural and Military Sciences of Chemical, Biological Warfare and Terrorism.* Commack, N.Y.: Nova Science, 2001.

Taylor, Maxwell, and John Horgan, eds. *The Future of Terrorism.* London: Frank Cass, 2000.

Taylor, Robert. "Bioterrorism Special Report: All Fall Down." *New Scientist,* May 11, 1996.

Teitelbaum, Joshua. *Holier Than Thou: Saudi Arabia's Islamic Opposition.* Washington: Washington Institute for Near East Policy, 2000.

Telford, Hamish. "Counter-Insurgency in India: Observations from Punjab and Kashmir." *Journal of Conflict Studies* 21 (2001): 73–100.

Terrorist Group Profiles. Washington: U.S. Government Printing Office, 1988.

Testas, Abdelaziz. "The Roots of Algeria's Religious and Ethnic Violence." *Studies in Conflict and Terrorism* 25 (2002): 161–183.

Thomas, Trent N. "Global Assessment of Current and Future Trends in Ethnic and Religious Conflict." In *Violence and Terrorism.* Edited by Bernard Schecterman and Martin Slann. Guilford, Conn.: Dushkin/McGraw-Hill, 1999.

"Three British Soldiers Killed in IRA Attacks in Netherlands." *Boston Globe,* May 2, 1988.

Tibi, Bassam. *The Challenge of Fundamentalism: Political Islam and the New World Disorder.* Berkeley: University of California Press, 1998.

———. *Islam between Culture and Politics.* New York: Palgrave, 2002.

Tikhonov, Valentin. *Russia's Nuclear and Missile Complex: The Human Factor in Proliferation.* Washington: Carnegie Endowment for International Peace, 2001.

Tishkov, Valery. *Ethnicity, Nationalism, and Conflict in and after the Soviet Union: The Mind Aflame.* Thousand Oaks, Calif.: Sage, 1996.

Toffler, Alvin. "Third Wave Terrorism Rides the Tokyo Subway." *New Perspectives Quarterly* 12 (1995): 4–76.

Toloyan, Khacig. "Martyrdom as Legitimacy: Terrorism, Religion and Symbolic Appreciation in the Armenian Diaspora." In *Contemporary Research in Terrorism.* Edited by Paul Wilkinson and A. M. Stewart. Aberdeen, UK: Aberdeen University Press, 1987.

———. "Terrorism and the Politics of the Armenian Diaspora." Paper presented to the Joint Convention of the International Studies Association and the British International Studies Association, March 28–April 1, 1989, at London.

"Totaling up the Devastation." *Dallas Morning News,* May 31, 2002.

Treaster, Joseph. "The Race to Predict Terror's Costs." *New York Times,* September 1, 2002.

Tripathi, B. K. "Terrorists Challenge in Punjab." In *Terrorism in India.* Edited by S. C. Tiwari. New Delhi: South Asian, 1990.

Trundle, Robert C., Jr. "Has Global Ethnic Conflict Superseded Cold War Ideology?" *Studies in Conflict and Terrorism* 19 (1996): 93–107.

Tucker, David. *Skirmishes at the Edge of Empire: The United States and International Terrorism.* New York: Praeger, 1997.

Tucker, Jonathan B. "Bioterrorism: Threats and Responses." In *Biological Weapons: Limiting the Threat*. Edited by Joshua Lederberg. Cambridge, Mass.: MIT Press, 1999.

———. "Chemical/Biological Terrorism: Coping with a New Threat." *Politics and the Life Sciences* 15 (1996): 167–183.

———. "Chemical and Biological Terrorism: How Real a Threat?" In *World Politics*. Edited by John T. Rourke. Guilford, Conn.: McGraw-Hill/Dushkin, 2002.

———. "Gene Wars." *Foreign Policy* 57 (1985): 58–79.

———. *Scourge: The Once and Future Threat of Smallpox*. New York: Atlantic Monthly, 2001.

Tucker, Jonathan B., ed. *Toxic Terror: Assessing Terrorist Use of Chemical and Biological Weapons*. Cambridge, Mass.: MIT Press, 2000.

Tucker, Jonathan B., and Amy Sands. "An Unlikely Threat." *Bulletin of the Atomic Scientists* 55 (1999): 46–52.

Tully, Mark, and Satish Jacob. *Amritsar: Mrs. Gandhi's Last Battle*. Delhi: Rupa, 1991.

Turbiville, Graham H. *Weapons Proliferation and Organized Crime: The Russian Security Force Dimensions*. Colorado Springs, Colo.: United States Air Force Institute for National Security Studies, 1996.

Ulrich, Christopher J., and Timo A. Kivimaki. *Uncertain Security: Confronting Transnational Crime in the Baltic Sea Region and Russia*. Lanham, Md.: Rowman and Littlefield, 2001.

Umnov, Alexander. "Islamic Fundamentalism, Ethnicity and the State: The Cases of Tajikistan, Pakistan, Iran and Afghanistan." In *Ethnic Challenges beyond Borders: Chinese and Russian Perspectives of the Central Asian Conundrum*. Edited by Yongjin Zhang and Rouben Azizian. New York: St. Martin's, 1999.

"U.N. Renews Anti-Terrorism Stance." *Dallas Morning News*, October 20, 1999.

United Nations Research Institute for Social Development. "Four Categories of Ethnic Conflicts." In *Ethnic Violence*. Edited by Myra H. Immel. San Diego: Greenhaven, 2000.

U.S. Army. Center for Strategic Leadership. *Report on the Executive Seminar on Special Materials Smuggling*. Carlisle Barracks, Pa.: U.S. Army War College, 1996.

"U.S. Asserts Right to Attack Governments Hosting Terrorists." *Dallas Morning News*, February 8, 1999.

U.S. Congress. General Accounting Office. *Chemical and Biological Defense: Emphasis Remains Insufficient to Resolve Continuing Problems*. Washington: General Accounting Office, 1996.

U.S. Congress. House of Representatives. Committee on Energy and Commerce. *Nuclear Weapons Facilities: Adequacy of Safeguards and Security at Department of Energy Nuclear Weapons Production Facilities*. 99th Congress, 2d session, 1986.

U.S. Congress. House of Representatives. Committee on National Security. *Terrorist Attack against United States Military Forces in Dhahran, Saudi Arabia: Hearings before the Committee on National Security*. 104th Congress, 2d session, 1996.

U.S. Congress. Office of Technology Assessment. *Proliferation of Weapons of Mass Destruction: Assessing the Risks*. Washington: U.S. Government Printing Office, 1993.

———. *Technologies underlying Weapons of Mass Destruction*. Washington: U.S. Government Printing Office, 1993.

———. *Technology against Terrorism: The Federal Effort.* Washington: U.S. Government Printing Office, 1991.

———. *Technology against Terrorism: Structuring Security.* Washington: U.S. Government Printing Office, 1992.

U.S. Congress. Senate. Committee on Armed Services. *Bomb Attack in Saudi Arabia.* 104th Congress, 2d session, 1996.

———. *Intelligence Briefing on Smuggling of Nuclear Material and the Role of International Crime Organizations, and on the Proliferation of Cruise and Ballistic Missiles.* 104th Congress, 1st session, 1995.

U.S. Congress. Senate. Committee on Foreign Relations. *Loose Nukes, Nuclear Smuggling, and the Fissile Materials Problem in Russia and the NIS: Hearings before the Subcommittee on European Affairs.* 104th Congress, 1st session, 1995.

U.S. Congress. Senate. Committee on Governmental Affairs. *Global Proliferation of Weapons of Mass Destruction: Hearings before the Permanent Subcommittee on Investigations, Part I.* 104th Congress, 1st session, 1996.

———. *Global Proliferation of Weapons of Mass Destruction: Hearings before the Permanent Subcommittee on Investigations, Part II.* 104th Congress, 2d session, 1996.

———. *Global Proliferation of Weapons of Mass Destruction: Hearings before the Permanent Subcommittee on Investigations, Part III.* 104th Congress, 2d session, 1996.

U.S. Congress. Senate. Committee on the Judiciary. *Biological Weapons Anti-Terrorism Act of 1989.* 101st Congress, 1st session, 1990.

———. *Foreign Terrorists in America: Five Years after the World Trade Center Bombing—Hearing before the Senate Judiciary Subcommittee on Terrorism, Technology and Government Information.* 105th Congress, 2d session, 1998.

———. *Terrorist Activity: The Cuban Connection in Puerto Rico.* 94th Congress, 1st session, 1975.

U.S. Department of Defense. *Advances in Biotechnology and Genetic Engineering: Implications for the Development of New Biological Warfare Agents.* Washington: U.S. Department of Defense, 1996.

———. *Report to Congress: Domestic Preparedness Program in the Defense against Weapons of Mass Destruction.* Washington: U.S. Department of Defense, 1997.

U.S. Department of Defense. Camp Detrick. Special Operations Division. *A Study of the Vulnerability of Subway Passengers in New York City to Covert Attack with Biological Agents.* Frederick, Md.: Special Operations Division, Commodity Development and Engineering Laboratory, 1968.

U.S. Department of Defense and U.S. Department of Energy. *Joint Report to Congress: Preparedness and Response to Nuclear, Radiological, Biological, or Chemical Terrorist Attack.* Washington: U.S. Department of Defense and U.S. Department of Energy, 1996.

U.S. Department of Health and Human Services. *Health and Medical Services Medical Support Plan for the Federal Response to Acts of Chemical/Biological (C/B) Terrorism.* Washington: U.S. Department of Health and Human Services, 1996.

———. *Proceedings of the Seminar on Responding to the Consequences of Chemical and Biological Terrorism, July 11–14, 1995.* Washington: U.S. Department of Health and Human Services, 1995.

U.S. Department of State. *Patterns of Global Terrorism 2002.* Washington: U.S. Department of State, 2002.

"U.S. Funding Biological Research in Russia." *Dallas Morning News,* August 10, 1997.

"U.S. Still Unprepared for Biological Attack, Exercise Shows." *Dallas Morning News,* April 26, 1998.

Uyangoda, Jayadeva. "Sri Lanka." *American Psychologist* 58 (1998): 771–777.

Van Creveld, Martin. *The Rise and Decline of the State.* New York: Cambridge University Press, 1999.

Van der Veer, Peter. *Religious Nationalism: Hindus and Muslims in India.* Berkeley: University of California Press, 1994.

Van Horn, Winston A., ed. *Global Convulsions: Race, Ethnicity, and Nationalism at the End of the Twentieth Century.* Albany: State University of New York Press, 1997.

———. *The Transformation of War.* New York: Free Press, 1991.

Varshney, Ashutosh. *Ethnic Conflict and Civic Life: Hindus and Muslims in India.* New Haven: Yale University Press, 2002.

Vatikiotis, P. J. "The Spread of Islamic Terrorism." In *Terrorism: How the West Can Win.* Edited by Benjamin Netanyahu. New York: Farrar, Straus, Giroux, 1986.

Vegar, José. "Terrorism's New Breed." *Bulletin of the Atomic Scientists* 54 (1998): 50–55.

Venzke, Ben N., ed. *The al-Qaeda Documents.* Alexandria, Va.: Tempest, 2002.

———. *First Responder Chem-Bio Handbook.* Alexandria, Va.: Tempest, 1998.

Vermaat, J. A. Emerson. "Terrorist Sympathizers in the Netherlands." *Terrorism* 10 (1987): 329–335.

Viorst, Milton. *In the Shadow of the Prophet: The Struggle for the Soul of Islam.* New York: Knopf, 1994.

Volgy, Thomas J., and Lawrence E. Imwalle. "Hegemonic and Bipolar Perspective on the New World Order." *American Journal of Political Science* 39 (1995): 819–834.

Volkan, Vamik. *Blood Lines: From Ethnic Pride to Ethnic Terrorism.* Boulder, Colo.: Westview, 1997.

Von Tangen Page, Michael. *Prisons, Peace and Terrorism: Penal Policy in the Reduction of Political Violence in Northern Ireland, Italy and the Spanish Basque Country, 1968–97.* New York: St. Martin's, 1998.

Waddy, Charles. *The Muslim Mind.* London: Longman, 1976.

Wade, Nicholas. "Going Public with VX Formula: A Recipe for Trouble?" *Science* 187 (1975): 414.

Walker, Edward. "No War, No Peace in the Caucasus: Contested Sovereignty in Chechnya, Abkhazia, and Karabakh." In *Crossroads and Conflict: Security and Foreign Policy in the Caucasus and Central Asia.* Edited by Gary K. Bertsch, Cassady Craft, Scott A. Jones, and Michael Beck. New York: Routledge, 2000.

Walker, Jenone. *Security and Arms Control in Post-Confrontation Europe.* Oxford: Oxford University Press, 1994.

Wallace, Paul. "Political Violence and Terrorism in India: The Identity Crucible." Paper presented to the Terrorism in Context Conference, June 8–10, 1989, at Middletown, Connecticut.

Waller, Douglas. "Nuclear Detection Teams Can Avert a Surprise Attack." In *Weapons of Mass Destruction*. Edited by Jennifer A. Hurley. San Diego: Greenhaven, 1999.

Walt, Stephen M. "International Relations: One World, Many Theories." *Foreign Policy* 110 (1998): 29–47.

Walzer, Michael. *The Revolution of the Saints: A Study in the Origins of Radical Politics*. Cambridge, Mass.: Harvard University Press, 1965.

Warburg, Gabriel R. *Islam, Sectarianism, and Politics in the Sudan since the Mahdiyya*. Madison: University of Wisconsin Press, 2003.

Warburg, Gabriel R., and Uri M. Kupferschmidt, eds. *Islam, Nationalism and Radicalism in Egypt and the Sudan*. New York: Praeger, 1983.

Ward, Richard H., and Cindy S. Moors, eds. *Terrorism and the New World Disorder*. Chicago: University of Illinois Press, 1998.

Wark, William B. "Managing the Consequences of Nuclear, Biological, and Chemical (NBC) Terrorism." *Low Intensity Conflict and Law Enforcement* 6 (1997): 179–184.

Watanabe, Manabu. "Religion and Violence in Japan Today: A Chronological and Doctrinal Analysis of Aum Shinrikyo." *Terrorism and Political Violence* 10 (1998): 80–100.

Watt, W. Montgomery. *Islamic Fundamentalism and Modernity*. London: Routledge, 1988.

Weaver, Mary Anne. *Pakistan: In the Shadow of Jihad and Afghanistan*. New York: Farrar, Straus and Giroux, 2002.

———. *A Portrait of Egypt: A Journey through the World of Militant Islam*. New York: Farrar, Straus and Giroux, 2000.

Webster, William H., and Arnaud de Borchgrave, eds. *Wild Atom: Nuclear Terrorism*. Washington: Center for Strategic and International Studies, 1998.

Wege, Carl Anthony. "Hizbollah Organization." *Studies in Conflict and Terrorism* 17 (1994): 151–164.

Weiner, Myron. *Sons of the Soil: Migration and Ethnic Conflict in India*. Princeton: Princeton University Press, 1978.

Weintraub, Pamela. *Bioterrorism: How to Survive the 25 Most Dangerous Biological Weapons*. New York: Kensington, 2002.

Weisbecker, J. C. "Protecting Nuclear Materials in the Terrorist Age: The International Challenge." *Brooklyn Journal of International Law* 12 (1986): 305–338.

Weisburd, David. *Jewish Settler Violence: Deviance as Social Reaction*. University Park: Pennsylvania State University Press, 1989.

———. "Vigilantism as Rational Social Control: The Case of Gush Emunim Settlers." In *Cross Currents in Israeli Culture and Politics*. Edited by Myron J. Aronoff. New Brunswick, N.J.: Transaction, 1981.

Weiss, Anita M., ed. *Islamic Reassertion in Pakistan: The Application of Islamic Laws in a Modern State*. Syracuse, N.Y.: Syracuse University Press, 1986.

Westerlund, David, ed. *The Worldwide Resurgence of Religion in Politics*. London: Hurst, 1996.

Whitaker, David J. *Terrorism: Understanding the Global Threat*. London: Longman, 2002.

Whitaker, David J., ed. *The Terrorism Reader*. New York: Routledge, 2003.

Whitby, Simon M. *Biological Warfare against Crops*. New York: Palgrave, 2001.

White, Jonathan R. *Holy War: Terrorism as a Theological Construct.* Gaithersburg, Md.: International Association of Chiefs of Police, 1986.

———. *Terrorism: An Introduction.* Belmont, Calif.: Wadsworth, 2002.

Whitsel, Bradley C. "Catastrophic New Age Groups and Public Order." *Studies in Conflict and Terrorism* 23 (2000): 21–36.

Whittle, Richard. "Bin Laden Deputy Reportedly Killed." *Dallas Morning News,* November 17, 2001.

Wickham, Carrie Rosefsky. *Mobilizing Islam: Religion, Activism and Political Change.* New York: Columbia University Press, 2002.

Wiener, Stanley L. "Terrorist Use of Biological Weapons." *Terrorism* 14 (1991): 129–133.

Wieviorka, Michel. "ETA and Basque Political Violence." In *The Legitimation of Violence.* Edited by David Apter. New York: New York University Press, 1997.

———. *The Making of Terrorism.* Chicago: University of Chicago Press, 1993.

Wijesekera, Daya. "The Cult of Suicide and the Liberation Tigers of Tamil Eelam." *Low Intensity Conflict and Law Enforcement* 5 (1996): 18–28.

———. "The Liberation Tigers of Tamil Eelam (LTTE): The Asian Mafia." *Low Intensity Conflict and Law Enforcement* 2 (1993): 308–317.

Wilcox, Philip C., Jr. "The Western Alliance and the Challenge of Combating Terrorism." *Terrorism and Political Violence* 9 (1997): 1–7.

Wilkening, Dean A. "BCW Attack Scenarios." In *The New Terror: Facing the Threat of Biological and Chemical Weapons.* Edited by Sidney D. Drell, Abraham D. Sofaer, and George D. Wilson. Stanford, Calif.: Hoover Institution Press, 1999.

Wilkinson, Paul. "Editor's Introduction: Technology and Terrorism." In *Technology and Terrorism.* Edited by Paul Wilkinson. Portland, Ore.: Frank Cass, 1993.

———. "Hamas—An Assessment." *Jane's Intelligence Review* 5 (1993): 31–32.

———. *Terrorism versus Democracy: The Liberal State's Response.* London: Frank Cass, 2001.

Wilkinson, Paul, ed. *Technology and Terrorism.* London: Frank Cass, 1993.

Williams, Andrew. *Failed Imagination? New World Orders of the Twentieth Century.* New York: Palgrave, 1999.

Williams, Mary E., ed. *The Terrorist Attack on America.* San Diego: Greenhaven, 2003.

Williams, Paul L. *Al Qaeda: Brotherhood of Terror.* Upper Saddle River, N.J.: Pearson, 2002.

Williams, Peter, and David Wallace. *Unit 731: Japan's Secret Biological Warfare in World War II.* New York: Free Press, 1989.

Williams, Phil, and Paul N. Woessner. *Nuclear Material Trafficking: An Interim Assessment.* Pittsburgh: Ridgway Center for National Security Studies, 1995.

———. "The Real Threat of Nuclear Smuggling." *Scientific American* 274 (1996): 40–44.

Willis, Michael. *The Islamist Challenge in Algeria: A Political History.* New York: New York University Press, 1999.

Willrich, Mason. "Terrorists Keep Out!" *Bulletin of the Atomic Scientists* 31 (1975): 12–16.

Willrich, Mason, and Theodore B. Taylor. *Nuclear Theft: Risks and Safeguards.* Cambridge, Mass.: Ballinger, 1974.

Wilson, Michele, and John Lynxwiler. "Abortion Clinic Violence as Terrorism." *Terrorism* 11 (1988): 263–273.

Wimmer, Andreas. *Nationalist Exclusion and Ethnic Conflict: Shadows of Modernity.* New York: Cambridge University Press, 2002.

Wippman, David, ed. *International Law and Ethnic Conflict.* Ithaca, N.Y.: Cornell University Press, 1998.

Woesnner, Paul N. "Chronology of Radioactive and Nuclear Materials Smuggling Incidents: July, 1991–June, 1997." *Transnational Organized Crime* 3 (1997): 114–209.

Woodward, Bob. *Bush at War.* New York: Simon and Schuster, 2002.

Woodworth, Paddy. *Dirty War, Clean Hand.* Portland, Ore.: Ork University Press, 2001.

Wright, Robert. "Be Very Afraid: Nukes, Nerve Gas and Anthrax Spores." *New Republic,* May 1, 1995.

Wright, Robin. "Ethnic Conflict." In *Nationalism and Ethnic Conflict.* Edited by Charles P. Cozic. San Diego: Greenhaven, 2000.

———. *The Last Great Revolution: Turmoil and Transformation in Iran.* New York: Vintage, 2001.

———. *In the Name of God: The Khomeini Decade.* New York: Simon and Schuster, 1989.

———. *Sacred Rage.* New York: Simon and Schuster, 1986.

Wright, Robin, and Igor Beliaev. "Religious Extremism—Links to Terrorism." In *Common Ground on Terrorism: Soviet-American Cooperation against the Politics of Terror.* Edited by Igor Beliaev and John Marks. New York: W. W. Norton, 1991.

Wright, Susan. "Recombinant DNA Projects Funded by U.S. Military Agencies." In *Preventing a Biological Arms Race.* Edited by Susan Wright. Cambridge, Mass.: MIT Press, 1990.

Wright, Susan, and Robert L. Sinsheimer. "Recombinant DNA and Biological Warfare." *Bulletin of the Atomic Scientists* 39 (1983): 20–26.

Wriston, Walter B. *The Twilight of Sovereignty.* New York: Scribner's, 1992.

Yaeger, Carl H. "Menia Muria: The South Moluccans Fight in Holland." *Terrorism* 13 (1990): 215–226.

———. "Sikh Terrorism in the Struggle for Khalistan." *Terrorism* 14 (1991): 221–231.

Young, Oran R. "The Perils of Odysseus: On Constructing Theories of International Relations." *World Politics* 24 (1972): 179–203.

Yusufzai, Rahimullah. "Conversation with Terror." *Time,* January 11, 1999.

Zacharias, Ravi K. *Light in the Shadow of Jihad.* Sisters, Ore.: Multnomah, 2002.

Zakaria, Rafiq. *The Struggle within Islam: The Conflict between Religion and Politics.* London: Penguin, 1988.

Zartman, I. William, ed. *Collapsed States: The Disintegration and Restoration of Legitimate Authority.* Boulder, Colo.: Lynne Rienner, 1995.

Zawati, Hilmi M. *Is Jihad a Just War? Peace and Human Rights under Islamic and Public International Law.* Lewiston, N.Y.: Mellen, 2002.

Zevelev, Igor. *Russia and Its New Diasporas.* Herndon, Va.: United States Institute of Peace Press, 2001.

Zilinskas, Raymond A. "Rethinking Bioterrorism." In *World Politics.* Edited by Helen E. Purkitt. Guilford, Conn.: McGraw-Hill/Dushkin, 2002.

———. "Terrorism and Biological Weapons: Inevitable Alliance?" *Perspectives in Biology and Medicine* 34 (1990): 44–72.

Zilinskas, Raymond A., ed. *Biological Warfare: Modern Offense and Defense.* Boulder, Colo.: Lynne Rienner, 2000.

Zinberg, Dorothy S. *The Missing Link? Nuclear Proliferation and the International Mobility of Russian Nuclear Experts.* Geneva: United Nations Institute for Disarmament Research, 1995.

Zirakzadeh, Cyrus E. *A Rebellious People: Basques, Protests and Politics.* Reno: University of Nevada Press, 1991.

Zisser, Eyal. "Hizballah in Lebanon—At the Crossroads." *Terrorism and Political Violence* 8 (1996): 90–100.

INDEX